Montaigne and the Origins of Modern Philosophy

Montaigne and the Origins of Modern Philosophy

✦

Ann Hartle

NORTHWESTERN UNIVERSITY PRESS
EVANSTON, ILLINOIS

Northwestern University Press
www.nupress.northwestern.edu

Printed in the United States of America

10 9 8 7 6 5 4 3 2 1

Library of Congress Cataloging-in-Publication Data

Hartle, Ann.
Montaigne and the origins of modern philosophy / Ann Hartle.
pages cm
Includes bibliographical references and index.
ISBN 978-0-8101-2965-8 (cloth) — ISBN 978-0-8101-2932-0 (pbk.)
1. Montaigne, Michel de, 1533–1592. Essais. 2. Montaigne, Michel de, 1533–1592—Philosophy. 3. Montaigne, Michel de, 1533–1592—Political and social views. 4. Philosophy in literature. I. Title.
PQ1643.H295 2013
844.3—dc23

2013025328

To Francis Slade

Teacher, Friend, True Philosopher

CONTENTS

ACKNOWLEDGMENTS

This book is dedicated, in gratitude and admiration, to Francis Slade, my teacher, friend, and exemplar of the integrity of the life of philosophy and the life of faith. His work on the origins of modern philosophy, especially the political philosophy of Machiavelli, has influenced my understanding of Montaigne at the most fundamental level. My thanks are due to John Kekes, Donald Livingston, and Donald Phillip Verene who read earlier versions of the manuscript and gave me their very helpful comments and suggestions. Erika Ahern's sharp editorial eye was most useful in making my expression clearer. I am grateful for her care and skill. The Emory University Research Committee funded a semester during which much of the research was done. Additional support from the Emory Philosophy Department and Emory College of Arts and Sciences for the completion of this work is gratefully acknowledged. A year spent at the Fox Center for Humanistic Inquiry of Emory University was invaluable to me in the earliest stages of this project. I am grateful to Martine Brownley, Keith Anthony, and their staff for their gracious support. The Seminar on "Montaigne and the Origins of Modern Philosophy" (sponsored by the Institute for the History of Philosophy of the Emory Philosophy Department through the generosity of the Marcus Foundation), which I conducted in June 2010, was an occasion for the development of these ideas in the company of learned and insightful colleagues. I thank the participants for their generosity and friendship. Finally, my debt to my husband, Robert, goes well beyond what I can express here.

Chapter 2, "Sticking to the Old Ways: Montaigne and Sacred Tradition," appeared in *Anamnesis: A Journal for the Study of Tradition, Place, and 'Things Divine,'* vol. 1, no. 1 (2011).

INTRODUCTION

What is modernity? What is modern philosophy? What is modern society? And what, if anything, does philosophy have to do with the possibility of a free society?

The purpose of this book is to show that Montaigne transforms philosophy itself, bringing it down from the heavens and into the streets, markets, and taverns of ordinary men and ordinary life. Thus, he "invents" or discovers society as a distinctly modern form of association and radically changes the nature of political power. The essay is philosophy made sociable.

My approach to the *Essays,* then, is philosophical rather than literary. True, the essays do not look anything like traditional philosophy, and Montaigne himself calls them "bizarre." Nevertheless, he does describe himself as a philosopher, "a new figure: an unpremeditated and accidental philosopher." My discussion of the language, style, and order of the essays is intended to show the ways in which these features of the essay form reveal Montaigne's radically new philosophical project. The essay is not simply a literary innovation: it is the expression of an unprecedented philosophical intention.

In *Michel de Montaigne: Accidental Philosopher* (2003), I argued that Montaigne should be regarded as an original philosopher, not simply as the inventor of the essay. I was also especially concerned to show that Montaigne is not a skeptic as most of his scholarly readers take him to be. The emphasis in that book, then, is on drawing a contrast between Montaigne and the "deliberate" philosophers of antiquity. In this book, I return to many of the same themes that emerged in *Accidental Philosopher* in order to explore them in greater depth. However, my emphasis here is on Montaigne's relationship to modern philosophy, and I believe that this relationship brings out his originality in a more radical way.

Thus, I approach Montaigne as a philosopher within the context of modernity rather than Renaissance humanism, although there is much in common between these contexts. Two major works on humanism and the Renaissance are especially compatible with my view of the *Essays.* Montaigne holds a central place in Tzvetan Todorov's account of the humanist tradition, a tradition that he traces into the eighteenth century.

In his *Imperfect Garden: The Legacy of Humanism,* Todorov argues that humanism offers the antidote to our deepest and most pressing moral and political problems: the dissolution of society, the disappearance of morality and the self, and the conflict between liberty and community. The humanists do not fall into the extreme either of the autonomy of the individual or the disappearance of individuality. The "humanist core" that he sees in the tradition of liberal democracy can combat the drift of democracy toward collapse into illiberal and inhuman forms of autonomy and isolation.

Montaigne also figures prominently in William J. Bouwsma's *The Waning of the Renaissance, 1550–1640*. The Renaissance saw three liberations: the liberation of the self in the affirmation of the uniqueness of every human being, the liberation of the cosmos from the constraints of the classical-medieval hierarchy of being, and the liberation of politics in the emergence of the concept of sovereignty. Montaigne's moral attitude, according to Bouwsma, displays "the re-ordered self" in the absence of natural hierarchy.

These conclusions are, in some ways, similar to my own. However, by approaching Montaigne as a modern philosopher, rather than as a Renaissance thinker, I believe it is possible to bring to light certain epistemological and political aspects of his thought that might otherwise remain unnoticed. Although I do not focus primarily on Montaigne's relationships to other modern philosophers, I do discuss them at certain points in order to elucidate Montaigne's thought.

In addition to the influence of Machiavelli, we find in the *Essays* intimations of such widely diverse philosophers as Descartes, Pascal, Bacon, Hobbes, Hume, and Rousseau. Montaigne appears as the incomparably rich source from which both rationalists and empiricists, liberals and conservatives, draw. Yet Montaigne himself is neither a rationalist nor an empiricist, neither a liberal nor a conservative. His "unpremeditated and accidental" philosophy transcends these distinctions. Indeed, both modern epistemology and modern political philosophy take on a somewhat different color when seen through the lens of Montaigne's philosophical project.

Montaigne's re-formation of philosophy is his radical break with the classical-medieval Aristotelian tradition. This rejection of Aristotelian philosophy is a fundamental principle of early modern philosophy. Montaigne undermines the foundations of Aristotle's metaphysics, politics, and ethics, so that the traditional hierarchy of being collapses. In his rejection of Aristotelian metaphysics, Montaigne combats especially the conceit that the philosopher is most fully human and therefore divine through his participation in the divine activity of contemplation. Modern philosophy understands itself as a human, not a divine, activity and therefore abandons contemplation as the philosophical act.

Montaigne sees the philosophical pretense to divinity as dangerous because it makes the philosopher inhuman, destroys his natural sympathy, and separates him from other men. The Aristotelian view identifies the philosopher with the act of contemplation: the man is essentially the philosopher. Only the philosopher attains the perfection of the human form. Montaigne, however, sets himself forth as a radical and devastating rebuttal to this understanding. He makes himself "a new figure: an unpremeditated and accidental philosopher." The essay is the form of this new mode of philosophy which separates the man from the philosopher: the man is not essentially but rather only accidentally a philosopher. The separation of the man from the philosopher is actually, then, the humanization of the philosopher through the recovery of a common humanity. The human good is found, not in the escape to the heavens of philosophical contemplation, but in the experience of everyday life in society with other men. Montaigne turns philosophy on its head.

So also, Montaigne separates the man from the prince. The prince's identification of himself with his mastery over others makes the prince inhuman. Montaigne overcomes the Aristotelian notion of natural mastery by separating the master from his power, bringing him down from his lofty throne to "essay" himself with other men. The separation of the man from the prince is actually, then, the humanization of the prince through his recovery of his common humanity. It is the basis for the principles of representative government and the freedom of society which are central to modern political philosophy. Montaigne effects both the separation of the man from the philosopher and the separation of the man from the prince through his discovery of the social.

The first part of this book (chapters 1 through 4) focuses on the reformation or refounding of philosophy through the separation of the man from the philosopher and the humanization of the philosopher through the subjection of reason to the experience of everyday life. The second part (chapters 5 through 7) focuses on the refounding or reordering of human life through the separation of the man from the prince and the humanization of the prince through the invention of society.

Why must philosophy be reformed? What is it about the philosophy of Aristotle—the philosophy of the schools—that distorts our being and that must be overcome if human beings are to be free? In chapter 1, I set out the first step in Montaigne's refounding of philosophy, his reversal of the fundamental principles of Aristotle's metaphysics and political philosophy. Form, end, and potentiality and actuality are all brought together in Aristotle's understanding of perfection: final cause is the perfection of form, the actualization of the potentialities that belong to the individual by virtue of his species. Human perfection must be understood in terms of the hierarchy of being in which the human is located below the divine and above the bestial. Man is perfected by striving for and attaining the divine. For Aristotle, there are two distinct kinds of perfection: intellectual excellence (or contemplation) and moral excellence, which requires the political realm for its complete actualization.

For Montaigne, however, perfection is the enjoyment of "our own" condition: he considers man as he is in himself, "without striving." Montaigne replaces contemplation (the divine activity) with judgment (the human activity that is all "one's own"). He also replaces the primacy of the political with his own "end," the domestic and private. Montaigne changes the meaning of "form" by particularizing form, especially in his notion of the "master-form" which is a form "all one's own." Final cause, or "end," becomes power and the production of effects. Aristotelian potentiality and actuality are replaced by possibility.

Aristotelian philosophy and medieval theology understand human desire as, ultimately, a desire for the divine and eternal. Montaigne's philosophical stance toward the temporal world is not one of escape to the eternal. But neither is it one of immersion in the temporal realm of practice. Montaigne is actually reordering the temporal realm. He rejects and reverses Aristotle, because Aristotle's foundations are weak: they rest on the presumption and pride of the philosopher in his own divinity. That is, the Aristotelian philosopher cannot separate the man from the philosopher.

Despite his rejection of Aristotle, are there intimations within the tradition inherited by Montaigne that might suggest the possibility of a free society? In chapter 2, I discuss Montaigne's relation to sacred tradition. The question of Montaigne's sincerity in matters of religion and religious belief is one that deeply divides his readers. The apparent absence of piety, the lack of concern with the "next world," and his attitude toward death, for example, lead some to hold that his frequent avowals of his Catholicism are merely a cover for atheism. Others consider him a skeptic-fideist who combines philosophical skepticism with unexamined faith. Most readers agree that his adherence to Catholicism is due to his conviction that, within the context of the civil wars of his day, the old religion is a source of political stability. I put aside the question of his personal sincerity and attempt instead to make sense of both the apparent absence of piety in the *Essays* and his claims of submission to the Church. Montaigne objects to the role of Aristotle's philosophy in medieval theology and in the schools: he separates out what he regards as essential to the tradition and thereby frees it from its dependence on ancient philosophy.

Montaigne attacks the Reformation not only for the threat that it poses to the social bond but also, and more fundamentally, for its understanding of the human being and of man's relationship to God. He sees the reformers as attempting to institute a purely spiritual and intellectual religion, disdaining the role of the senses and images in worship. Montaigne's understanding of the human world can be described as a sacramental and incarnational metaphysics. He finds the miraculous in the lowliest details of ordinary life. Here again, he reverses Aristotle, who locates the divine in the highest and most rare.

What precisely is the philosophical act that frees the philosopher from the traditional hierarchy and makes possible the existence of society? In chapter 3, I first examine the nature of the new philosophical act in which the philosopher is separated from the man. For Montaigne, the philosophical act begins in the world of thought, not in the world of things. Hence, it begins in the condition of error because the mind is not (as Aristotle held) receptive of what is, but rather generates and produces out of itself.

The mind's capacity for "representation," as Montaigne holds, manifests the "unruliness of thought." The mind represents to itself both what is and what is not, the true as well as the false. Invention enables Montaigne to discover the possible: his task is to tell "what can happen" rather than what has happened. Montaigne's descriptions of reason have led many of his readers to conclude that he is a skeptic: reason is weak, self-interested, and biased. However, Montaigne discusses another kind of reason as well: "reason inflexible and impassive." This reason is without self-interest and can, therefore, settle the conflict between mastery and slavery.

The philosophical act is ultimately the act of judgment in which reason, representation, and invention are brought together under the will. Montaigne says that the essays are the tests of his judgment. Judgment here replaces Aristotle's contemplation. Montaigne's judgment does not contemplate "the thing itself"; it subjects the thing itself, making it his own. Freedom of judgment is the mark of the "self-ordered soul" which is "strong in itself." Montaigne does not judge by the standard of what ought to be (Aristotle's final cause): he judges what is, as it is, in its imperfection. His judgment of other men is unique, for he does not judge them by the standard of himself. Thus, he removes himself, his self-interest and self-esteem, from the act of judgment. That is the separation of the man from the philosopher.

Chapter 4 completes my presentation of the philosophical act and of Montaigne's reformation of philosophy. His unpremeditated and accidental philosophy is the separation of the man from the philosopher. The man is not essentially a philosopher: he does not participate in the divine but is simply a man like all other men. Traditional philosophy, in contrast, dehumanizes the philosopher because it destroys his sympathy with other men.

How, then, does Montaigne "humanize" the philosopher? The essay is the perfect form for unpremeditated and accidental philosophy because it makes philosophy sociable. I examine five features of the essay form in order to show how the essay is sociable. First, Montaigne's practice of quotation brings ancient philosophy into ordinary conversation. Second, he writes the essays in French rather than Latin, the language of the schools. He uses only the language of the streets, markets, and taverns of France. Third, he sometimes goes beyond the limits of propriety in speaking about the body and the sexual, thus overcoming the shame of the private. Fourth, the use of testimony and stories enlarges his experience and allows him to test or essay himself against other men. Fifth, in spite of the apparent disorder of the essays, Montaigne follows the everyday order of shepherds and shopboys who, unlike the learned, never fail to understand each other.

The essays look unphilosophical because there are no syllogisms, arguments, or conclusions. That is because judgment is not a conclusion but an act. Montaigne's judgment reorders the mind to the lowest rather than the highest. The act of judgment reverses the traditional order by submitting philosophy to the everyday, to the social, and thus to experience. That is why the last essay is "Of Experience."

In chapters 5, 6, and 7, I take up the political, social, and moral aspects of Montaigne's reordering of human association. Just as the man must be separated from the philosopher in order to recover his humanity through submission to the social, so the man must be separated from the prince in order to recover his humanity through submission to the social.

Why must the man be separated from the prince? Why is it that the rule of one man over another cannot be based on natural inequality? In chapter 5, I discuss the separation of the man from the prince as the overcoming of natural mastery, the inequality that, for Aristotle, justifies the rule of one man over another. The first essay, "By Diverse Means We Arrive at the Same End," serves as my example of Montaigne's practice of essaying and as the structure for presenting an account of his political project. In particular, I explore the unspoken presence of both Homer and Aristotle in the stories about Alexander the Great. In the two stories Montaigne recalls here, Alexander believes himself to be divine and displays extreme cruelty. In contrast, Epaminondas, a figure largely invented by Montaigne, exemplifies the separation of the man from the prince. Montaigne's words about himself, also in this first essay, spoken from the position of the philosopher-prince, point to the fundamental principles of his new political philosophy: forgiveness and promise-keeping. These two principles demand a new foundation for human society.

Montaigne therefore rejects Aristotle's foundation of "the common good," for he sees it as really the pretext for the actions of vicious men. Since the good cannot be pursued in common, he asserts: "let each one seek it in his particularity." If the standard of the common good is abandoned, then the new standard for the exercise of power must be the limitation of evil, violence, and force. Montaigne acknowledges that the prince must sometimes submit to the demands of necessity and that vicious means may be required to preserve the state. The limit on the power of the prince, however, is the freedom and independence of society from the political.

How do the *Essays* actually bring about the invention of society? What is the fundamental reform of mores that must occur, and how do the *Essays* effect that reform? In chapter 6, I discuss Montaigne's "domestic and private" end. Society is the domestic and private brought out into the public realm. That is the action of the *Essays:* Montaigne reveals himself in public without the justification of great deeds, specifically by exposing those aspects of private life that are normally hidden or shameful.

By revealing himself in public, he overcomes the shame of the private. He transforms the meaning of honor by associating courage with truthfulness rather than simply with valor in combat. Open speaking about oneself is, he says, the "cure" for pride. Montaigne criticizes the French legal system for the burdens it imposes on the people in all their domestic affairs; he also suggests that these burdens should be lifted and the trades and negotiations of the people be made "free, gratuitous, and lucrative." Such a reform would free the private sphere from the control of the political. But Montaigne also offers the possibility of a much deeper reform through the project of the *Essays,* that is, the reform of the nobility at the deepest level of mores.

In fact, Montaigne reorders the traditional virtues and vices in accordance with the requirements of social life. Cruelty becomes "the extreme of all vice." Lying and ambition are also among the worst vices, while those vices associated primarily with the body are ranked as lesser vices. Truth becomes "the first and fundamental part of virtue," and Montaigne offers himself as the primary example of its practice.

Montaigne's self-revelation is the generous gesture that lies at the origin of a free society. Not only does this gesture invite the nobility to imitate him, but it also serves as the act of trust and confidence that invites a reciprocal trust and confidence of the people. Montaigne insists that he is nothing more than a common man. He gives a voice to the people and shows that they are not naturally slaves.

What are the conditions for the preservation of a free society? Is the notion of the radical autonomy of the individual sufficient to constitute the social bond? Or is character of a certain kind necessary to make possible both community and individual freedom? In chapter 7, I discuss the character of the free individual as it is displayed in the *Essays:* the "self-ordered soul," who is neither master nor slave. The free, self-ordered individual is necessary for the existence of a free society.

In "Of the Education of Children" Montaigne says that he has only one new lesson for the young man who is to be brought up as a free man: his new lesson is "the ease of virtue." Virtue in the traditional sense involves the mastery of reason over the passions, which means struggle within the soul at least until this mastery has become a habit. Montaigne, however, experiences no such struggle. Rather, he enjoys the harmony of soul and body. His two descriptions of his production of virtue within himself—"unlearning evil" and "training the disposition"—show that naturalness can actually be acquired. That is to say, one's natural disposition or nature can be changed. The new foundation of virtue is the ease of goodness rather than the strength of self-mastery.

Montaigne's new character can be set out in terms of the virtues of generosity and integrity. Generosity is the virtue which prompts him to reveal himself in public. It can be seen especially in the way he judges other men, and thus it is the virtue associated with the philosophical life itself. Generosity is Montaigne's replacement for Aristotelian magnanimity. Integrity means "knowing how to belong to oneself." Thus, it suggests both the independence of the individual from political association and the limits on what can be demanded of him. This virtue is manifested in Montaigne's description of his own association with princes: he wants nothing from them, serves them freely, and owes them nothing. He does not seek his own good in public affairs for he already possesses it in himself.

In Montaigne's character we can discern the ways in which the social is the limit on the power of the prince. First, Montaigne is one of the very few modern philosophers who treat friendship as an important topic of moral and political philosophy. The stories of friendship in the *Essays* are often about opposition to tyranny, a point made very forcefully in his friend La Boétie's *On Voluntary Servitude*. Second, Montaigne's views on education focus on the freedom and independence of the young nobleman from his prince. Liberal education, especially the study of history, forms the judgment and puts before its students examples of noble character. Third, the frankness and openness of Montaigne's speech show how important freedom of speech is to a free society. Montaigne not only tolerates but also even welcomes opinions that are different from his own. Indeed, he claims that he is "perfect in forbearance" of disagreement. Thus, unpremeditated and accidental philosophy is the philosopher's mode of participation in and preservation of a free society. Fourth, the universal Church stands as both Montaigne's model for society and as an independent authority which limits the power of the state over the individual.

In the conclusion, I bring out more explicitly the way in which Montaigne's transformation of philosophy and his invention of society are the same act. Philosophy becomes invisible—unpremeditated and accidental—as the common man emerges into the light of the good. Modern philosophy originates in this single, hidden act.

NOTE ON THE TEXTS

References to the French text of the *Essais* are to the edition by Pierre Villey and V.-L. Saulnier, 3 vols., 2nd ed. (Paris: Presses Universitaires de France, "Quadrige," 1992). The English translation is that of Donald Frame, *The Complete Essays of Montaigne* (Stanford, Calif.: Stanford University Press, 1943). The citation (VS16, F9), for example, refers to p. 16 of the Villey-Saulnier edition and to p. 9 of the Frame translation. In some instances, I have emended Frame's translation. I have also consulted the translation by M. A. Screech, *The Essays of Michel de Montaigne* (London: Penguin, 1991).

No English translation of *mœurs* of which I am aware captures precisely the scope of meaning that Montaigne wants to convey. Frame sometimes translates it as "behavior" (F409) and Screech as "ways of life" (S614). I have settled on "mores" in order to try to capture both the very broad meaning of "ways of life" and the more narrow, moral dimension of "behavior."

Montaigne and the Origins of Modern Philosophy

Part One

✦

The Transformation of Philosophy

Chapter One

Reversing Aristotle

In his discussion of Montaigne's ancient sources, Hugo Friedrich says that "traces of readings in Aristotle are weak in the *Essais* . . . It cannot be established to what extent he actually read Aristotle; certainly it was not a thorough study."[1] It is true that the number of explicit references to and discussions of Aristotle in the *Essays* would give that impression. A quick survey of the index for Frame's translation reveals many more references to Cicero, Plato, and Seneca than to Aristotle. When Montaigne decides to tell his ways of being in public, he calls upon the help of ancient philosophy and discovers, to his surprise, that his ways of being conform to many different philosophical discourses and examples. So it is to be expected that philosophers and philosophical schools of all kinds should appear in the pages of the *Essays:* he uses them as fragmented and approximate expressions of what he is, but no single philosophical teaching can capture what he is.

However, Montaigne is "a new figure" of the philosopher, a profoundly original philosopher with a philosophical project that is entirely new and all his own. Therefore, it is necessary to look past the quotations in order to identify that original project. What is new and original in Montaigne can be discovered primarily through his relationship to Aristotle. He uses the Aristotelian vocabulary of form and final cause, perfection and imperfection, but he transforms the meaning of these terms. This transformation pervades the *Essays* even when Aristotle himself is not mentioned.

The philosophy of Aristotle, as appropriated by Scholastic theologians such as Thomas Aquinas, was the teaching that dominated the universities.[2] "The god of scholastic knowledge is Aristotle; it is a religious matter to discuss any of his ordinances, as with those of Lycurgus at Sparta. His doctrine serves us as magisterial law. . . . Nothing in it is discussed in order to be placed in doubt, . . . his authority is the end beyond which it is not permitted to inquire" (VS539, F403). Therefore, accepted philosophical beliefs are never questioned but are discussed only to be supported and confirmed. Montaigne criticizes the philosophy of the schools because it accepts Aristotle's teaching as truth "with all its structure and apparatus of arguments and proofs, as a firm and solid body, no longer shakable, no longer to be judged." However, Montaigne regards this foundation as weak. "The reason why we doubt hardly anything is that we never test our common impressions. We do not probe the foundation [*le pied*], where the fault and weakness lies; we dispute only about the branches. We do not ask whether this is true, but whether it has been understood this way or that." This presumption is both the constraint on the liberty of our judgments and the tyranny over our beliefs. "It is very easy, upon accepted foundations, to build what you please; . . . By this path we find our reason well founded, and we argue with great ease." Aristotle's first principles have become our presuppositions, and "whoever is believed in his presuppositions, he is our master and our God; he will plant his foundations so broad and easy that by them he will be able to raise us, if he wants, up to the clouds" (VS539–40, F403–4).

The centrality of Aristotle for Montaigne's philosophical project is indicated by the fact that the very first presentation of his intention, in "To the Reader," is framed in terms of Aristotle's four causes: formal, final, material, and efficient (e.g., *Meta.* 1.3, 983a25–32; *De An.* 2.4, 415b). The end Montaigne has proposed for himself is domestic and private, not public service or his own glory. "My powers are not capable of such a design." He will present himself in his simple, natural, ordinary manner, without striving, for he wants to be seen in his natural form, which includes all his defects. He himself, he says, is the matter of his book. Efficient cause is implicit in the immediate inference that he is also the maker of his book and is explicit in his reference to his power. It is important to note that, in each case, Montaigne weakens the meaning of the cause. His end is merely domestic and private, not the lofty goal of public service and glory. His form is not perfect but deficient and defective. Because he himself is the matter of his book, the reader is warned: "It is not reasonable to spend your leisure on so frivolous and vain a subject" (VS3, F2).

Montaigne questions the classical foundations of metaphysics and epistemology in the "Apology" within the context of his discussion of whether it is possible to know even what is most near to us, our own selves. We do not know how a "spiritual impression" can penetrate a body and we do not understand the nature of the connection between "these wonderful springs of action," soul and body (VS539, F402). Montaigne here criticizes Aristotle's account of causality. In his *Physics* (1.7, 190b16–191a22), Aristotle says that matter, form, and privation are the principles of natural things. Montaigne ridicules the idea that privation can be a principle: "And what could be more inane than to make emptiness itself the cause of the production of things? Privation is a negative; by what notion can he have made it the cause and origin of the things that are?" (VS540, F403). Aristotle claims that what makes the body move is "entelechy" or actualization. Montaigne calls this a "frigid invention," for it refers to "neither the essence, nor the origin, nor the nature of the soul, but merely notes its effect" (VS543, F406).

Both privation and entelechy refer to Aristotle's teaching concerning final cause. Final cause is the completion or perfection of a being in accordance with its nature or form. Final cause moves the being toward its perfection. In that sense, it is really first, for it initiates movement. Privation implies a lack of something that must be there if the being is to become a complete and perfect member of its species. Therefore, privation entails "striving" for the perfection of form, for the good. Final cause, then, is the good.

Form is "what" a thing is. All of the members of a species have the same form. Thus form is universal. Form is actuality: it is the realization of the being in the activities that are proper to it (e.g., *Meta.* 9.8, 1050b2). So, for example, the form of the eye is sight. Final cause is the completion of form: the final cause of the eye is also sight. Both the "what" and the "why" of the eye are sight. Aristotle says that "if the eye were an animal, the soul would be sight" (*De An.* 2.1, 412b18–20). As sight is the actualization of the eye, so the soul is the actualization of the body. The actualization or realization of form is the movement from potentiality to actuality. The perfection, the completion of the form of any being, is simply to be a perfect member of its species, capable of the activities proper to that species. This understanding of being and becoming entails a grounding in the eternal and the divine as first unmoved mover, as necessary being, and as pure actuality.

Montaigne breaks with Aristotle on every major aspect of his metaphysics: form, final cause, potentiality and actuality, perfection, the good, and the eternal and divine. And he reverses Aristotle's understanding of philosophy itself: he reverses the philosophical act. Montaigne uses the vocabulary of form and end, perfection and imperfection, because these are the terms available to him: he has no new words in which to express his originality. But he transforms the meaning of these terms in a way that allows him to display just what is new in his thought and to introduce notions of diversity, power, and freedom that amount to an understanding of philosophy, of nature, and of politics radically different from Aristotle's.[3]

The Particularization of Form

Montaigne changes the meaning of form entirely by particularizing form. He often refers to the great diversity and variety of forms, especially in reference to men and to human action: "the perpetual variety of forms of our nature" (VS973–74, F744).[4] Nature, he says, has become variable and particular to each man (VS1049, F803). There is, then, not simply one single human form. The clearest instance of the particularization of form occurs in his introduction of the idea of the "master-form" in "Of Repentance." "There is no one who, if he listens to himself, does not discover in himself *a form all his own,* a master form" (VS811, F615, emphasis added). The description "all one's own" emphasizes the *possession* of the form by the particular, in contrast to the notion of the particular "participating" in the universal form of human nature.

At the beginning of his essay on Cato the Younger, Montaigne explains the way in which he regards other men in terms of the particularity of form: "Because I feel myself tied down to one form, I do not oblige everybody to espouse it, as all others do. I believe in and conceive a thousand contrary ways of life; and in contrast with the common run of men, I more easily admit difference than resemblance between us. . . . I consider [each man] simply in himself, without relation to others; I mold him to his own model" (VS229, F169). He does not judge other men by the standard of a common, universal human form or nature. Rather, he sees each man as he is in himself, in his own form.

The way in which Montaigne changes the meaning of "form" calls into question the relationship between the individual and the species and introduces a new notion of particularity. For Montaigne, particularity cannot be grounded simply in the body. He particularizes form itself and claims that there is greater variety among minds than among bodies: "Variety is the most general fashion that nature has followed, and more in minds than bodies, inasmuch as minds are of a substance suppler and susceptible of more forms" (VS786, F598). Whereas for Aristotle, the particular is not the object of knowledge because knowledge is the apprehension of the universal form, the *Essays* are a philosophical attempt to reveal the intelligibility of a particular human being.

This is why there is little talk of essences and universals in the *Essays.* I believe that there is only one place where Montaigne refers to his "essence." In "Of Practice" he tells us: "What I chiefly portray is my thoughts, a subject unformed, which is not able to manifest itself in action. I am barely able to couch them in this airy body of words. . . . These are not my deeds that I write, this is me, this is my essence" (VS379, F274). They are *his* thoughts, *his own* thoughts. And they are "unformed." He seems to be suggesting a contrast between the universal essence of man as "reason" (man defined as "the rational animal") and the particularization of essence (each man as his own thoughts). This amounts to the particularization of the mind in contrast to the Aristotelian view of mind as the same in all men: it is the same because it is simply a receptivity to the world. It seems, then, that whereas for Aristotle the mind is public, for Montaigne it is private: one's own.

Final Cause and Infinite Desire

Francis Slade argues that "the repudiation of end in the sense of *telos*" is "foundational for all modern philosophy."[5] In the tradition, final cause or "end" is completion, the completion of form. "End" does not refer to a temporal finish, the last moment in a temporal sequence, but rather to a condition in which nothing is lacking for the perfection of the being in question. For Aristotle, the end of human life, the human good, is happiness, which he describes as both final and self-sufficient. All men by nature desire happiness, and all of their actions, whether they deliberately intend it or not, are directed to that end.

In "Of the Inconsistency of Our Actions" Montaigne presents the traditional philosophical notions of consistency and perfection as the direction of all of one's actions to a single end. Whoever has not directed his entire life to a certain end (*fin*) cannot order his particular actions. It is necessary to have the "form" of one's whole life, and a certain "design" of one's life, in one's head. Our projects go astray because they have no determinate direction and end (*but*) (VS337, F243). It is, in fact, a very rare achievement to direct all of one's actions to a single end. Very few men, perhaps a dozen among the ancients, have actually attained such perfection. We see, then, that Aristotle's account of human action does not capture the lives of most men for it judges by the standard of "what ought to be," not by what is in its imperfection.

To locate human happiness in a self-sufficient perfection not only misjudges what is, but also fails to account for the nature of human desire. Montaigne says that the sages distinguish between desires that come from nature and desires that come from the unruliness of our imagination: those of which one can envision the end (*bout*) are nature's, whereas those whose end (*fin*) we cannot reach are our own, that is, produced by the imagination (VS1009, F771). He calls this a "subtle" distinction, suggesting that it is merely verbal. In fact, there is no end to our desires, or at least to those that involve the soul and not only the body. In "On Some Verses of Virgil"

Montaigne advises those men who are astonished at the "unnatural and incredible" sexual appetite of women to look at themselves where they will find the same insatiability. "It would be, perhaps, more strange to see there some stop [*arrest*]; this is not a passion simply corporeal; if one finds no end [*bout*] in avarice and ambition, there is none either in lust. It lives still after satiety, and it is possible to prescribe neither constant satisfaction nor end [*fin*]: it goes always beyond what it possesses" (VS885, F675). Desire without end means that there is no permanent satisfaction and no completion or fulfillment of desire; rather, desire extends through the whole of life and ceases only in death. All satisfaction is temporary and temporal. Montaigne says that death is the end (*bout*) but not the end (*but*) of life; "this is its end [*fin*], its extremity, not its object" (VS1051–52, F805). Death is the finish, the stop, of life. Montaigne here conflates the meanings of *bout, but,* and *fin.* When he says that death is the end of life, he uses the term *fin* for "extremity," meaning the last point in time. The sense of the extreme as the last temporal moment shows the infinite character of desire, because that last moment is not a completion or perfection or actualization.

For Aristotle, the desire of the philosopher, implicit in the beginning of philosophy in wonder, is satisfied in contemplation. But for Montaigne, the desires of the mind are without end. In "Of Experience" he writes: "There is no end [*fin*] to our investigations; our end [*fin*] is in the other world." The pursuits of the mind are "without end [*terme*], and without form," and the movement of the mind is "irregular, perpetual, without a model, and without end [*but*]" (VS1068, F817–18). Our end is in the other world and therefore there is no end, in the sense of perfection and completion, in this world.

Montaigne contrasts those Christian ascetics and contemplatives who desire permanent union with the eternal and divine in this life with "that brattish rabble of men that we are," distracted by our desires and thoughts. These ascetics are "venerable souls, exalted by ardent piety and religion to constant and conscientious meditation on divine things," who anticipate, "by dint of keen and vehement hope, the enjoyment of eternal food, final end [*but final*] and last stop [*dernier arrest*] of Christian desires, sole constant and incorruptible pleasure" (VS1114, F856). Even the final end of Christian desires is the "last stop."

Power: Producing Effects

Montaigne replaces Aristotelian ends with effects, transforming the meaning of human action from the actualization of potentiality to the production of effect. In book 1 of the *Metaphysics* Aristotle explains that final cause is "the counterpart" to efficient cause, for final cause is "the purpose of a thing and its good—for this is the goal of all generation and movement" (1.3, 983a25–32). Efficient cause cannot be understood apart from final cause, because movement is initiated by the end. The end is the beginning; final cause is the naturally given end, the good. The rejection of final cause means that efficient cause is now cut off from its connection with final cause and thus from its role in the attainment of the good. Efficient cause, then, becomes "power." In Montaigne's metaphysics, beginnings are not ends. Aristotle's "entelechy" or actuality is no longer the essence, origin, or nature of the soul but only its "effect."

Montaigne replaces end with effect in the very first essay, "By Diverse Means We Arrive at the Same End [*Fin*]." The most common way to soften the heart of the avenging conqueror is through submission, but there are times when defiance has the "same effect [*effect*]." It might plausibly be argued that strong souls are moved by esteem, whereas weak, common souls are moved by compassion; in some cases, however, astonishment brings about a "like effect [*effect*]" (VS7–8, F3–4). By diverse means we produce the same effect.

Montaigne uses the Aristotelian vocabulary of ends and perfection to speak about his own project, but his meaning is very different. In the first sentences of "To the Reader," he says that his end is domestic and private: it is the end he has "proposed" to himself. In "Of the Power of the Imagination" he says that his end is to tell what can happen, not what has happened (VS105, F75). The end proposed for the *Essays* will be arrived at exactly and fully: in order to "perfect" his work, he must only be faithful to what he is (VS805, F611). Even though his work would have been "better" had he done it elsewhere, it is "perfect" because it is his own (VS875, F667). In each of these cases, he is talking about his own project, the end "proposed" by himself to himself. He transforms the meaning of "end" from the perfection and completion of nature to the projection of the will, that is, to the production of effects.

Montaigne notices that men ordinarily jump to inquire into the causes of things without first inquiring into the truth of things. These thinkers ask why something is the case instead of whether it is the case at all. "Following this custom, we know the foundations and causes of a thousand things that never were" (VS1027, F785). In particular, we look for "powerful and weighty causes and ends," while the true causes escape us by their littleness. Many famous impressions, accepted as true, spring from "empty beginnings and frivolous causes." The beginnings of all things, he says, are always "weak" (VS1020, F780). They must be weak because they are not ends; the end is not inherent in the beginning. In the search for such true causes, "a very prudent, attentive, and subtle inquirer is needed, impartial and unprejudiced" (VS1029, F787). Montaigne is concerned not simply with finding the "true" causes but also with imagining or inventing possible causes. Origins are not ends but merely spontaneous beginnings with no intelligent direction. Therefore, the connection between beginnings and effects is not inevitable: a given action might have been caused by any number of motives or springs. Alexander's rage at the captain Betis, for example, might have been caused by disdain, by envious spite, or by the natural impetuosity of his anger. In another example, the softening of the heart of the avenging conqueror might be accomplished through submission, but sometimes is brought about by defiance. With respect to Montaigne's own disposition, he notes that his innocence and goodness could be due to his father, his nurse, his earliest upbringing, or to "some other cause." His strong propensity to compassion might be due to the circumstances of his baptism, or to pride, or to nature. In all of these cases, and many others, Montaigne seems interested only in setting out possible causes. His invention of possible causes and his apparent indifference to identifying the one true cause show that the origins are not determinative and that one cause can replace another.

This indeterminacy of the origins is the condition for power as the production of effects. Montaigne's meaning can be seen more clearly in Hobbes's definition of philosophy. In chapter 11 of the *Leviathan,* Hobbes claims that there is no such thing as the "greatest good" of the ancient philosophers: "I put for a general inclination of all mankind, a perpetual and restless desire of power after power, that ceases only in death."[6] Hobbes defines philosophy in the *Leviathan,* chapter 46: "By philosophy is understood the knowledge acquired by reasoning from the manner of the generation of anything to the properties; or from the properties to some possible way of generation of the same; to the end to be able to produce, as far as matter and human force permit, such effects as human life requireth."[7] Desire is satisfied temporarily when we produce and thereby possess the effects that we want.

This understanding of philosophy is the basis for modern science and modern politics: it explains why modern philosophy is a refounding. Causes and origins can be replaced. The goal is not to understand the causes but to produce the desired effect, not to understand the "why" but to produce the "that." To understand philosophy as simply the search for the true causes of things concedes authority to nature, that is, to natural ends as causal. The search for possible causes, however, liberates the mind from nature and gives the determination of ends to man himself. The invention of possible causes is the act that frees man from the power of natural causes. For modern philosophy, "thought defines itself as access to indefinite possibilities, thus to what it may be able to cause to be . . . Understanding itself as freedom from the actual, i.e., as not determined by ends, thought comes into view as power, the power to create forms, forms which have no actuality except as thoughts."[8]

Potentiality and Actuality: Possibility

For Aristotle, fulfillment, completion, and perfection are brought about through the actualization of potentialities. Human action is actualization. Potentialities are given by nature and determined by species, and actualization occurs through the agency of final cause. Form, then, is actuality (*Meta.* 9.8, 1050b2). Therefore, nothing genuinely new can ever emerge in the world. The limits of what can happen are set; differences among members of the same species are simply degrees of actualization of the same form.

For Montaigne, human action is not actualization but the production of effects. Potentiality and actuality are replaced by possibility. The genuinely new can emerge only as the possible, which can be understood in two ways. It can be limited to what has already happened: what has happened *can* happen. Alternatively, the possible can be understood as what has never been seen before. Montaigne says that his "end" is to tell not what has happened but what can happen, what is possible to happen (VS105–6, F75). This suggests that he is not limiting the possible to what has happened, to what has been seen before, but that he is concerned with bringing out the new. The new can only emerge, or appear, against the background of the old, the familiar. This is why Montaigne is an "accidental" philosopher. He is using ancient philosophy, and Aristotle in particular, as the background for what he is bringing into existence. The possible can only be what had been thought to be impossible or, at least, what had never before been thought to be possible.

The central role of possibility in Montaigne's philosophical project makes sense of the fact that, in the *Essays,* extremes seem to replace essences. For example, cruelty is the "extreme of all vice," and the extreme of that extreme is the enjoyment of the spectacle of another man's suffering. We might expect, then, to see the essence of vice in cruelty and the essence of cruelty in extreme cruelty. But Montaigne does not say that. Extremes seem to be the limits of what is possible: extreme cruelty is "the uttermost point that cruelty can attain" (VS432, F316). Montaigne is especially interested in the limits of the human soul. "It is very hard," he says, "to assign limits to the achievements of the faculties of the soul" (VS723, F546). Montaigne, then, is open to possibilities of the soul that would have looked impossible from the perspective of Aristotle's understanding of nature.

Perfection and Hierarchy

Final cause is inseparable from form because final cause is just the perfection or the realization of form. In contrast to this Aristotelian picture, Montaigne emphasizes his deformity and his imperfections. In "To the Reader" he says that he wants to be seen in his simple, natural, and ordinary form, "without striving." Therefore, his defects will be an important aspect of his self-portrait (VS3, F2). In "Of Cripples" he tells us that he is astonished at his own deformity (VS1029, F787). He is a particular, "very ill-formed" (VS804, F610). The *Essays* do not conceal such imperfections any more than does his portrait which displays, not a perfect face, but his own face (VS148, F108).[9]

The *Essays* begin with Montaigne's "end," the end that he has proposed to himself: "I have set myself no end but a domestic and private one. I have had no thought of serving either you or my own glory. My powers are inadequate for such a purpose" (VS3, F2). The *Essays* end with his judgment of human perfection: "It is an absolute perfection and God-like to know how to enjoy our own being rightly. We seek other conditions because we do not understand the use of our own, and go outside ourselves because we do not know what it is like inside. Yet there is no use our mounting on stilts, for on stilts we must still walk on our own legs. And on the loftiest throne in the world we are still sitting on our own rump" (VS1115–16, F857).

Human perfection is simply the enjoyment of "our own" condition. Montaigne intends to contrast this perfection with the philosopher's attainment of the divine condition as well as with the condition of the prince who sits on "the loftiest throne in the world." The "end" as the domestic and private is the locus of human perfection. This notion of human perfection amounts to a removal of man from the ancient, traditional hierarchy in which he is located between the divine, which is above him, and the bestial, which is below him. In this hierarchical view, man's perfection must be seen as the attainment of the divine condition. Therefore, Montaigne's valuation of the human as such might be seen as simply a kind of "lowering" of the standards of thought and action.

His insistence that he shows himself "without striving" lends itself to that interpretation, for he appears to demand less of himself than philosophical and moral perfection would require. There is no struggle within himself between the higher and lower parts of his being.

However, Montaigne's restoration of the human should not simply be interpreted as a kind of lowering of the standards of human perfection. This estimation fails to recognize the radical newness of Montaigne's project and persists in the framework of the tradition: it judges man as a being within and entirely determined by his place in the natural hierarchy. From that perspective, Montaigne's perfection does indeed look like imperfection. In fact, however, Montaigne is introducing a new notion of perfection that cannot be measured by the old standards, even though it must be articulated in the terms of those old standards. This new notion of perfection is the free and entire possession of what is one's own, "to enjoy our own being rightly." Philosophy "belongs" to man. To fully possess our "end" is to enjoy our own being: possession means that there is no distance between what is and what ought to be.[10]

Montaigne's description of the perfection of the *Essays* manifests this new notion of human perfection: "For this purpose of mine [*mien dessein*], it is also appropriate for me to write at home, in a backward region, where no one helps me or corrects me, where I usually have no contact with any man who understands the Latin of his Paternoster and of French a little less. I would have done it better elsewhere, but the work would have been less my own; and its principal end and perfection is to be precisely my own" (VS875, F667). He writes the essays at home, and therefore they are his own. They would have been better had he written them elsewhere, but they are perfect because they are precisely his own.

Unlike a perfection "all one's own," Aristotelian perfection implies hierarchy. Human beings either attain the perfection of the human form or they fall short in varying degrees. From this perspective, the lower is the imperfection of the higher. Again, this presupposes a common human essence or complete form against which the individual is to be measured. But for Montaigne, the low is not the imperfection of the high. He relates men to one another not in terms of sameness of essence but in terms of accidental similarity. In the first essay, for example, the lowly "common herd" is accidentally similar to the lofty princes, for the astonishment of the people is accidentally similar to the esteem of the princes. Or, to put it somewhat differently, the weakness of the people is accidentally similar to the strength of the princes, because both produce the same effect. Also, Montaigne describes himself as accidentally similar to the ancient philosophers: his weak mores conform "by accident" to many of the teachings and examples of ancient philosophy. That is why he is "an unpremeditated and accidental philosopher" (VS546, F409).

The Good: Contemplation and Politics

The Aristotelian notions of final cause, perfection, and the good are impossible to separate. Final cause is the good and final cause is perfection. The good for man, or happiness, is the activity of the soul in accordance with virtue (*NE.* 1.7, 1098a1–16). Since there are two kinds of virtue, intellectual and moral, Aristotle holds that there are two distinct kinds of perfection for man: the theoretical and the practical. The "good life" can be either the life of the philosopher, that is, the life of contemplation, or the life of complete moral virtue, which manifests itself most fully in the ruler who, above all, must exercise practical wisdom. Each of these ways of life is the outcome of man's uniqueness within the whole of nature, within the natural hierarchy. Man is unique by virtue of his reason.

Montaigne's view of the uniqueness of man is very different. In the "Apology for Sebond" Montaigne examines an essentially Aristotelian-Thomistic view of nature that is hierarchical.[11] God is revealed in the book of nature, and man—on account of his reason—is the part of nature that most clearly reveals God. Whereas this understanding of nature sees human reason as unique and therefore as that which makes man to be in the image of God, Montaigne says that what is unique to man is the "unruliness of thought and freedom of imagination," which make it impossible for man to remain within the bounds of nature (VS459–60, F336).

The second characteristic that is unique to man among all the animals, according to Montaigne, is shame. Adam and Eve eat of the tree of the knowledge of good and evil. It is pride that makes them want to be God: their desire is not limited by their place within nature but is rather an infinite desire to become divine through the knowledge of good and evil (which is philosophy). When they realize what they have done, they cover their genitals. They cover the very parts that produce the human and thus they reveal their shame at being merely human. Man is the only animal that hides himself in the act by which he generates another member of his species (VS484, F356–57).

It should be noted here that Montaigne's picture of man's uniqueness strongly suggests belief in original sin. The original sin, the sin at the origins, is pride, and this manifests itself in both philosophy and politics, the two ways of life which Aristotle regards as the good for man. Montaigne does not see either philosophy or politics as innocent. His refounding of both reveals the way in which he comes to terms with pride.

With respect to Aristotle's first and highest mode of the good life, that is, philosophy, Montaigne replaces Aristotelian contemplation with judgment. Contemplation is the receptivity of the mind to being and presupposes a kind of harmony between the mind and the world. The mind receives the forms of things without the matter: the form in the mind and the form in the thing are identical (*De An.* 3.4, 430a). Montaigne's "unruliness of thought and freedom of imagination" presuppose no such harmony. For Montaigne, the mind is not receptive but rather productive and generative. Judgment does not gaze at "the thing itself," but subjects it and makes it "one's own." (These metaphysical and epistemological aspects of Montaigne's reversal of Aristotle will be taken up in chapters 3 and 4.)

With respect to Aristotle's second and lesser notion of happiness, that is, moral virtue or the life of politics, Montaigne reverses Aristotle's ordering of the private and the political. For Aristotle, the good of moral virtue is the final cause or end of politics. Aristotle says that the city comes into existence for the sake of mere life but that it exists for the sake of the good life, the life of moral excellence (*Pol.* 1.2, 1252b25–35). The city emerges out of the pre-political forms of association, the family, and the village. These pre-political associations are imperfect: they achieve their perfection only in the city, which is complete and self-sufficient. The city, then, is the final end or completion of the pre-political. Montaigne, on the other hand, begins the *Essays* in "To the Reader" with his statement that his "end" is the domestic and private. His powers are not great enough for the end of public service or glory. That is, he reverses the Aristotelian order: he reorders philosophy to the imperfect and incomplete domestic and private association.

According to Hannah Arendt, the Greek and Roman world, and even the Christian world of the Middle Ages, knew only two realms: the public and the private. Arendt's account of the distinction and the relation between the realms of the public and private is Aristotelian in its major outlines. For Aristotle, the city is the public space for the practice and display of virtue. The private sphere remains hidden, unworthy to appear in public. The private realm is that of the household where biological needs are met through a kind of activity called "labor." Labor is tied to the life-processes of the body, including the labor of childbirth. Thus, the household is the domain in which the human bondage to necessity can be most clearly seen. Because the private realm of the household deals with the biological and the necessary, it remains hidden from public view. From the perspective of the distinctly human, higher activities, the private is identified with the shameful. The ordinary daily functions of the body are hidden on account of what seems like an instinctual sense of shame. This includes, of course, the very act by means of which the species is continued.

The public realm, on the other hand, is the place of self-disclosure and, thus, of honor and glory. The public realm is also the realm of freedom, which means, first of all, freedom from necessity and labor. It is only within the public sphere that action, as distinguished from labor and work, can take place. Action is the specifically human mode of association, the way in which men are related to each other, not through the medium of material things but directly, through deeds and speech. It is here that men rise above the merely biological to the specifically human practice of virtue or excellence. Therefore, the public sphere is the place where men compete and distinguish themselves, where they display their uniqueness and superiority. The city is the space in which virtue appears in deeds and speech. It is only the political relationship that allows for the full exercise of virtue: prudence, justice, and courage come into their perfection in the greater scope for action that only the political can provide.

Arendt explains that "society" is the new, modern form of human association that comes about when the private realm rises into the public sphere. "The emergence of society . . . from the shadowy interior of the household into the light of the public sphere, has not only blurred the old borderline between private and political, it has also changed almost beyond recognition the meaning of the two terms and their significance for the life of the individual and the citizen."[12]

Montaigne not only reorders philosophy to the domestic and private, he also brings the domestic and private out into the public realm. In so doing, he refuses to hide out of shame for mere life. This emergence of the private into the public is the bringing into being of modern society.

For Aristotle, the good of politics is the "common good," a good that can only be achieved in common (*Pol.* 3. 6–7). Montaigne says that philosophy has not been able to find a way to the good that is commonly shared. Therefore, "let each one seek it in his particularity" (VS622, F471). Montaigne rejects the notion of the common good as the foundation of politics: his "end" is instead domestic and private. We should, consequently, expect that the good is to be found in the domestic and private, but the domestic and private brought into the public, that is, the social. To that end, he reorders the virtues and vices in accordance with the requirements of social, rather than political, life. (These moral and political aspects of Montaigne's reversal of Aristotle will be discussed in chapters 5, 6, and 7.)

The Eternal and the Temporal

For ancient philosophy as well as for Christian theology, human desire is ultimately desire for the divine, for eternity and immortality. The human good is the transcendence of the human: the completion and perfection of the human consists in the attainment of the divine condition. For Aristotle, even sexual desire is ultimately the desire for immortality, the desire to share in the eternal. The desires of the philosopher are fulfilled in contemplation, which is a sharing in the activity of the eternal and the divine. Although Aristotle does not consider politics a divine activity, we see in his pupil Alexander (who believed himself descended from the gods) the desire of the prince for immortal glory.

The infinite desires of the philosophers, Christian contemplatives, and princes all appear on the very last pages of the *Essays*. There, Montaigne refers to the philosophers who want to "get out of themselves and escape from the man." He says of this desire: "That is madness: instead of changing into angels, they change into beasts; instead of raising themselves, they lower themselves." Of the Christian ascetics who "scorn to give their attention to our beggarly, watery, and ambiguous comforts," he says: "these are two things that I have always observed to be in singular accord: supercelestial thoughts and subterranean conduct." And of Alexander's pretensions to divinity, he says: "I find nothing so humble and so mortal in the life of Alexander as his fancies about his immortalization." When the oracle of Jupiter Ammon had placed Alexander among the gods, Philotas wrote to Alexander congratulating him on his elevation: "As far as you are concerned, I am very glad of it; but there is reason to pity the men who will have to live with and obey a man who exceeds and is not content with a man's proportions" (VS1115, F856–57).

For Montaigne, Alexander's apotheosis is a delusion and therefore also the very reverse of human perfection: absolute perfection is, rather, to know how to enjoy our own being rightly. "We go out of our condition" only because we do not know what it is like inside ourselves. Human perfection is not the attainment of the divine condition but the enjoyment or complete possession of our own condition. But what does this mean? Would we not necessarily already have taken complete possession of our own condition as created and temporal beings? Montaigne rejects the attempt and even the possibility of becoming divine, of rising above the human condition by our own agency. He does the opposite: he brings the eternal into the temporal. And this amounts to a valuing of the temporal in a new way.

Montaigne's "stance," the standpoint from which he looks at the world of human things in the *Essays,* is entirely new. He neither immerses himself in the busyness of this world nor escapes to the eternal. That is to say, he takes neither a theoretical nor a practical attitude toward the human things. He transcends Aristotle's distinction between the theoretical and the practical. Montaigne's stance, or attitude, comes through especially in "Of Vanity." There he tells us that he really knows very little about the actual workings of his household, even though he has retired there and is devoted to it as his inheritance from his father. He is ashamed, he says, that he doesn't even know the names of some of the most common implements, or how wine is made. He is not immersed in the running of his chateau or in the economic details of his livelihood. On the other hand, he insists that "this is not a philosophical scorn for transitory and mundane things" (VS953, F728). So his attitude toward the everyday is not an attitude either of utility or of action within the practical world. Yet he has no philosophical disdain for these ordinary and common things. The ordinary and common is, in fact, the focus of his attention as a philosopher.

There is, then, a kind of theoretical or contemplative stance that Montaigne takes in the *Essays*. But this is not the attempt to contemplate the divine, the eternal and unchanging. Rather, he looks at the human things, especially human action, examining them from different angles. That examination is the contemplative element in his thought. However, he does not look at the temporal realm from the perspective of eternity for, from that perspective, the temporal appears as nothing. "Of Vanity" expresses his stance so well because he seems to say: yes, the world, the temporal, and the fleeting are all vanity, but this is what we are, and there is value in the temporal world, there is good in what we are.

Montaigne's "contemplative" stance toward the temporal, however, includes an element of action, for he also reorders the temporal. He does not just ponder the world as it is, but transcends the Aristotelian distinction between the theoretical and the practical. He does not act within the flow of time, but stands, as it were, in a middle position between the eternal and the temporal.[13] In reordering time, he stands above time. Yet he is not directing time to the eternal. Rather, he brings the eternal into the temporal.

I will discuss three aspects of the *Essays* that display Montaigne's new stance toward the eternal and the temporal. First, although he tells many stories, he includes no extended narrative of either his own life or of human history in general. Second, Montaigne refers to himself as "a new figure" of the philosopher: the new appears in time as a "figure." Third, in spite of his insistence on his changeability, he also claims that he is, in some sense, consistent.

The Absence of Narrative in the Essays

The rejection of final cause introduces the possibility of a new kind of freedom with respect to the temporal order, for the temporal is no longer ordered to the eternal. Montaigne's rejection of final cause is reflected in the way in which he presents eternity and time in the *Essays*. Final cause binds thought and action to the eternal, connecting the moments of time by ordering them to the end. The end is the origin: it is there from the beginning, guiding the temporal sequence, making the temporal sequence intelligible. The temporal is subordinated to the eternal and ordered to the eternal. For Montaigne, man cannot attain "the perfection of being" that belongs only to the eternal and divine. On the other hand, Montaigne's stance toward the temporal does manifest a new kind of freedom that follows from the rejection of final cause. Ends are no longer given by nature but are chosen as his purposes. Francis Slade puts this precisely: "It is this reduction of end to purpose that makes possible the argumentative strategy employed against teleological explanation. . . . Nature must be construed as *end-less* for modern freedom. . . . Ends are constituted by our choice. They are our 'projects.'"[14] The difference between ends and purposes is that "ends exist independently of our willing them to be; they do not originate in our willing them to be. Purposes take their origin from our willing them; purposes would not be if agents did not give them being. . . . [Aristotle's] happiness is the end of human life whatever the purposes of human beings may be. Happiness is the end not because I choose happiness and make it my purpose, but because of what I am, the intrinsic character, or nature, of the human being itself."[15]

Narrative implies final cause. "Narrative, presenting the interplay between purpose and end, is the classic form that allows us to contemplate human life in its completeness and incompleteness. . . . The narrative arts presuppose the ontological priority of ends to purposes because without that priority, there is nothing to be revealed about the adequacy or inadequacy of human purposes to the completeness of human life, for in action a human being 'purposes' the realization of his life as a whole, complete in itself."[16]

Narrative is made coherent in terms of some notion of completion, and that means change that is directed to an end. Montaigne says: "There is nothing so contrary to my style as an extended narrative" (VS106, F76). Men and events are presented in the *Essays* without regard to their place in an unbroken historical process and are given a new non-temporal order by the mind. Thus, although the *Essays* are full of stories, there is no concern for chronological order and no extended narrative either of

Montaigne's own life or of human history. What we are told about Montaigne's life is given to us in fragments scattered throughout the work without regard to their place in any temporal sequence.

Compare the *Essays* to the presentation of Augustine's life in the *Confessions.* The nine narrative books begin with his conception and end with the death of his mother. In his reflections on this beginning and end, he emphasizes the bodily or biological aspect of his relationship to his parents, "the parents of my flesh," by whose bodies he came into this life: "the father from whom, and the mother in whom, You fashioned me in time" (1.6). Thus, the nine narrative books present the natural, biological life cycle of the human species, the way in which one generation gives birth to the next and then goes out of existence. We see, then, the fleeting character of the life of individuals, held by the bonds of necessity to the merely biological and thus to time and mortality. This is the inheritance of original sin and the condition of trial and temptation. In the later books on memory, time, and Genesis he presents the temporal character of all created things, but also the possibility of the transcendence of the temporal flow and the promise of eternal life. Narrative is transcended in the eternal now of God's vision.

In Augustine's narrative, we see the interplay of divine and human action. God, who is eternal and unchanging, acts in time, directing Augustine to his end. That end is completeness, wholeness, found only in the eternal union with God in the next world. While Augustine is seeking happiness in lower things, God is secretly bringing him to the point of his conversion. The action of God looks like a cause, a necessarily superior cause that enters into the natural realm of causality and overrides all other causes. This interplay of divine and human action, which must result in the victory of divine grace, raises the question of human freedom in a new way. Augustine's choices are not ultimate. Therefore, his freedom must be made compatible with divine agency.

In contrast with Augustine's *Confessions,* Montaigne is not appealing to the action of God within his life in order to explain who he is. When the factor of freedom is introduced into the picture of Montaigne's life, any idea of an extended narrative must be abandoned. His freedom must be displayed in the discrete moments of time rather than in a story that holds the moments together in a temporal order of change directed to an end. The intelligibility of a particular human being therefore cannot be revealed in the story of his life. The absence of an extended narrative of Montaigne's life points to his freedom from final cause.

Narrative is the attempt to tell what has happened in chronological order. Montaigne's end is to tell not what has happened but what can happen (VS105–6, F75). He is not concerned with the actual but with the possible. Therefore, his relation to time cannot be expressed in narrative. There is no ordered movement in time, for there is no final cause of human action. His "transpositions of chronology" mean that his stories have their place in the *Essays* "according to their opportunity, not always according to their age" (VS964, F736). Their timeliness is dependent on his purposes. Montaigne is imposing his own order on the temporal.

The presence of Montaigne's father in the *Essays,* like the presence of Augustine's mother in the *Confessions,* points to the origins and the biological dimension of human life, the way in which the generations of men come into being and go out of being. Perhaps the strangest of the "transpositions of chronology" involving his father appears at the beginning of the "Apology" in Montaigne's account of how he came to translate Sebond's book. The way in which he presents the chronology of his translation does not follow the natural temporal order. Montaigne's father was given Sebond's book as a gift by one of his learned houseguests and, "a few days before his death," he asked his son to translate it into French. Montaigne did the translation with which his father was very pleased and so ordered it to be printed. "And this was done after his death" (VS440, F320). Since the *Theologia Naturalis* is a work of nearly a thousand pages, how could he have translated it within a few days? In the dedicatory epistle to the translation, he lets it be known that he had been working on the translation some months before his father's death (a fact that he does not mention in the *Essays*). M. A. Screech estimates that the translation would have taken at least a year. Stranger still, the dedication to his father wishes him a long life, yet it is dated on the very day of his father's death, June 18, 1568.[17] Now, perhaps this is all just a mistake on Montaigne's part and nothing should be made of it. But if it is not a mistake, then we are faced with a deliberately incomprehensible chronology. The temporal order is thrown off so that the chronology does not match the natural order of things. He is imposing his own order on these events, a non-natural order which concerns the life and death of his father, his own origin. There is a strange sense here in which his father is "reborn," a sense in which he is reversing the beginning and the end.

Montaigne is subjecting the temporal to himself, taking power over the temporal order. Human agency is not captured in narrative, because action is not actualization. Action is a new beginning and has the power to wipe out the past. So there is no story behind his actions. The absence of narrative shows that Montaigne is complete at every moment, and at every moment has the power to make a new beginning.

A New Figure

Montaigne describes himself as "a new figure: an unpremeditated and accidental philosopher." His choice of "figure" to express what is new about him brings to mind both medieval and ancient meanings of that term. In his essay "Figura," Erich Auerbach goes through the history of "figure" beginning with ancient poetry where the term first arises as an expression for "form" and conveys the meaning of "new form."[18] The term has a rich and varied history among the ancients, but "the meaning which the Church Fathers gave the word . . . was of the greatest historical importance."[19] The figural involves concrete historical persons or events that are related to each other but that do not simply represent anything in any abstract way. "Figural interpretation establishes a connection between two events or persons, the first of which signifies not only itself but also the second, while the second encompasses or fulfills the first. The two poles of the figure are separate in time, but both, being real events or figures, are within time, within the stream of historical life." So, for example, the persons and events of the Old Testament prefigure the Incarnation and the Gospels, which in turn are a promise of the kingdom of God at the end of time.[20]

Figural interpretation "removes the concrete event, completely preserved as it is, from time and transposes it into a perspective of eternity." The figures, then, have an eternal character and must be understood from the eternal divine perspective. "The future is represented figurally by past events" but for God there is no "difference of time."[21] Figure entails an "immediate vertical connection with a divine order."[22]

That the two events or persons are not simply related horizontally, in a temporal relationship of before and after, is due to the fact that "every future model, though incomplete as history, is already fulfilled in God and has existed from all eternity in His providence." The figures are "the tentative form of something eternal and timeless; they point not only to the concrete future, but also to something that has always been and will always be. . . . which is at all times present, fulfilled in God's providence, which knows no difference of time" because all of the moments of time are present to God at once. The figure is both a fragmentary temporal reality and a veiled eternal reality.[23]

Auerbach contrasts this understanding of time with the modern view in which "the provisional event is treated as a step in an unbroken horizontal process." From the perspective of the figural system, "the interpretation is always sought from above; events are considered not in their unbroken relation to one another, but torn apart, individually, each in relation to something other that is promised and not yet present."[24] As Peter Burke explains in *The Renaissance Sense of the Past,* "this kind of interpretation clearly worked against the sense of the past, for it depends on taking men and events out of their historical context, and putting them into a spiritual one."[25]

In describing himself as a new figure, Montaigne is both preserving and transforming the ancient and medieval meanings of "figure." Figure replaces Aristotelian form. Whereas form is eternal and universal, a figure is a concrete particular that is related to other particulars not through sameness of essence but through the accidental similarity of discrete and fragmentary stories: Montaigne finds that he is accidentally similar to the examples of many different philosophers. Whereas figure in the medieval sense is directly related to the divine, Montaigne is a new figure and exemplar, not of God, but of the philosopher.

Montaigne takes from the medieval notion of figure the possibility of the transcendence of the temporal by a particular, a kind of transcendence that would not have been thinkable or possible for the ancients. He is a new possibility, the new type of the philosopher, an unpremeditated and accidental philosopher. He brings together and uses the fragments of the philosophers of the past in order to reveal himself. All of ancient philosophy is ordered to him: he transcends the temporal by bringing the fragments of ancient philosophy under his own judgment and directing them to his own purposes. It is as if the new had been there all along. Ancient philosophy had always expressed, in a fragmentary way, what he is.

Change and Consistency

Montaigne's stance toward the temporal and the significance of the absence of narrative can also be seen in what he says about his changeability and his consistency. On the one hand, he claims that he is constantly changing: "I do not portray being; I portray passing. Not the passing from one age to another, or, as the people say, from seven years to seven years, but from day to day, from minute to minute" (VS805, F611). In "Of the Inconsistency of Our Actions" he says that only about a dozen men among the ancients managed to achieve perfect consistency. Striving for perfection means directing all of one's actions to a single end. Following Aristotle's account of final cause, the perfection or complete actualization of form requires the rule of reason in the soul: this rule of reason brings about consistency of action because reason is such that it directs all action to a single end. Montaigne, however, presents himself "without striving." He includes himself among the common herd of men who are constantly moved and changed both from without and within: "Not only does the wind of accident move me at will, but, besides, I am moved and disturbed as a result merely of my own unstable posture; and anyone who observes carefully can hardly find himself twice in the same state" (VS335, F242). The rejection of final cause would mean that change has no natural direction and therefore may or may not be consistent with previous or subsequent events. There is constant change, but it does not go anywhere. Each moment is discrete and unconnected to any other moment.

On the other hand, in spite of this picture of radical change, Montaigne says that he is consistent. In "Of the Useful and the Honorable" he gives an account of his actions as negotiator between princes: "If anyone follows and watches me closely, I will concede him the victory if he does not confess that there is no rule in their school that could imitate this natural movement and maintain an appearance of liberty and license so constant and inflexible on such tortuous and varied paths, and that all their attention and ingenuity could not bring them to it" (VS795, F603). Montaigne's consistency cannot be captured in the rules of any philosophical school because it has gone beyond the limits of ancient philosophy and cannot be judged by its standards. His consistency is just his liberty and license: it is not due to final cause. But because it is without striving, his conduct appears natural.

Montaigne is, in some way, holding all of his actions together. His liberty and license are, paradoxically, "constant and inflexible." All of his actions are free, undetermined by an end. He produces these actions out of himself. Each action is a new beginning, yet his actions are not random but consistent. In some sense, he is always the same since the "springs of action" are always the same. He concludes "Of the Inconsistency of Our Actions" with a discussion of the fact that vicious motives sometimes underlie virtuous-looking actions. "In view of this, a sound intellect will refuse to judge men simply by their outward actions; we must probe the inside and discover what springs set men in motion. But since this is an arduous and hazardous undertaking, I wish fewer people would meddle with it" (VS338, F244). Montaigne's actions are consistent from the inside, from the consistency of his free will. This is a consistency of beginnings, of "springs" rather than ends, a kind of consistency that is possible on account of the rejection of final cause. Why does Montaigne say that the discovery of the springs of action is a hazardous undertaking? Perhaps he means that the rejection of final cause is desirable but dangerous because it implies a new understanding of human agency and a new kind of freedom: the human will is now free from the causality of naturally given ends.

The New as What Was Always There: Replacing the Foundations

What are we to make of the absence of narrative, the strange transpositions of chronology, the claim that he is a new figure, and his puzzling treatment of his own consistency? What is the meaning of his stance toward the temporal? The movement of the essay form is not to ascend to the eternal but rather to go back to the beginning and change the foundation. Montaigne is ordering the temporal, subjecting it to his own purposes, so as to accomplish his refounding. That is, he is going back to the origins and replacing them. The new is really what was there all along. Replacing the old foundations would have to be this kind of act if everything is, somehow, to remain the same and yet be radically different.

Montaigne adopts this stance toward eternity and time because the production of the genuinely new requires freedom from both the past and the eternal. If change is grounded in the eternal, as it is for Aristotle, then the coming into being of the new is impossible. The new order that Montaigne imposes on time is the order of the possible: time is ordered not to the eternal but to the possible, which escapes the categories of potentiality and actuality. He can impose his own order on time because beginnings are not ends.

For Aristotle, the necessary condition for philosophy is leisure. It is only when all of the needs of life have been provided for that the theoretical life can occur (*Meta.* 1.2, 982b20–25). Leisure is the setting aside of time, removing it from the workaday world, and taking the theoretical attitude toward the world. The philosopher sets himself apart from the everyday. He is engaged in an activity that is higher than the activities of everyday life. For Montaigne, however, leisure must be understood in terms of his stance: neither immersed in busyness nor escaping to the eternal. Montaigne brings philosophy back down into the temporal realm. "Unpremeditated and accidental" philosophy brings philosophy into the immediacy of the moment.

The essay that Montaigne places last is "Of Experience." He ends, then, not in the eternity of contemplation but in the temporality of experience. He reverses Aristotle's order, the order of philosophy itself. Montaigne reverses Aristotle, because Aristotle's foundation is weak. Montaigne replaces the weak foundation with his own good foundation. This is the act of philosophy, the act of refounding. Aristotle's foundation is weak because it is the presumption of the philosopher and the pride of the philosopher. Assuming the Aristotelian notion of perfection as the completion of the human form, only the philosopher is fully human or, to put it differently, only the philosopher bears the entire form of human nature. For Montaigne, on the contrary, "*each man* bears the entire form of the human condition" (VS805, F611).

Aristotle does not separate the philosopher from the man. The man who philosophizes is essentially a philosopher, and therefore he is divine. In contrast, Montaigne's unpremeditated and accidental philosophy is the separation of the man from the philosopher: the philosopher is only accidentally a philosopher.

Chapter Two

Sticking to the Old Ways: Montaigne and Sacred Tradition

How is it possible for the philosopher to see himself as just a man? To what can he turn in order to ground his recovery of a common humanity? What is it that allows Montaigne to see the possibility of society? I argue that, in spite of his radical break with the philosophical and theological tradition, Montaigne finds in the core of sacred tradition—the tradition freed from Aristotle—the intimations of a new form of human association.

The Presence of Sacred Tradition in the *Essays*

Readers of Montaigne are sharply divided over the question of whether or not he was a sincere Catholic. Those who claim that he was indeed sincere generally defend their view on the basis of evidence external to the *Essays*. Although there are allusions to various Christian beliefs in the *Essays*, the work clearly lacks what might be called a pious tone, so defenders of his sincerity must point to his religious practices that he mentions in his *Travel Journal*. Many of his readers, then, see him as a "skeptic-fideist," that is, as someone who believes what faith teaches but who also denies that we can have knowledge of these truths of the kind that theology seeks to attain.[1]

Those who claim that Montaigne is really an atheist, or at least an unbeliever, dismiss his professions of faith and his allusions to Christian belief as mere window-dressing intended to conceal his true opinions. Many, if not most, readers of Montaigne interpret his adherence to Catholicism as a purely prudential and practical position stemming from his conviction that Catholicism could provide social and political stability. Thus, according to this view, he holds to the Catholic side in the civil wars of his day simply because it is the tradition of his country, not because he sees any inherent value in the content of that tradition.[2]

The problem with this approach is that it requires the reader to simply dismiss a great deal of what Montaigne actually says and about which he claims to be truthful. In effect, it amounts to saying that he doesn't really mean what he says. In some cases, this judgment is based on what appear to be contradictions in his writings. The interpreter then simply dismisses one of the apparently contradictory claims. But on what grounds? The effort to make a philosopher consistent by dismissing a significant portion of what he says is ultimately arbitrary. If there are contradictory claims in his writings, then the first task of the interpreter is to attempt to understand how they might be reconciled.

I propose to set aside the question of Montaigne's sincerity and to consider the *Essays* themselves, with their apparent contradictions and lack of piety, in an effort to understand Montaigne's position on religion in general and on Catholicism in particular.[3] I will argue that Montaigne is bringing philosophy and faith together in a new way. The medieval theologian begins with the articles of faith as the first principles of his science. He then seeks to understand what he already believes: theology is "faith seeking understanding." Thus, philosophy serves as the "handmaiden" of theology. In "Of Prayers" Montaigne says that he has heard certain writings reproached for being "purely human and philosophical, with no admixture of theology." Nevertheless, a purely human consideration is precisely his project: "I set forth notions that are human and my own, simply as human notions considered in themselves, not as determined and decreed by heavenly ordinance and permitting neither doubt nor dispute; matter of opinion, not matter of faith; what I reason out according to me, not what I believe according to God" (VS323, F234).[4]

On the other hand, in a remarkable statement of submission from a philosopher who prizes his freedom of judgment, Montaigne says that he submits his essays "to the judgment of those whose concern it is to regulate not only my actions and my writings, but even my thoughts. Equally acceptable and useful to me will be condemnation or approval, since I hold it as execrable if anything is found which was said by me, ignorantly or inadvertently, against the holy prescriptions of the Catholic, Apostolic, and Roman Church, in which I die and in which I was born. And therefore, always submitting to the authority of their censure, which has absolute power over me, I meddle rashly with every sort of subject, as I do here" (VS317–18, F229).[5]

Montaigne, then, liberates philosophy from its status as the servant of theology. However, it is his submission to the Church (in which he was born and in which he will die) that gives him the freedom to think and write as he does in the *Essays:* in the context of his submission to the Church, philosophy becomes "unpremeditated and accidental." And in this unpremeditated and accidental way, certain aspects of religion in general and of Catholicism in particular are woven into the fabric of the *Essays:* the sacraments, the Mass, the angelus bell, and many allusions to the New Testament appear, unobtrusively, throughout the work. So, while Montaigne does not engage in arguments concerning the nature of the Trinity or the Incarnation, he does treat Catholicism as an integral part of everyday life in ways that might remind us of a Brueghel painting. Of course, this does not prove that he was a sincere believer, but it does indicate that he is, in some way, bringing the content of faith into his own practice of philosophy. The beliefs and practices of the Church are present as the familiar, as what was always there, the unpremeditated source of his emergence into the public as a philosopher.

Montaigne's adherence to Catholic tradition is more than formal, that is, it is based not only on the conviction that tradition as such is a force for stability, but also on the goodness and truth of the content of that tradition. Montaigne's innovations incorporate the possibilities or intimations that are available to him in Christian faith. Divine revelation means that certain things that were unthinkable, and that were therefore impossible, for ancient philosophy can now be possibilities for thought. The way in which Montaigne avails himself of the possibilities offered by Christian belief is to transform this world, to open up possibilities for human thought and action in this life.

Montaigne's project of displaying the possible as the object of philosophical thought is precisely the description of the role of reason in relation to faith as set out by Thomas Aquinas. Reason, Thomas says, cannot demonstrate the truths of faith. If the truths of faith could be demonstrated by reason, the intellect would be compelled, whereas faith must be free and must, therefore, include an act of the will. The task of reason with respect to faith is to remove the obstacles to belief by showing that "what faith proposes is not impossible."[6] Thus, the phenomenon of faith offers to philosophy the possibility of a kind of thought that is free and open to the possible. Faith opens the way for the transformation of the activity of philosophy. In contrast to the Aristotelian account of knowledge as the mind's reception of forms, faith is a new kind of intellectual assent that requires an act of the will. Montaigne's philosophical act transforms this possibility of the role of the will in thought into the fundamental act of the mind in bringing society into being.[7]

Sacred Tradition and the Permanent Things

Throughout the *Essays,* Montaigne insists on his changeability, instability, and inconsistency. However, there is one way in which he remains constant from the very beginning: "Now from the knowledge of this mobility of mine I have accidentally engendered in myself a certain constancy of opinions, and have scarcely altered my original ones. . . . Thus I have, by the grace of God, kept myself intact [*entier*], without agitation or disturbance of conscience, in the ancient beliefs of our religion, in the midst of so many sects and divisions that our century has produced" (VS569, F428). His religion ("in which I die and in which I was born") is the basis of the unity of his life.

In "Of Vain Subtleties" Montaigne distinguishes between two kinds of good Christians. Simple people, who are less curious and learned, believe simply through reverence and obedience. Great minds, on the other hand, have reached a deep level of understanding of the Scriptures and the Church through long study and investigation. Both of these types, the lowly and the learned, are good Christians. But "in the middle range of mental vigor and ability, error in opinion is engendered; those in this range follow the first plausible meaning, and have some claim to regard our sticking to the old ways—those of us who are not versed in these matters by study—as simplicity and stupidity." Montaigne then places himself among those who stick to the old ways, but neither from simplicity nor through study and learning. These believers have reached "the extreme limit of Christian intelligence" for they stick to the old ways, but in a manner different from both the great minds and the simple. This captures the essence of Montaigne's adherence to sacred tradition.

In *Tradition: Concept and Claim,* Josef Pieper discusses the concept of tradition in terms of the distinction between sacred tradition and tradition in the broader sense of what is in any way handed down, that is, the distinction between "The Tradition" and "traditions." Pieper argues that "there is in the last analysis only *one* traditional good that it is absolutely necessary to preserve unchanged, namely the gift that is received and handed on in the *sacred* tradition."[8] This is because what is believed in sacred tradition concerns "the center of the world" and the core of human existence.[9] Sacred tradition, as Pieper presents it, is not primarily about unreflective modes of behavior or ways of doing things. It primarily concerns belief—belief about what might be called the metaphysical and, in particular, about the relation of the human to the divine.

The character of sacred tradition is such that it becomes intertwined with all aspects of life so that what is truly essential to it can be difficult to discern. On the one hand, it requires great caution to undertake the smallest changes even in customs that do not appear to be directly related to the essence. Pieper explains, "It is common for the essence of what must be preserved to become overgrown and entangled with the concrete forms of historical life, and a change in the outer may very well threaten the pure preservation of the essence, so that anyone who carelessly discards or makes light of the 'outer' traditions commits a dangerous act." On the other hand, it is this distinction between the essence of sacred tradition and its nonessential accretions that sometimes make possible even significant changes in custom. Pieper explains that "the explicit respect for the unimpeachable character of the sacred tradition presupposes the possibility of relativizing other traditions and in fact makes it possible and reasonable." Thus, a true appreciation of sacred tradition is not to be confused with any form of ideological conservatism. "Genuine consciousness of tradition makes one positively free and independent in the face of conservatisms, which worry obsessively about the cultivation of the 'traditions.' Certainly, a 'cultivation of tradition' that attaches itself to a historically accidental external image of what has been handed down becomes a positive hindrance to a real transmission of what is truly worth conserving, which perhaps can occur only under changed historical forms. It is possible to imagine a real transmission of what is in the last analysis worth handing down, which a dogmatic conservatism could not even recognize."[10]

Montaigne acknowledges this distinction between the changeable and the permanent things. In his essay "Of Custom" he cautions those who would introduce changes in the civil laws, but he also defends both the public status of the Church and its immunity from innovation: "It seems to me very iniquitous to want to subject *public and immutable institutions* and observances to the instability of a private fancy (private reason has only a private jurisdiction), and to attempt against divine laws what no government would endure against civil laws" (VS121, F88, emphasis added). He criticizes the English who, in his own lifetime, have changed several times "not only in political matters, in which people want to dispense with constancy, but in the most important subject that can be, [that is], religion" (VS579, F436).

Montaigne's radical reform of both philosophy and politics must be seen in light of the distinction between sacred tradition and non-sacred traditions. Not only does he introduce a new order within the philosophical and political spheres, but also his understanding of the essence of sacred tradition demands that new order.

The Errors of Reformation

Montaigne's adherence to sacred tradition often becomes explicit in response to the threat that the Reformation poses to Catholicism: in his lifetime, the reformers' attack on the Catholic Church had brought about the condition of civil war in France. Montaigne opposes the Reformation for many reasons, but above all because he sees it as the dissolution of the social bond.[11] Beneath this, however, lies a deeper opposition to the Protestant understanding of the human being and of the relationship of the human to the divine.

The Church is a "public and immutable" institution. The "innovations of Luther" were already shaking "our ancient belief," and the teaching concerning "personal consent" would inevitably lead to atheism (VS439, F320). The teaching concerning personal consent goes precisely against the authority of sacred tradition. So also does the practice of private interpretation of the Bible. The Protestant principle of personal consent, including private interpretation of Scripture, also means the privatization of religion. As Francis Slade writes: "Christianity cannot live in the privacy of the heart. It is the religion of publicness. To cease to profess it publicly is 'to lose the Faith.' This is because Christianity is the religion of truth."[12] Tradition has an inherently public status and claim to authority. "Private reason" can have only a private status.

Montaigne regards the Protestant attempt to reform morals as superficial, and even dangerous, because it is based on new opinions: "Those who in my time have tried to correct the world's morals by new opinions, reform the superficial vices; the essential ones they leave as they were, if they do not increase them" (VS811, F615). Yet, Montaigne suggests that he himself is engaged in a project of reform: "Oh what an easy and applauded route those superficial men take, compared with ours!" (VS888, F677). His reform, however, is not by new opinions but by old opinions. New opinions cannot reach to the essential level at which mores begin.

The most fundamental level of Montaigne's criticism, then, concerns the way in which the Reformation understands the human being himself. "As for those who, in recent years, tried to construct for us a system of religious practice that is all contemplative and spiritual, they should not be astounded if there are some who think that religion would have melted away and slipped through their fingers if it did not hold fast among us as a mark, title, and instrument of division and faction rather than by itself" (VS930, F710). His comments on Numa, the Roman king and legislator who tried to attach the piety of his people to a purely intellectual religion, actually pertain to the Reformation: "The human spirit cannot keep on floating in this infinity of formless ideas; they must be compiled for it into a definite picture after its own pattern. The divine majesty has thus let itself be somewhat circumscribed within corporeal limits on our behalf; his supernatural and heavenly sacraments show signs of our earthly condition; his worship is expressed by perceptible rituals and words; for it is a man that believes and prays" (VS513, F381).[13]

The reformers' attempt to institute a purely spiritual and intellectual religion is manifested clearly in the attack on images. In *The Stripping of the Altars: Traditional Religion in England 1400–1580,* historian Eamon Duffy demonstrates that "iconoclasm was the central sacrament of reform." The eradication of sacred images is "the sacrament of forgetfulness" and thus one of the most important instruments for the destruction of the traditional religion.[14] Against the iconoclasts, Montaigne defends the use of images, especially the crucifix: "I leave aside the other arguments that are employed on this subject. But I could hardly be made to believe that the sight of our crucifixes and the pictures of that piteous agony, the ornaments and ceremonious movements in our churches, the voices attuned to the piety of our thoughts, and that stirring of the senses, do not warm the souls of the people with religious emotion very beneficial in effect" (VS513–14, F381). Montaigne says of the sign of the cross: "it is a sign that I revere and continually use" (VS319, F231). For Catholics at the time of the Reformation, "the Crucifix was the icon of Christ's abiding solidarity with suffering humanity."[15]

The stance of the Reformation toward the human being might be considered a form of rationalism. The Reformation's entirely spiritual and intellectual form of religion, with its disdain for the senses and for images as idolatry, betrays a misunderstanding both of what it means to be human and of who God is. Montaigne recognizes that his adherence to the Catholic faith in contemporary religious conflicts might appear unreflective and irrational simply because the faith is inherited. But he rejects explicitly what he regards as a presumptuous prejudice: "How fantastic seemed to me the imagination of those who in recent years had the habit of reproaching each and every man in whom there gleamed some light of intelligence and who professed the Catholic religion, with dissimulation; and who even maintained, thinking to do him honor, that whatever he said for appearance, he could not help having his belief within reformed according to their measure. . . . They may take my word for it: if anything were to have tempted my youth, ambition for the risk and difficulties that attended this recent enterprise would have played a good part in it" (VS320, F231–32). In admitting that ambition for the risk and difficulties of the Reformation might have tempted him, Montaigne suggests that he himself is engaged in a project of reform. At the same time, however, he implies that, whatever innovations he himself intends, they will not be based on the rejection of the old ways, but rather on the foundation of the sacred tradition.

In "It Is Folly to Measure the True and the False by Our Own Capacity" Montaigne makes Pieper's point about the way in which sacred tradition holds together: even what appear to be trivial and therefore dispensable matters are actually very important. "Now, what seems to me to bring as much disorder into our consciences as anything, in these religious troubles that we are in, is this partial surrender of their beliefs by Catholics. It seems to them that they are being very moderate and understanding when they yield to their opponents some of the articles in dispute. But, besides the fact that they do not see what an advantage it is to a man charging you for you to begin to give ground and withdraw, and how much that encourages him to pursue his point, those articles which they select as the most trivial are sometimes very important. We must either submit completely to the authority of our ecclesiastical government, or do without it completely. It is not for us to decide what portion of obedience we owe it. Moreover, I can say this for having tried it. In other days I exercised this freedom of personal choice and selection." But now he accepts fully the authority of "our ecclesiastical polity." The observances of the Church have "a massive and very solid foundation" (VS182, F134–35).

Separating the Essential from the Nonessential

Montaigne's opposition to the Reformation is crucial to understanding his stance toward sacred tradition. However, he also breaks with the Catholic tradition insofar as he sees it to be dependent upon classical philosophy, especially Aristotle, and classical values. This break comes through especially in his relationship with his father, from whom he inherited his Catholicism, his goodness, and his fortunate disposition. Throughout the essays he praises his father as "the best father that ever was" (VS440, F320); yet, Montaigne points to two important ways in which he himself differs from his father.

At the beginning of the "Apology for Sebond" he recounts that he had translated Sebond's book on natural theology into French at his father's request. His father had been given the book by Pierre Bunel, a very learned man, who had been a guest in his house. Montaigne's father was "inflamed with that new ardor" for letters and "sought with great diligence and expense the acquaintance of learned men, receiving them at his house like holy persons having some particular inspiration of divine wisdom, collecting their sayings and discourses like oracles, and with all the more reverence and religion as he was less qualified to judge them; for he had no knowledge of letters, any more than his predecessors." The son says: "Myself, I like them well enough, but I do not worship them" (VS439, F319). By saying that he does not worship learning Montaigne points to and rejects the Aristotelian teaching concerning the divinity of the intellect, a teaching that, strictly speaking, medieval theology also rejects (since nothing within the created world is divine), but which is nevertheless preserved in the theological claim that man is in the image of God by virtue of his intellect. Montaigne distances himself from his father's almost religious reverence, which also reflects the tradition's view, for human knowledge.

The second way in which Montaigne breaks with his father concerns the status of public service. In "Of Husbanding Your Will" Montaigne tells us that he warned the magistrates of Bordeaux, who had elected him mayor, that he does not have the same attitude toward public service as his father had. His father had grown old and sick because the weight of public affairs had lain so heavily upon him. "He was like that; and this disposition in him sprang from a great goodness of nature: there never was a more charitable and public-spirited soul." However, "this course, which I commend in others, I do not love to follow, and I am not without excuse. He had heard it said that we must forget ourselves for our neighbor, that the particular was not to be considered at all in comparison with the general" (VS1006, F769). Montaigne suggests that his father had identified his activities as mayor with the theological virtue of charity. Further, he implies that this is what his father had been taught, perhaps in connection with the admonition of Christ to love one's neighbor as oneself.

The two ways in which Montaigne breaks with his father seem to be about philosophical contemplation and political life, the two kinds of human perfection put forward by Aristotle and adopted, albeit in a transformed way, by medieval Christian thought. For Aristotle, human perfection is twofold: the philosophical act of contemplation in which the human being participates in the divine, and the life of moral virtue displayed in the activity of politics. Medieval theology had adopted the classical view of the world, especially the Aristotelian hierarchical account of being, and classical philosophy had become thoroughly intertwined with Christianity. The contemplative life of the philosopher was preserved in the ascetic and contemplative life of the monastery. The classical moral virtues persist while the theological virtues are added on to make a complete picture of the moral life. And the Aristotelian standard of "the common good" is preserved as the end of politics, so that the political realm remains the locus of the human good in this world.

Montaigne's separation of the core of sacred tradition from the philosophy of Aristotle shows itself with respect to both forms of human perfection. Philosophy becomes unpremeditated and accidental, a merely human, not a divine, activity. The pride of the philosopher is thus overcome. The philosopher is just a man, like any other. This "lowering" of philosophy and the philosopher makes the invention of society possible, for society requires the overcoming of the Aristotelian hierarchy. The social, rather than the political, becomes the locus of the human good.

Repentance of the Intellect

Montaigne's overcoming of the pride of the philosopher entails what might be called a "repentance of the intellect," a kind of repentance that is understood in relation to the God who reveals himself in the Bible. In *Mystery and Philosophy,* Michael B. Foster contrasts the God of the Bible with the idea of the divine in Greek philosophy. God in the Bible is hidden, in contrast to the unhiddenness of being for Greek philosophy. The God of the Bible makes himself known, but only by an act of will or grace: "It is not his nature to be unhidden."[16] Foster claims that "belief in a divine Revelation seems to involve something like a repentance in the sphere of the intellect."[17] The philosopher, such as Aristotle, who thinks that the mind can not only know the divine but is itself also divine in the act of contemplation, is guilty of pride; it is this pride of the philosopher that Montaigne repents of. The requirement of repentance of the intellect is "alien to our main philosophical tradition which has inherited from Greek philosophy the belief in the divinity of the intellect."[18]

Montaigne's essay "Of Repentance" is often cited to prove that his adherence to Catholicism is superficial at best, for he seems to deny that he has any need to repent. It is true that he says "I rarely repent" (VS806, F612), and "if I had to live over again, I would live as I have lived" (VS816, F620). But he also says: "I know no superficial, halfway, and perfunctory repentance. It must affect me in every part before I will call it so, and must grip me by the vitals and afflict them as deeply and as completely as God sees into me" (VS813, F617). He does repent, then, but only deeply and completely.

There are two places in the *Essays* in which Montaigne suggests such repentance, and both have to do with a "descent" to the simple and lowly. Montaigne sticks to the old ways: he has come through error and has arrived at "the extreme limit of Christian intelligence." Of those who have come through error, some have become violent and immoderate in the defense of the Catholic side in the civil wars. Others, however, have returned to the old ways "with marvelous profit and confirmation, as at the extreme limit of Christian intelligence, and . . . enjoy their victory with consolation, active gratitude, reformed conduct, and great modesty" (VS312–13, F227). Sticking to the old ways means being one with the simple and thus giving the appearance of stupidity. Repentance of the intellect necessarily entails moral reformation—a real outward, as well as inner, conversion—because the pride of the philosopher is only overcome in recognition of his common humanity and his oneness with the most lowly human beings.

In "It Is Folly to Judge the True and the False by Our Own Capacity" Montaigne tells of his youthful attempt to exercise his "personal choice" with respect to the beliefs of the faith. However, he came through that error and acknowledged the authority of the Church. Looking back on that time of his life, he writes: "It is foolish presumption to go around disdaining and condemning as false whatever does not seem likely to us; which is an ordinary vice in those who think they have more than common ability. I used to do so once; and if I heard of returning spirits, prognostications of future events, enchantments, sorcery, or some other story that I could not swallow, . . . I felt compassion for the poor people who were taken in by these follies. And now I think that I was at least as much to be pitied myself" (VS178–79, F132). His openness to the testimony of the simple and his submission to the simplicity of the old ways manifest his complete and deep repentance.

The Dialectic of Faith and Reason in the "Apology for Sebond"

The "Apology for Sebond" is the strongest evidence for those who hold that Montaigne is a skeptic-fideist, i.e., that he is a skeptic on the philosophical level and a believer who believes "simply," without any support from reason. Montaigne wrote this apology as a response to two criticisms commonly made to the theologian Sebond's *Natural Theology, or The Book of Creatures* and other such works in natural theology. (Montaigne reports that someone told him that Sebond's book was actually a kind of distillation of the teachings of Thomas Aquinas.)[19]

In the "Prologue" to his work, Sebond claims that God has revealed himself both in the Bible and in nature and that it is possible to prove the truths of faith by reason. The first objection to Sebond's theology is put forward in the name of piety by those who think of themselves as believers. They say that "Christians do themselves harm in trying to support their belief by human reasons, since it is conceived only by faith and by a particular inspiration of divine grace" (VS440, F321). The second objection is put forward by unbelievers and atheists. Sebond's arguments, they say, are "weak and unfit to prove what he proposes," and these unbelievers set out to shatter Sebond's arguments with ease (VS448, F327). Those who see Montaigne as an atheist place him on the side of the second objection. Those who see him as a skeptic-fideist place him on the side of the first objection. Montaigne, however, refutes both objections and he also finds something true in each objection, so that any interpretation of the "Apology" that places him simply on either side must be inadequate.

The two objections, as formulated by Montaigne, are usually regarded as opposites, as the opposing and contradictory voices of belief and unbelief. Frédéric Brahami, for example, says that "the second objection is diametrically opposed to the first" and that "these two radical positions, that of belief and that of unbelief undermine the synthesis of Sebond."[20] But when these objections are exposed more fully, they show themselves to be related to each other and even dependent on each other at a deeper level. The first objection defines faith in terms of its origin: faith is "belief that is conceived only by faith and by a particular inspiration of divine grace." God inspires those whom it pleases him to inspire: that is why they believe, and others do not. There is a direct communication by God to the mind of the believer. Faith, then, is taken to be private, inarticulate, and incommunicable. The second objection is a reaction against the possibility of faith but it also accepts this understanding of what faith is. Unbelief must see faith as a private experience, an experience that it ultimately regards as illusory because it is publicly indefensible.

Rationality prides itself in being both public and common. In the first place, it is completely transparent and communicable: when the demonstrations of Euclidean geometry are displayed, for example, they can be understood by any rational human being and they receive universal assent. The truths of faith, of course, do not receive universal assent. Secondly, rationality is universal, the defining characteristic of the human species, whereas particular inspiration is not universal. Therefore, on this view of reason, faith (understood as particular inspiration) cannot give a public account of itself. It is defenseless before the court of reason. The first and second objections, then, share the same understanding of the meaning of faith. It is this shared understanding that gives rise to the dialectic of the two objections, and it is this shared understanding that Montaigne is most deeply concerned to refute.

Montaigne's defense of the mind's place in the life of faith leads him directly into the second objection. In the process of responding to the understanding of faith in the first objection, he just suddenly finds himself speaking in the voice of unbelief. He says: "I have already, without thinking about it, half involved myself in the second objection" (VS448, F327). The way in which Montaigne falls into the second objection and the way he characterizes reason from the very beginning of his response suggests that, once reason is invited in, it claims for itself an authority that ultimately admits no other authority. Now it must be said that this presumption of reason is very similar to the position taken by Sebond's natural theology: man is said to be in the image of God by virtue of his reason. This, of course, is why Montaigne's "defense" of Sebond seems ambiguous and even ironic: an attack on reason is an attack on the second objection but, at the same time, it is an attack on Sebond's entire project of natural theology. In attacking the arrogance of reason, Montaigne is acknowledging what is true in the first objection, namely, that Christians do themselves harm by seeking to support their faith by reason, if reason is presumed to be the autonomous reason of the second objection. So also, in refuting the first objection and thus demanding public evidence of faith, he acknowledges what is true in the second objection, namely, the indefensibility of claims to private inspiration.

Montaigne's skeptical response to the second objection leads to the conclusion that reason, to which we had turned for a common ground, is so highly particularized that it cannot serve as the common, public ground we were seeking. The logic of his response to the first objection drove Montaigne to the common, public, universal ground of reason. But autonomous reason, instead of being the solid rock on which to build anything common, turns out to be a mere dream or, worse, a nightmare that dissolves into chaos.

Where, then, does Montaigne himself stand on the question of the relation of faith and reason, at least insofar as his stand is revealed in the dialectic of the two objections? Is he, in fact, a skeptic-fideist? We can begin to answer this by returning to the issue of his sincerity in calling this essay a "defense" of Sebond. The tendency has been to see Montaigne's apology for Sebond as either completely ironic or as unselfconsciously ambiguous and self-contradictory because, if he is either an atheist or a skeptic fideist, then he must deny any harmony or compatibility between faith and reason, and compatibility is Sebond's most fundamental assumption.

If we see the two objections in their relation to each other and follow the movement of Montaigne's thought as he works his way through the objections and their shared understandings of reason and faith, we find that he is in fact defending a transformed version of Sebond's assumption. Montaigne calls this essay an apology for Sebond because he does affirm the harmony of faith and reason—but not faith as defined in the first objection and not reason as assumed in the second objection. Faith as defined in the first objection is incomplete, imperfect, and even presumptuous: it is unexamined belief and it must be completed and in some way transformed in its dialectic with reason. The autonomous reason of the second objection is proud and presumptuous: it must be reformed in its dialectic with faith.

In "Of Vain Subtleties," as we have seen, Montaigne refers to the error of those who regard his "sticking to the old ways" as due to simplicity and stupidity. It turns out that his sticking to the old ways is "the extreme limit of Christian intelligence." In "It Is Folly to Measure the True and the False by Our Own Capacity" he comes to see that his skepticism concerning the testimony of the simple was pitiable because it was due to the presumption of the learned that what they have never experienced themselves must be impossible. Now Montaigne is subject neither to the unthinking credulity of the simple nor to the arrogant presumption of the learned.

That same movement of thought is just what occurs in the dialectic of the two objections in the "Apology." From simple inarticulate belief, he ascends through doubt to autonomous rationality and then descends through doubt to the truth of faith. Of course he cannot simply return to or deliberately adopt the stance of unthinking belief as if he had never ascended from it. He ends up in a kind of middle position that transcends both simple credulity and learned skepticism, and that, in philosophical terms, would be called "learned ignorance."

Perhaps this is what T. S. Eliot has in mind when he says that "what makes Montaigne a very great figure is that he succeeded . . . in giving expression to the skepticism of *every* human being. For every man who thinks and lives by thought must have his own skepticism, that which stops at the question, that which ends in denial, or that which leads to faith and is somehow integrated into the faith which transcends it."[21] Montaigne's skepticism is integrated into the faith which transcends it. The faith that has transcended and transformed doubt is not an unthinking and inarticulate faith but Montaigne's way of living the examined life as a Christian.

At the beginning of his reply to the second objection, Montaigne says that the means he will take to beat down the pride and presumption of those who advance the second objection is "to make them feel the inanity, the vanity, and the nothingness of man" (VS448, F327). How will he do this? "St. Augustine, arguing against these people, has good cause to reproach them for their injustice in that they hold those parts of our belief to be false which our reason fails to establish. And to show that there can have been plenty of things whose nature and causes our reason cannot possibly establish, he puts before his adversaries certain known and indubitable experiences into which man confesses he has no insight." Presumably, Montaigne is referring to the *City of God* (especially book 21, chapter 5), where Augustine makes this argument and gives examples, mostly from Pliny, of natural marvels. But Montaigne does not propose to follow Augustine's procedure. Rather, he says, "we must do more, and teach them that to convict our reason of weakness, there is no need to go sifting out rare examples" (VS449, F328). "Doing more than St. Augustine" might plausibly be understood to imply a defense of a thoroughgoing skepticism. But seen within the dialectic of faith and reason, "doing more than St. Augustine" means showing the ordinary to be extraordinary. Montaigne's movement of thought reveals the strange in the familiar, the extraordinary in the ordinary. The world is restored through true faith to its astonishing strangeness. A world created out of nothing, a world in which the Word was made flesh, is revealed as such in the philosophical activity that ends in wonder at the most familiar.[22]

Sacramental and Incarnational Metaphysics

The way in which Montaigne holds fast to sacred tradition amounts to nothing less than a reordering of the mind and of being itself. He sticks to the old ways because his understanding of the world is what might be called a sacramental and incarnational metaphysics: the reversal of the Aristotelian order and the relocation of the divine in the lowest rather than the highest. The Catholic tradition brings into everyday life its sacramental and incarnational metaphysics: the everyday world is thoroughly intertwined and imbued with the sacred.

Montaigne says: "In my opinion, from the most ordinary, common, and familiar things, if we could put them in their proper light, can be formed the greatest miracles of nature and the most marvelous examples, especially on the subject of human actions" (VS1081, F829). The "proper light," the way in which the most ordinary, common, and familiar things can be seen as marvelous and miraculous, is that they embody the sacred. Indeed, this is what happens in the *Essays:* the familiar becomes astonishing. The everyday is not astonishing because of something extraneous being brought into it. The everyday shows the presence of God not through reason, not in the highest, but in the lowest and most hidden human actions. Sacred tradition gets down into the lowest aspects of "mere" life. The everyday is the incarnation of the sacred.

In his "Notes Towards the Definition of Culture," T. S. Eliot describes the conditions for the kind of common culture that Montaigne presupposes: "While we believe that the same religion may inform a variety of cultures, we may ask whether any culture could come into being, or maintain itself, without a religious basis. We may go further and ask whether what we call the culture, and what we call the religion, of a people are not different aspects of the same thing: the culture being, essentially, the incarnation (so to speak) of the religion of a people."[23] The situation that Eliot describes is one in which "the culture of an artist or a philosopher is distinct from that of a mine worker or a field labourer; the culture of a poet will be somewhat different from that of a politician; but in a healthy society these are all parts of the same culture."[24] Specifically, the mode of being of Europe cannot be understood apart from its Christian culture: "It is in Christianity that our arts have developed; it is in Christianity that the laws of Europe have—until recently—been rooted. It is against a background of Christianity that all our thought has significance."[25] Eliot's account of the way in which culture is the incarnation of religious belief, the embodiment, as it were, of religion in everyday life, articulates how culture can be the source of unity through the metaphysical beliefs of religion that penetrate to the deepest levels of everyday life.

What I have called Montaigne's sacramental and incarnational metaphysics can be seen especially in the way the sacraments are present in the *Essays*. The sacraments are related to incarnational metaphysics because they gather the everyday materials of life itself (water, bread, and wine) and make these elements sacred. Montaigne brings baptism, penance, extreme unction, and the Eucharist into the flow of his thought and expression in a way that is so "natural" that it is easy to miss their significance. His father had him held over the baptismal font by villagers of the lowest condition in order to attach him and oblige him to them (VS1100, F844). In the sacrament of extreme unction (the last rites), the priest anoints all of the five senses in the sign of the cross. Montaigne says that, when he becomes very ill, "I reconcile myself with God by the last Christian offices, and find myself thereby more free and unburdened" (VS982, F751). He mentions that the Mass is still celebrated in the chapel in his house, while all of the churches around his house have been emptied and ruined by the reformers (VS966, F738). The *Essays* have the sense of confession, and Montaigne refers to his work as a public confession (VS846, F643). His repentance is both deep and complete for it is a repentance of the intellect and of the will.

The apparent absence of piety in the *Essays* leads most readers to conclude that Montaigne is insincere in his professions of faith. I would argue, on the contrary, that this absence is in fact meant to make the sacred fit into the flow of everyday life. When he says, for example, that "we are Christians by the same title that we are Perigordians or Germans" (VS445, F325), he does not intend to reduce Catholicism to the status of custom but rather to acknowledge the way in which the divine, as sacred tradition, is embedded in the accidents of human life.

The clearest expression of the presence of the sacred in the everyday concerns the Eucharist. As Eamon Duffy says of the Mass on the eve of the Reformation: the body on the communion cloth is "the emblem and the instrument of all truly human embodiment."[26] Our own being is neither divine nor angelic, but embodied. The domestic and private are the anchor of that embodiment and the locus of the human good.

In "To the Reader" Montaigne elaborates on what he means by his domestic and private end. His essays are the means by which his friends and relatives will "nourish" more completely and vividly their knowledge of him after he dies.[27] This allusion to food is then taken up again at the very end of the *Essays,* where Montaigne mentions food in a very unusual way. Speaking of those Christian ascetics and contemplatives who despise the bodily pleasures, Montaigne says that they anticipate, "by dint of keen and vehement hope, the enjoyment of eternal food, final end and last stop of Christian desires, sole constant and incorruptible pleasure" (VS1114, F856). These are the ascetics whose "transcendental humors" frighten him. Here, he brings them down to the everyday, to this world, in this extraordinary reference to the Beatific Vision—the supposed purely spiritual and intellectual pleasure of the contemplation of God—as eternal food. Montaigne describes even this purely spiritual and intellectual joy of the vision of God in terms of the everyday enjoyment of the pleasures of eating.

According to Eamon Duffy, "the rhythms of the liturgy on the eve of the Reformation remained the rhythms of life itself."[28] The sacramental and incarnational character of the *Essays* accounts for the way in which Montaigne's Catholicism is almost invisible in this work. The sacred and the mundane are linked in such a way that the everyday is permeated with the divine, which is therefore not easily distinguished from the lowliest actions. Pascal's thought also moves within this hiddenness of the divine: "Just as Jesus remained unknown among men, so the truth remains among popular opinions with no outward difference. Thus the Eucharist and ordinary bread."[29] The sacred is just "in there" with the everyday, but this does not destroy its character as sacred and divine. As C. S. Lewis puts it: "Common bread, miraculous bread, sacramental bread—these three are distinct, but not to be separated."[30] What is revered in the sacrament is what is already present in common matter. Sacred tradition is hidden first in everyday life (bread and wine) and is made visible, that is, public, in the sacramental life of the Church.

Oakeshott's view of religion might well serve as a description of Montaigne's own stance toward sacred tradition: "Religion, then, is not . . . an interest attached to life, a subsidiary activity; nor is it a power which governs life from the outside with a, no doubt divine, but certainly incomprehensible, sanction for its authority. It is simply life itself, life dominated by the belief that its value is in the present, not merely in the past or future, that if we lose ourselves, we lose all."[31] To say that religion is life itself is to say that we do not need to transport ourselves into the "other world" or to the "supernatural" realm in order to experience the divine in our lives. Rather, the divine is present in our lives in this world.

Refounding Society

Montaigne insists that the Church is a public institution that constitutes the social bond: it is the Church that makes society possible. The nature of the society that Montaigne regards as possible is a union of men that is determined not by territory, but by the universal bonds of truth and of goodness. Montaigne's adherence to the old ways is not merely formal: the truth and goodness required for the social bond are the essential content of sacred tradition. It is this essential core that Montaigne preserves and brings to light in his invention of modern society.

Montaigne says that, whereas the ancient philosophers taught that religion is merely a human contrivance to bind society together, our sovereign creator has "freed our belief" and "based it on the eternal foundation of his holy word" (VS579, F437). The basis of the classical forms of human association is a lie, albeit a "noble lie." The foundation of Montaigne's new form of society is truth. Not only does Christianity claim to be true, but it also holds that truth to be accessible to all men, to the most simple peasant woman as to the most learned theologian. Thus, the pride of the philosopher (that he is among the few who possess the truth) is overcome in the submission of the philosopher to the old ways of the simple.

Although Montaigne claims that the *Essays* are entirely human, with "no admixture of theology," there is one instance in which he does, in fact, call upon the help of theology. In "Of Cruelty" he defends his sympathy with the animals, a sympathy that makes him appear weak. "And so that people will not laugh at this sympathy that I have with them, Theology herself orders us to show some favor in their regard; and considering that one and the same master has lodged us in this place for his service, and that they, like ourselves, are of his family, she is right to enjoin upon us some respect and affection toward them" (VS433, F316). Montaigne is here elaborating on the principal theme of this essay: cruelty is the extreme of all vice. Although cruelty had always been regarded as a vice in both classical and Christian morality, Montaigne is the first to claim that it is the extreme of all vice. His reordering of the virtues and vices is intended to foster the social virtues by overcoming the distance—of which cruelty is the outward expression—between weak and strong through sympathy and compassion.

In the "Apology for Sebond," especially in his reply to the first objection, Montaigne is highly critical of the cruel conduct of those who call themselves Christians on both sides in the civil wars of his day. They use religion as a pretext for giving vent to their vicious passions, their cruelty, ambition, hatred, and avarice. So also, in "Of Coaches," he describes the extreme cruelty of the Spanish conquerors toward the people of the New World. "Would it be as a testimonial to their justice or their zeal for religion? Truly, those are ways too contrary and hostile to so holy an end. If they had proposed to extend our faith, they would have reflected that faith is not spread by possession of territory but by possession of men" (VS913, F697).

In "Of Cruelty" it is sympathy that ultimately shows itself to be the goodness that he inherits from his father. And it is sympathy rather than the strength of virtue that serves as the new basis for morality. Sympathy looks weak—and that is why he must call in the help of theology to defend himself from the derision of the strong—but it is actually divine. In "The Nature and Meaning of Sociality" Oakeshott argues that "God is the only principle of sociability which will explain the facts of life. Society becomes possible [only] by religion." Thus, Oakeshott interprets "God is Love" to mean "God is the only principle of sociality."[32]

For Montaigne, the spiritual power of the Church is inextricably linked to the transformation of the relation between the nobility and the people. It is, after all, his baptism that unites him to the poorest of the poor. Montaigne's father had sent him to the poorest village in his neighborhood to be nursed and had him held over the baptismal font by villagers of the lowest condition in order to attach and oblige him to them. "His plan," Montaigne says, "succeeded not at all badly. I give myself willingly to the little people, whether because there is more glory in it, or through natural compassion, which has infinite power over me" (VS1100, F844). Glory, natural compassion, and the grace of baptism are indistinguishable in him, and therefore he shares in the life of both the lowest and the highest in society. Eamon Duffy insists on "the social homogeneity of late medieval religion."[33] As he demonstrates: "Rich and poor, simple and sophisticate could kneel side by side, using the same prayers and sharing the same hopes." In spite of the differences of sophistication about the faith, "they did not have a different religion."[34]

The Church offers the possibility of a union among men that transcends natural and social inequality and is based on a foundation of truth. In both "It Is Folly to Measure the True and the False by Our Own Capacity" and "Of Vain Subtleties," Montaigne's turn to the lowly and common is identified or associated with his return to the Church and a renewed grasp of the meaning of the Church. In both of these accounts of his submission to sacred tradition, Montaigne descends, as it were, to the simple and identifies himself with their beliefs. The Church is "that great common way" (VS520, F387). The distinction between the learned and the common herd does not obtain within the Church for there "we are all the vulgar" (VS570, F429). As Roger Scruton observes: "When religious faith declines it becomes difficult for intellectuals to believe that they really belong to the same community as ordinary people."[35]

Montaigne is, I believe, the only modern political philosopher who defends the Catholic Church in its universality, the only one who does not recommend that it be subordinated to the state, or that it merely be tolerated as one among many religions within the state. By his allegiance to the Church as the universal bond, Montaigne does indeed weaken the national bond. From the point of view of the universal bond, the national bond is secondary and appears arbitrary. The Church transcends the limits of the political and stands as an independent authority and, therefore, as a limit on the power of the state.

The universal and common bond has its source in a universal and common city. Rome is "the only common and universal city. The sovereign magistrate who commands there is acknowledged equally elsewhere. It is the metropolitan city of all Christian nations; the Spaniard and the Frenchman, every man is at home there. To be one of the princes of that state one need only be of Christendom, wherever it may be" (VS997, F763). In his *Travel Journal,* Montaigne makes a similar claim: Rome is "the most universal city in the world, a place where strangeness and differences of nationality are considered least; for by its nature it is a city pieced together out of foreigners; everyone is as if at home. Its ruler embraces Christendom with his authority; his princely jurisdiction is binding on foreigners in their own homes just as here. At his own election and that of all the princes and grandees of his court the consideration of their origin has no weight."[36] The Church is the society in which the origins do not matter.

The Church is the proof of the possibility of society and is also the only possibility for multicultural society. This means, however, that society cannot be understood in terms of the boundaries of territory and language. The society of men is a union that is not limited by space and time. "We embrace both those who have been and those who are not yet" (VS976, F746). As Pieper maintains: "We should not forget that the common possession of the sacred tradition creates a fundamental *unity* of all mankind, really a unity in relation to that foundation of spiritual life that—hidden but very real—first makes communication among human beings possible and worth attempting."[37]

In his essay "Where Is Christendom?" Etienne Gilson reflects upon his travels in the United States, Europe, and the Soviet Union. Recalling the moment when he entered a church in Chicago, he asks "Where was I? Neither in America nor in France, nor at any geographical point on earth. Yet I had surely reached a journey's end, since I was at home: I was in Christendom." Wherever there is a parish church, there is Christendom.[38] Gilson explains the basis for this sentiment: "The same Mass, the same priests, the same communion in the same God given by the same priests to the faithful of the same faith—all this creates, at every moment and in every place, an immense spiritual society which knows neither geographic barriers nor political boundaries and in which the Christian always feels that he is at home."[39]

This universal society of Christendom is not to be identified simply with the Church itself. "As subject to the State, we Christians are all members of a society of which the State is seeking the common temporal end; as subject to the Church, we are all members of a society of which the Church is seeking the common spiritual end, and the very temporal part of the Church is integrally directed to this end; as members of Christendom, we are part of a third social group, one that is neither quite the State nor quite the Church, but one that is formed by the various members of the various states in so far as they are aware of belonging to the same Church and of being all disciples of Christ."[40] This third level of society might be described as the common culture of Christendom.

Montaigne expresses this sentiment when he writes: "If I were afraid to die in any other place than that of my birth, if I thought I would die less comfortably away from my family, I should scarcely go out of France; I should not go out of my parish without terror" (VS978, F747). He is, however, careless about where he will die because he is "at home" everywhere and "at home" in this world. In fact, Montaigne (who did not want his death to say anything that his life had not already said) died in his home at Mass at the elevation of the Host.

Montaigne refounds philosophy and human society by bringing out the core of sacred tradition, by discovering and bringing to light what was always there but hidden. The new is really the old. In this way, he changes the relationship between the eternal and the temporal as it was understood by ancient philosophy and as it was inherited by medieval theology. The temporal is not subsumed under the eternal. Rather, in Montaigne's incarnational metaphysics, the eternal is brought into time.

Chapter Three

The Philosophical Act (I): Judgment

For Montaigne, the philosophical act is neither contemplation nor practical wisdom, neither escape to the eternal nor immersion in the immediacy of practice. Rather, the philosophical act is judgment, purged of the self of the philosopher. Judgment subjects reason to the good. The philosophical act overcomes the traditional hierarchy and brings the new out of the old. In redefining this act, Montaigne surmounts the presumption of Aristotle, the pride of the philosopher, and separates the man from the philosopher.

To claim that the philosophical act is judgment is also to deny that Montaigne is a skeptic. The outcome of skepticism is not true judgment but the suspension of judgment. Although in some ways Montaigne's practice of essaying resembles the skeptical practice of weighing opposing perspectives on a given topic, his goal is neither suspension of judgment nor the imperturbability that results from it. And although Montaigne is cautious in giving assent, he does make judgments throughout the essays. Further, his judgment is not passively receptive: it effects a reordering of the human world.[1]

In chapter 2 I offer a reading of the "Apology for Sebond," the essay which provides the strongest evidence for the claim that Montaigne is a skeptic. In spite of his high praise of skepticism and the skeptics in that essay, Montaigne goes beyond traditional skepticism to be open to the possible and the astonishing character of the familiar. This aspect of his thought will be brought out more fully in chapter 4. In chapters 5, 6, and 7, I discuss the moral and political judgments that are central to Montaigne's philosophical project. Here again, in spite of his remarkable tolerance for differences of opinion, the freedom and autonomy that he introduces are not grounded in moral skepticism.

Beginning in Thought

The *Essays* present a man immersed in the world of thought, a man who must achieve his own mind within the world of inherited opinion.

Montaigne brings forth something new against the background of that inherited world. He brings forth the possible out of what would have seemed impossible.

The world of inherited opinion is a confused world in which true and false are mixed together with no obvious way to distinguish them. Montaigne shows us three conditions of error and falsehood which the philosophical act must overcome. The contexts in which he presents these conditions reveal the nature of the philosophical act in its overcoming of error and falsehood.

First, true opinions are mixed in with false opinions. Montaigne says that he is able to sift the true from the false. In "Of Presumption" he writes: "This capacity for sifting truth, whatever it may amount to in me, and this free humor not to subject my belief easily, I owe it principally to myself: for the most firm imaginations that I have, and the most general, are those which, in a manner of speaking, were born with me. They are natural and all mine. I produced them crude and simple, of a production bold and strong, but a little troubled and imperfect. Since then I have established and fortified them by the authority of others, and by the sound discourse of the ancients, with whom I found my judgment conformed: these have assured me a firmer grip on them and have given me the enjoyment of them and a more entire possession" (VS658, F499). He can distinguish the true from the false because his most firm and general "imaginations" were produced by himself, or generated by his own mind. They are his first beliefs. What he has always believed is true because he has always believed it. His study of the ancient philosophers has only confirmed these first opinions and made them more "his own." This, in fact, just looks like presumption: what is his own is true and ancient philosophy simply confirms him in this presumption. The philosophical act, then, must overcome, in some way, this most basic form of presumption. In returning to his first opinions, Montaigne actually introduces something new.

The mind's activity of generation is central to Montaigne's understanding of the philosophical act. "I let fly my caprices all the more freely in public, inasmuch as, although they are born with me and without a model, I know that they will find their relation to some ancient humor; and someone will not fail to say: 'That is where he got it' " (VS546, F409). His caprices are original. That is, they are born with him, generated by his mind, and not copied from anyone else: they are "without a model." But they resemble the sayings of ancient philosophy, and that is why he is "an unpremeditated and accidental philosopher." His caprices are new, but he does not want them to appear to be new. Rather, he is content to let them appear to be old for he is bringing the new out of the old.

Montaigne provides the second formulation of the condition of error in "Of Vain Subtleties." He always presents himself as a nameless type that must be articulated in the terms of the ancient hierarchy but that cannot really be accounted for within that hierarchy. There are, he says, two kinds of good Christians: the simple who accept without question the beliefs of the Church, and the learned who have made a profound study of the Church and Scripture and have penetrated into the meaning of what is believed. Then there is a third type: those who "stick to the old ways" but not on account of simplicity and stupidity and not on account of study. Unlike the reformers who reject the tradition, this third type does stick to the old ways, but in a way that is different from both the simple and the learned. This third type has reached "the extreme limit of Christian intelligence." This, we assume, is Montaigne himself. However, in this "middle region" of men, the region between the simple and the learned, error is "engendered." Those who "stop at the appearance of the first sense" assume that men like Montaigne, who stick to the old ways, do so out of simplicity and stupidity. They mistake the cause because they cannot get beyond first appearances. This means that first appearances are, or can be, misleading. The error here pertains to causes. They assume that the same effect must be produced by the same cause. The "middle region," then, offers two opposing possibilities: error and the extreme limit of Christian intelligence.

In this essay, Montaigne offers several other presentations of his status as a nameless third type.[2] First, there are two kinds of good men: the simple peasants and the philosophers who are strong and enriched by learning. Then there are the "half-breeds" who have disdained ignorance of letters but are unable to reach the status of the philosophers: "their rear-end between two stools, like me, and so many others." These half-breeds are "dangerous" and "trouble the world." Montaigne, however, has pulled himself back as far as possible to the first condition of ignorance. Second, Montaigne considers an "abecedarian ignorance" that precedes knowledge and a "doctoral ignorance" that comes after knowledge, "an ignorance that knowledge generates and engenders, just as it undoes and destroys the first" (VS312–13, F226–27). Third, Montaigne concludes this essay with the claim that his mind has "opened up a passage," and that it is easy to discover "an infinite number of examples" in which high and low are similar. The third, middle way, however, offers two different possibilities: error or the limit of Christian intelligence. The *Essays*, he says, would not appeal either to common, vulgar minds or to singular, excellent minds, but "they might get by in the middle region."

Of the two possibilities offered to the middle region of men (among whom Montaigne counts himself), one is associated with violence and danger, the other with "descending," as it were, to the lowest condition. Simple souls are "good Christians," and great minds who have studied the Scriptures are "good Christians." Of those in the middle region, some who have renounced the error of the Reformation have become extreme and violent in the defense of their side in the civil wars. Others, like Montaigne, stick to the old ways and "enjoy their victory with consolation, active gratitude, reformed conduct, and great modesty." They have come to a deeper understanding of Scripture and of "the mysterious and divine secret of our ecclesiastical polity." So also, both the simple peasants and the philosophers of his day are "good men." The half-breeds, those in the middle region, are dangerous and trouble the world. Montaigne pulls back, as far as possible, to the condition of ignorance.

If error is "stopping at the appearance of the first sense" (or in Frame's translation: "following the first plausible meaning"), then Montaigne is presenting the discovery of truth as getting beyond the appearance of the first sense to the true meaning. Going beyond the appearance of the first sense means testing our common impressions. Montaigne criticizes the philosophy of the schools for its unquestioned acceptance of the teachings of Aristotle; his criticism makes much of the fact that we never question our "common impressions." Our imagination is prone to receive "impressions of falsehood by frivolous appearances" (VS1034, F791).

Montaigne discusses one of the most important instances of "stopping at the appearance of the first sense" in "Of Cruelty." He here describes himself as merely innocent and good, rather than as virtuous. He is, therefore, lower in rank within the moral order than both the perfectly virtuous man, whose rule over the passions is absolute, and the imperfectly virtuous man, who must struggle with the passions. Montaigne's own, third condition of goodness and innocence is, he says, "so close to imperfection and weakness that I do not very well know how to separate their confines and distinguish them. The very names of innocence and goodness are for this reason to some extent terms of contempt" (VS426, F310). Stopping at the appearance of the first sense means misunderstanding the nature of goodness, mistaking it for weakness, and assuming that it is caused by weakness. This confusion of goodness with weakness and imperfection is based on the Aristotelian hierarchy of strong over weak. Montaigne's refounding replaces the weak with the good, thus overcoming error by establishing the strength of goodness.

The third condition of error and falsehood is brought about through what Montaigne calls "the violent prejudice of custom." He begins "Of

Custom" with an account of the "power" of custom. Habit or custom "is a violent and treacherous schoolmistress." She gains her power and authority over us stealthily, little by little. After a mild and humble beginning, "she soon uncovers to us a furious and tyrannical face against which we no longer have the liberty of even raising our eyes" (VS109, F77). Montaigne tells us that, at one time, he was charged with the responsibility of defending a certain custom, the content of which he does not specify. His approach was to uncover the origin of this custom, presumably because the origin would show him the reason and the justification for it. To his great surprise, he found the origin so weak that he became almost disgusted.

There are, he continues, two kinds of reaction to the discovery of the weakness of the origins of custom: "Our masters"—presumably the philosophers and theologians who are "directors of conscience"—make no attempt to defend custom on the basis of reason; they simply take refuge in the ancientness of usage. The Cynics, on the other hand, simply abandon custom and return to nature as the standard of reason. Montaigne, however, is a third type: "Whoever wants to [essay himself in the same way and] get rid of this violent prejudice of custom will find many things accepted with undoubting resolution, which have no support but in the hoary beard and the wrinkles of the usage that goes with them; but when this mask is torn off, and he refers things to truth and reason, he will feel his judgment as it were all upset, and nevertheless restored to a much surer status" (VS117, F84–85).[3] Unlike our masters, he does not simply defer to the authority of custom on account of its hoary beard. Unlike the Cynics, he does not simply abandon custom by returning to some version of original nature. His judgment is "restored" to a much surer status. The beginnings of all things, he says, are always "weak" (VS1020, F780). They must be weak because they are not ends; the end is not inherent in the beginning. To "restore" means to lead things back "to their true end" (VS118, F85).

The very meaning of "essaying," then, is the overcoming of the violent prejudice of custom. Essaying is exposing the weakness of the beginnings and the disproportion of those beginnings to the power of custom. Custom is the violence that is exerted over the mind, the violence that the philosopher must first recognize and then combat. But Montaigne also says that the opinions of the Cynics, who reject the authority of custom, are "barbarous." Therefore, Montaigne breaks with custom in an unusual way. He refounds custom, not by violently overturning everything, but by replacing its foundation: he replaces the weak with the strength of the good. Thus is his judgment restored to a much surer status.

Thought begins in conditions of error and falsehood because the mind is not receptive of "what is." For Aristotle, thought is measured by being: the mind is like a blank writing tablet, ready to receive the forms of things. In contrast, Montaigne does not claim that his mind receives the forms of things. Rather, he says, his mind "generates" and "produces" out of itself. The origin of thought is the mind itself.

In the Aristotelian tradition, the highest activity of the mind is contemplation because contemplation is a participation in the activity of the divine (*Meta.* 12.7, 1072b13; *NE.* 10.7, 1177a13–1177b8). It is the divine that establishes the hierarchy, and the divine is the highest in the order of things. Despite his great admiration, Montaigne cannot stomach the ecstasies of contemplation reported of Socrates (VS1115, F856), that he stood in a trance for an entire day and night in the midst of the army, "overtaken and enraptured by some deep thought" (VS1109, F852).

The contrast between the traditional notions of knowing and contemplation as essentially receptive activities and Montaigne's presentation of the mind as generating and producing comes through clearly in "Of Idleness." He intends by this title to bring to mind the traditional idea of leisure as the condition for contemplation. Idleness, in the tradition, is the opposite of leisure, which is time devoted to the divine in worship and contemplation. Leisure is not idleness because it involves activity, the highest activity; it is "useless" in the best sense, that is, it is not directed to an end outside itself but is an end in itself. Idleness, on the other hand, is useless in the worst sense: it is not good in itself but good for nothing.

In this essay, Montaigne tells of his withdrawal from the affairs of politics into the solitude of his study. He intends to let his mind "entertain itself in full idleness and stay and settle in itself, which I hoped it might do more easily now, having become weightier and riper with time." But that is not what happens. He finds instead that his mind "gives birth to so many chimeras and fantastic monsters, one after another, without order or purpose [*propos*]." He decides that "in order to contemplate their ineptitude and strangeness" at his pleasure, he will put these chimeras and monsters in writing, "hoping in time to make my mind ashamed of itself" (VS33, F21). Montaigne is playing on the traditional notions of leisure and contemplation, conflating leisure with idleness. Contemplation is not the beholding of form but the generation of chimeras and fantastic monsters, "unformed" productions of his own mind. The activity of the mind in idleness is not the measuring of the mind by eternal being but the mind entertaining itself in time. By emphasizing the role of time, he distances himself from the philosopher's escape to the eternal.

Because he says that he puts these fabrications in writing, it would seem that the *Essays* are just these productions of his own mind. But why should his mind be ashamed of itself? Shame suggests a moral and social dimension of his thought. The mind alone with itself is the mind withdrawn from the affairs of the world and from other men. Montaigne wants to make his mind ashamed of its chimeras, which have no order or purpose because they have no "definite subject" and "no fixed end" (VS32, F21). By putting the mind's fantastic productions into writing, he exposes them to public view and therefore exposes himself to the possibility of shame. Perhaps he is suggesting that the proper place of the mind's activity is the world of human affairs and that he must order his thought to that world.

Representation

The generative power of the mind, and thus the source of error and falsehood, is manifested in the capacity for representation. This capacity is one of the very few things that is said to be unique to man in the long comparison of man with the other animals in the "Apology." The ability to have the images of things in the mind without the matter, that privilege in which our soul glories, is not peculiar to man but is shared by the beasts (VS481, F354). Representation, however, shows that man is not constrained within the natural hierarchy. "If it is true that man alone, of all the animals, has this freedom of imagination and this unruliness of thought, that represents to him that which is, that which is not, and that which he wants, the false and the true, this is an advantage that is sold him very dear and in which he has very little to glorify himself, for from it springs the principal source of the evils that press him" (VS459–60, F336).

Representation is the source of evils because it gives us both the true and the false, both what is and what is not. Representation is not the mind's reception of the intelligible forms of things. A form can only be what is and what is true, whereas a representation is produced by the mind itself. If the capacity to receive the intelligible forms of things were distinctively human, then man would remain within the order and limits of nature. His capacity for thought would be located in a continuous ascent from sensation, which he shares with all animals, to contemplation, which he shares with the divine. But the human mind does not docilely receive the forms of things as they are; it also actively represents its own productions to itself and the world, and the capacity for representation means freedom and unruliness. "We have emancipated ourselves from [nature's] rules to abandon ourselves to the vagabond freedom of our fancies" (VS58, F39).

Montaigne writes: "Others form man; I tell of him, and *represent* a particular one, very ill-formed" (VS804, F610).[4] A form is an essence, a universal, fully achieved in a single end or notion of perfection. Montaigne, in contrast, represents a particular. Whereas forms must be articulated only in their perfection, representation allows for the expression of imperfection: this particular is "very ill-formed." Since form is perfect, it is what the thing ought to be. Montaigne's representation of himself is true because it is not in terms of what ought to be but of what is: "what is" is particular and imperfect. Yet the power of representation replaces the power of the universal; for Montaigne, the imperfect particular stands for all men: "each man bears the entire form of the human condition" (VS805, F611).

Imagination and Invention

Montaigne's essay on the imagination is entitled "Of the Power of the Imagination." In his view, "that faculty is all important, at least more important than any other" (VS1087, F833).[5] While the imagination is all-important and powerful for him, Montaigne's memory is "monstrously deficient." There is almost no trace of memory in him, and in this he is unique. "I do not think there is another one in the world so monstrously deficient. All my other faculties are low and common; but in this one I think I am singular and very rare, and thereby worthy of gaining a name and reputation" (VS34, F21). This apparently ironic assertion about himself is usually not taken seriously but is attributed to his penchant for self-deprecation. After all, his book is filled with hundreds of quotations and borrowed stories, all from the storehouse of his memory. But if we take him at his word, then this monstrous deficiency must tell us something about the mind itself.

Montaigne's lack of memory frees him from the past, from the inherited, from learning, and from custom. Therefore, he stands in a relation of distance from ancient philosophy and history. His mind is not held under the unexamined authority of the tradition. As Tzvetan Todorov says of Montaigne: "The activity of the mind itself must be freed from the grip of tradition in order to rely solely on its own forces."[6] That is why Montaigne is free to invent with respect to the stories taken from the histories. Absence of memory is freedom from the actual, from what has happened.

Montaigne's mind, then, is not memory. Most people, he says, make no distinction between memory and mind and therefore assume that deficiency of memory is deficiency of understanding (VS34, F22). The identification of mind with memory would seem to refer to the Socratic formula, "knowledge is recollection," and to the Augustinian formula, "memory itself is mind." These formulations attempt to capture the experience of discovery in the process of learning something new. It is as if we are discovering something that was already there, already present in the mind. What seems new is not really new. The new is in fact eternal. Knowledge is, in the tradition, ultimately recollection of the eternal unchanging forms.

Kierkegaard gives us an especially clear description of the alternatives in his *Philosophical Fragments:* either all learning is recollection, as Socrates had concluded, or the moment of learning, in time, must have "decisive significance."[7] For "viewed Socratically, any point of departure in time is *eo ipso* something accidental, a vanishing point, an occasion."[8] The moment in time is merely the occasion for remembering. From the Socratic viewpoint, "the temporal point of departure is nothing, because in the same moment I discover that I have known the truth from eternity without knowing it, in the same instant that moment is hidden in the eternal, assimilated into it."[9]

Montaigne's "monstrously deficient" memory means that his mind is not subsumed under the eternal: the action of his thought is a true beginning and not merely an occasion for remembering. That is the only way in which the new can emerge in his thought. Discovery is not remembering but inventing. In compensation for the imperfection of his memory, Montaigne has been given invention (VS35, F22).

The *Essays* are at the center of Grahame Castor's analysis of the meaning of "invention" in his *Pleiade Poetics: A Study in Sixteenth-Century Thought and Terminology.* The principal conclusions of this analysis are that invention is most closely associated with the faculty of the imagination, and that invention is not the creation of something entirely new but a discovery of something that was already present but hidden. Castor says that "the sixteenth century made no absolute distinction between the process of imagining and that of inventing."[10] "Invention" and "imagination" are more or less interchangeable terms for Montaigne.[11] Castor describes invention as, in some ways, a pre-rational activity, because invention seeks out particulars that are appropriate to a general topic. The function of the imagination is to assemble images and present them to reason. "Imagination and invention were thus the servants of reason; but this was a rather ambiguous relationship, for the reason was to a very large extent dependent upon them in its dealings with things outside itself. They were the powers which reason employed in order to move outwards, beyond itself, the means whereby it was able to act upon external things, and to enter into a relationship of knowledge with them."[12] Montaigne says that "we hold [not only the past but] even present things by the imagination" (VS996, F763). Thus, imagination and invention replace memory in the activity of knowing. And it is through the imagination that reason is able to exercise power.

Although invention later came to mean something like creation, "in the sixteenth century . . . invention was still quite definitely a finding, a discovery, or a finding out, rather than a creating."[13] This means that "the concept behind *invention* is not so much that of producing something entirely new, *ex nihilo,* as it were, but rather that of coming into and revealing for the first time something which already exists."[14] To invent was "to come into something which already existed and to make it manifest for the first time."[15] This understanding of invention is also found in Ullrich Langer's *Invention, Death and Self-Definitions in the Poetry of Pierre De Ronsard.* According to Langer, in the Renaissance "any discovery is only a discovery of that which is already there, both in the universe and in the mind. Therefore it would simply make no sense to say that the mind may construct anything essentially different from all that precedes or surrounds it." Langer maintains that "the only certain statement about *invention* in the Renaissance is that it does not designate the creation *ex nihilo,* by a transcendent and separate subject, of an essentially distinct object. The rhetorical sense must be located anywhere between an 'accidental coming-upon' and a 'discovery through research' of something already there. . . . Any analysis of 'newness' will be relativized by this conservative meaning of invention in a full universe."[16]

Castor says that "in talking of invention Montaigne is quite obviously dealing with a group of ideas which he considers to be familiar to his readers, and which requires no special elaboration on his part. Therefore Montaigne never deliberately sets out to explain what he means by *invention;* there was no need for him to do so."[17] It is true that Montaigne does not usually define his terms, and to that extent he does rely upon the accepted meaning of terms. But he also bends and turns language out of its ordinary course: his invention gives unaccustomed significance to words (VS873, F665). The "new" has a stronger sense for Montaigne than it does for Castor, the sense of the possible, and so we must take Castor's analysis of invention in the *Essays* a step further.

Invention cannot be distinguished from discovery, because the imagination is generative. It does not receive images from "external things" to present them to reason but generates images or representations. To say that invention is discovery is not to say that it finds what is already there actually or potentially, but rather that it discovers the possible and the new in thought itself. To discover possibilities is to bring them forth from the mind. In other words, Montaigne does not *remember* what was always already there. He *invents* it, and that is how he introduces the new.

Castor rightly points out that the change in thought represented by the prominence of invention must be understood in contrast to Aristotle's understanding of thought. But he sees this as a kind of falling off: "The weakening, or coarsening, of Aristotle's ideas can be seen in the movement of thought from 'potentiality' to 'possibility,' where the idea of an existent (unexercised) power, which is expressed in the Latin *potential* . . . is watered down to that of mere accidental perhaps-ness."[18] "Possibility" is "a falling-away from Aristotelian 'potentiality.' "[19]

Possibility would have the sense of a weakening of Aristotelian potentiality only if one accepts the truth of form and final cause. Potentiality is relative to final cause: potentiality is a mode of being such that, when it is actualized, the completion and perfection of the thing in question comes closer to fulfillment. Potentialities are given by nature; they are given with form. Possibility means the absence of form. In other words, potentialities are discovered in things, whereas possibilities are invented by the mind. Truth is no longer the conformity of the intellect to the object of knowledge, such that the form in the object is the same as the form in the intellect. Truth becomes a matter of judgment.

In a world without forms, in a world of accidental similarities, imagination and invention are essential to seeing things as they are and to judging men and their actions. One of the most important functions of invention in the *Essays* is the discovery of the possible causes and accidental similarities of human actions. Invention allows him to get beyond the appearance of the first sense. For example, in "By Diverse Means We Arrive at the Same End" Montaigne goes beyond "the appearance of the first sense" by calling into question the first plausible explanation of why the princes are moved only by esteem and not by compassion. The first credible meaning is that the princes are strong souls who revere only virtue and strength, whereas the common people are weak and are therefore moved not by esteem but by compassion. Montaigne finds two stories that show that the common people can be moved by astonishment at heroic virtue. Esteem and astonishment produce the same effect of mercy. In those two particular instances, the entire natural hierarchy of strong and weak is called into question. Montaigne concludes "Of Vain Subtleties" with the claim that, once "a passage is opened to the mind," our invention can find infinite examples of the similarity of high and low and of the appearance of the nameless middle region of men to which he himself belongs. This nameless middle region is the space in which the new can appear.

Reason

Montaigne's descriptions of reason, especially in the "Apology," have led most commentators to the conclusion that he is a skeptic. Reason appears to be weak and powerless, unable to know anything or to find the causes of anything. This would amount to a return to the position of the ancient skeptics, who called for the suspension of judgment as the only legitimate response to the weakness of reason. But Montaigne does make judgments all the time, and so it is necessary to distinguish among the different senses of reason that emerge in the *Essays* in order to determine what allows him to make these judgments.

Montaigne says: "I always call reason that appearance of intellect that each man forges in himself. That reason, of which, by its condition, there can be a hundred contradictory ones about one and the same subject, is an instrument of lead and of wax, stretchable, pliable, and adaptable to all biases and measures; all that is needed is the ability to mold it" (VS565, F425). Each man forges reason in himself: reason is produced, generated, within each individual man. Therefore, reason has "many forms" (VS1065, F815). In contrast with the Aristotelian-Thomistic view of reason as universal and the same in all men, Montaigne presents reason as inherently biased and contradictory. It is not the case that any rational human being would arrive at the same conclusions on the basis of reason. Reason is, in its very origins, self-interested. Reason is an instrument for measuring, but it is not a fixed, unchanging measure or rule because it is private and particular, adaptable to all measures.

There is, however, another description of reason that is very much at odds with this notion of biased reason. In "Of the Disadvantage of Greatness" Montaigne says: "There are few things on which we can give a sincere judgment, because there are few in which we have not in some way a private interest. Superiority and inferiority, mastery and subjection, are forced into a natural envy and contention; they must pillage one another perpetually. I do not believe either one about the rights of the other; let us leave it to reason, which is inflexible and impassive, when we are able to end it" (VS918, F701). Reason can become "inflexible and impassive" and can also make sincere and unbiased judgments when we are able to bring it to an end.

But what does it mean to end reason? First, it seems that reason has no natural end in the Aristotelian sense, for the conflicts of self-interested and biased reason are perpetual. Therefore, reason must be brought to an end, directed to an end, by the will. Ends have become effects. The effect with which Montaigne is here concerned, the impetus for his raising the possibility of an inflexible and impassive reason, is the resolution of the conflict between mastery and subjection.

Second, if reason is to be brought to an end, or made to produce a certain effect, its origin in the private individual must be overcome and self-interest must be transcended. Reason inflexible and impassive, then, has a public status. The possibility of the transcendence of private interest is associated here with "sincere judgment."

Third, bringing reason to an end means freeing it from the limitations of experience. In a discussion of the uncertainty of judgment with respect to political matters, Montaigne writes: "Machiavelli's arguments, for example, were solid enough for the subject, yet it was very easy to combat them; and those who did so left it no less easy to combat theirs. In such an argument there would always be matter for answers, rejoinders, replications, triplications, quadruplications, and that infinite web of disputes that our pettifoggers have spun out as far as they could in favor of lawsuits . . . For the reasons have little other foundation than experience, and the diversity of human events offers us infinite examples of all sorts of forms" (VS655, F497). Therefore, proofs and reasons that are founded on experience and fact have no end (VS1032, F790).

But how can reason be independent of experience? What else is there on which to ground our conclusions? At the beginning of his reply to the second objection to Sebond's natural theology, Montaigne refers to the way in which Saint Augustine argues against those who reject Christian belief because it cannot withstand reason's scrutiny. Augustine's approach is to try to demonstrate the weakness of reason by pointing to the many "known and indubitable experiences" into which we have no insight and of which we do not know the causes. Montaigne finds this mode of argument insufficient. "We must do more" than Augustine. Rare examples are not necessary to convict reason of weakness: Montaigne will show that even the most familiar is impenetrable to reason. Montaigne rejects Augustine's mode of argument because it is based on experience (VS449, F328). This rejection is what makes the "Apology" appear so skeptical. But that, I would argue, is not Montaigne's ultimate intention. Rather, in making the causes of the familiar suddenly unknown, he opens the question of possible causes.

Reason inflexible and impassive is not based on experience, because experience is merely what has been; it is the actual, not in the Aristotelian sense of actuality but in the sense of simply what has happened in the past. Reason inflexible and impassive, however, is based not on experience but on possibility, not on what has happened but on what might happen. "So in the study that I am making of our behavior and motives, fabulous testimonies, provided they are possible, serve like true ones. Whether they have happened or no, in Paris or Rome, to John or Peter, they exemplify, at all events, some human capacity. . . . There are authors whose end it is to tell what has happened. Mine, if I could attain it, would be to talk about what can happen." Hence, his attitude toward testimony, even fabulous testimony, is not rejection, as is the practice of the philosophers and theologians of "exquisite and exact conscience," and not acceptance, as is typical of the simple, but a kind of openness to the possible. "I refer the stories that I borrow to the conscience of those from whom I take them. The reflections are my own, and depend on *the proofs of reason, not of experience*" (VS105–6, F75, emphasis added).

This openness to the possible accounts in some measure for the fact that Montaigne stays closer to the simple than to the learned. The learned tend to reject as impossible anything that is not familiar to them. This is the presumption of the learned. They tend to identify the possible with the probable, whereas the simple, who do not presume to know the causes of things, are more open to the strange and unfamiliar. In one of the very rare places in the *Essays* in which Montaigne points to a radical change within himself, he cites the beliefs of the simple in such things as enchantments, prognostications, and returning spirits: "I used to feel compassion for the poor people who were taken in by these follies. And now I think that I was at least as much to be pitied myself. *Not that experience has since shown me anything surpassing my first beliefs, and that through no fault of my curiosity; but reason has taught me* that to condemn a thing thus, dogmatically, as false and impossible, is to assume the advantage of knowing the bounds and limits of God's will and of the power of our mother nature" (VS179, F132, emphasis added). Reason inflexible and impassive is not limited by experience: "How many things of slight probability there are, testified to by trustworthy people, which, if we cannot be convinced of them, we should at least leave in suspense! For to condemn them as impossible is to pretend, with rash presumption, to know the limits of possibility" (VS180, F133). It is not experience but reason that teaches him to be open to the possible.[20] Reason surpasses his first beliefs and thus becomes inflexible and impassive. This, then, is the first moment of the philosophical act: the ascent of reason from first beliefs and the freedom of reason from the limitations of experience.

Judgment

The second moment of the philosophical act is the act of judgment, in which reason is subjected to the good and the good becomes his own: judgment is what is all one's own. The *Essays* are quite literally the *essais,* the tests, of Montaigne's own judgment (VS301, F219; VS653, F495).[21]

In his essay on the education of children, he works out the distinction between mere learning and true education in terms of the difference between simply borrowing from the ancients, which is only an exercise of memory, and forming one's own judgment. The student should be taught what to do with the pieces borrowed from others: "he will transform and blend them to make a work that is all his own, to wit, his judgment. His education, work, and study aim only at forming this" (VS152, F111).

Within the tradition, contemplation is regarded as the highest human activity because, in contemplation, the mind escapes the temporal and is united with the divine, eternal, and unchanging: the human becomes divine. The *Essays,* however, are not directed to the divine, eternal, and unchanging, but to the human, temporal, and changing. Montaigne cannot stomach the contemplative ecstasies of Socrates. But he admires the Socrates "who brought human wisdom back down from heaven, where she was wasting her time, and restored her to man, with whom lies her most proper and laborious and useful business" (VS1038, F793).

Unlike contemplation, judgment is human, a purely human activity concerned only with the human. The *Essays* are about human beings and human action: in them, Montaigne encounters the human itself and as such. He considers it "purely," judging it as it is in itself, without relation to anything else. To judge within the traditional hierarchy, by contrast, is to judge by the standard of what is above. Man is between the divine and the bestial and judges himself by the standard of the divine. To judge man as he is in himself and to identify judgment as the defining human activity is to change everything about what it means to be human.

Contemplation is the ecstatic beholding of the thing itself, but judgment is the subjecting of the thing itself, thus making it one's own. Montaigne's praise of Socrates for bringing philosophy back down from the heavens reveals the way in which contemplation has been transformed. "It is only for first-class men to dwell purely on the thing itself, consider it, and judge it. It belongs to the one and only Socrates to become acquainted with death with an ordinary countenance, to become familiar with it and play with it. He seeks no consolation outside the thing itself; dying seems to him a natural and indifferent accident. He fixes his gaze precisely on it, and makes up his mind to it, without looking elsewhere" (VS833, F632).

In contrast, the disciples of Hegesias, who were inflamed by fine arguments for immortality, "do not consider death in itself; they do not judge it. It is not there that they fix their thoughts; the goal to which they run is a new existence" (VS833, F632). To dwell on "the thing itself," to fix one's gaze on it, is not to contemplate it but to judge it, subject it, make up one's mind to it. Socrates was "always one and the same, and raised himself, not by sallies but by disposition, to the utmost point of vigor. Or, to speak more exactly, he raised nothing, but rather brought vigor, hardships, and difficulties down and back to his own natural and original level, and subjected them to it" (VS1037, F793).

The Socrates of Montaigne's invention does not contemplate the thing itself; he judges it, subjects it to himself, by bringing it down and back to what is his own. He makes the thing itself his own, and what is his own is natural to him. He *makes* it natural. That is what it means to restore philosophy to man.

Georges Poulet explains what judgment is for Montaigne in just this way: "Judgment is the act by which the mind makes something its own. It is an act of the mind . . . the motion of the mind by which it envelops and unites the self and the object. . . . Far from being an adhesion of the mind to things, judgment is an integration of things within the mind by the mind. . . . This freedom of judgment is of value only when it is transformed into a choice and into an act."[22]

Freedom of Judgment: The Self-Ordered Soul

Montaigne asks himself: "And then, for whom do you write?" The learned, who pass judgment on books, recognize only erudition and art and value only learning. Common and popular souls, on the other hand, cannot recognize the grace and the weight of lofty and elevated discourse. These two human types almost exhaust the possibilities; nevertheless, there is a third. "The third type into whose hands you fall, that of souls ordered and strong in themselves, is so rare that for this very reason it has neither name nor rank among us: it is time half lost to aspire and strive to please them" (VS657, F498). The third type has no name *because* it has no rank. In pointing to the fact that this type has no rank among us, Montaigne implies that his project involves a transcendence of the traditional hierarchy, the traditional order of high and low, strong and weak. The strength of the self-ordered soul is not measured by its perfection within the hierarchy but by its freedom of judgment: "Indeed there are few souls so regulated, so strong and well-born, that they can be trusted to their own conduct, and who are able, with moderation and without temerity, to sail in the liberty of their judgments beyond the common opinions" (VS559, F419–20). Freedom of judgment must be distinguished from unruliness of thought. Although the self-ordered soul is free and not bound by the common opinions, he acts with moderation. "Our mind is an erratic, dangerous, and heedless tool; it is difficult to impose order and moderation [*mesure*] upon it. And in my time those who have some rare excellence beyond the others, and some extraordinary quickness, are nearly all, we see, incontinent in the license of their opinions and conduct [*mœurs*]. It is a miracle if you find a sedate and sociable one" (VS559, F419). To judge is to order. Order is not given by nature: the origin of order is the mind itself.[23] The self-ordered soul imposes order and measure upon itself. This is Montaigne's new kind of strength. The self-ordered soul is strong in itself because it has subjected reason to the good and made the good its own.

Subjecting Reason to the Good

Montaigne begins "Of Cruelty" with the distinction between goodness and virtue: "It seems to me that virtue is something other and nobler than the inclinations toward goodness that are born in us. Souls naturally regulated and wellborn follow the same path, and show the same countenance in their actions, as virtuous ones. But virtue means something greater and more active than letting oneself, by a happy disposition, be led gently and peacefully in the footsteps of reason" (VS422, F306). Goodness looks weaker than virtue: it seems to be nothing more than a "natural mildness and easygoingness" in contrast with the strength of virtue that requires struggle and self-mastery. Yet, goodness shows "the same countenance" as virtue.

Montaigne explains the origins of his goodness and why he holds most vices in horror. "I hold them in horror, I say, from an attitude so natural and so much my own that the same instinct and impression that I brought away from my nurse I have still retained. Nothing has been able to make me alter it, not even my own reasonings, which, having in some things broken away from the common road, would easily give me license for actions which this natural inclination makes me hate" (VS428, F312). Montaigne goes further: "It is a monstrous thing that I will say, but I will say it all the same: I find in that area, in many things, more restraint and order in my morals than in my opinions, and my lust less depraved than my reason" (VS428, F312). In "Of Cruelty" goodness is identified with sympathy, a natural inclination.

Montaigne's reason gives him license for vicious actions that his inclinations make him hate. His judgment, however, affirms his inclinations.

He hates cruelty and judges it the extreme of all vice: "Among other vices, I cruelly hate cruelty, *both by nature and by judgment,* as the extreme of all vices" (VS429, F313, emphasis added). Reason is brought to an "end" by judgment, which rejects reason's justifications of cruelty.[24] Reason must instead be directed to the good, subjected to the good by judgment. Montaigne's judgment affirms his earliest impressions and natural inclinations to goodness or sympathy. Now, through judgment, he has a "more secure possession" of them than he did as a young child.

This is Montaigne's new strength, the strength of the self-ordered soul. It is not the mastery of reason over the passions but rather the harmony of judgment and natural inclination. However, not all natural inclinations are good. Montaigne hates cruelty by nature, yet there are others—"bloodthirsty" souls—who seem to have an inclination to cruelty. "Nature herself, I fear, attaches to man some instinct for inhumanity" (VS433, F316). Cruelty, "so unnatural a vice," nevertheless seems to dwell in us by nature (VS790, F599). Natural inclinations themselves must be judged.[25] This act of choosing well among natural inclinations is the freedom of the self-ordered soul. Through judgment Montaigne chooses his natural disposition, his "nature." His disposition is no longer simply "given." Whatever Montaigne's "original" nature or natural disposition, he presents it as good solely because he has made it good.

After confessing the monstrous fact that his reason would give him license for actions that his inclinations make him hate, Montaigne asks: "Could it possibly be true that to be wholly good we must be so by some hidden, natural, and universal property, without law, without reason, without example?" (VS428, F312). Goodness, he says, is hidden. Therefore, we must get beyond the appearance of the first sense in order to see it. Goodness is also natural because it is a natural inclination chosen and affirmed by judgment: it has been made his own in a new way. Third, goodness is universal because it includes the entire man: it is his integrity and consistency. Finally, goodness is a property, a possession of the individual, not an end for which the individual must strive. It is not caused by law, reason, or example. Rather, through judgment a man makes the good his own, his possession, his property. In his possession of the good, the self-ordered soul becomes sociable, as is reflected in the way he judges other men.

Judging "What Is": Imperfection

Judging is, in the tradition, held to be the subsuming of a particular under a universal, determining that a particular is an instance of a certain kind, and that it is the same as other particulars in an essential way. A particular man, then, is judged by the standard of the universal "man," by the standard of the perfection of the human form. In the first essay, Montaigne concludes: "Truly man is a marvelously vain, diverse, and undulating subject. It is hard to found any constant and uniform judgment on him" (VS9, F5). When his friends ask for his judgment of their actions, he avoids generalizations: "So I reveal to my friends, by their outward manifestations [*productions*], their inward inclinations. I do not attempt to arrange this infinite variety of actions, so diverse and so disconnected, into certain types and categories, and distribute my lots and divisions distinctly into recognized classes and sections" (VS1076, F824). On the whole, he finds universal judgments to be useless. "These universal judgments that I find so common signify nothing. They are like men who salute a whole people in a crowd and in a body. Those who have a real acquaintance with them salute them and notice them by name and individually. But that is a risky undertaking" (VS936, F715). Montaigne refers to this as "risky" perhaps because it undermines the standard of the perfection of form in judging men and their actions.

In fact, we "strengthen and enlighten our judgment by reflecting on this continual variation of human things" (VS297, F216). In the formation of judgment, the study of history is of the greatest importance. History, he says, is "the skeleton of philosophy, in which the most abstruse parts of our nature are penetrated." The student should be taught "not so much the histories as how to judge them. That in my opinion, is of all matters the one to which we apply our minds in the most varying degree" (VS156, F115). Learning how to judge the histories means something more than learning the "facts" given by the historians: it means probing the inside to the springs of human action.

The way in which judgment acts in the *Essays* has to do first with determining "what is," whether something is actually the case. This is usually assumed in the rush to universal judgments about why something is the way it is. In determining whether something is, in fact, the case, judgment is a very different kind of act from the act of ascertaining why a thing is the way it is. Judgment must first overcome the presumption of custom. It must resist the attraction to the universal—a very difficult resistance, indeed—because human beings believe, following Aristotle, that they know particulars only through the universal. How is it even possible to see something as a particular?

For Montaigne, judgment as the determination of "what is" includes two related aspects. First, to see "what is" as it is means to see it without the measure of what it ought to be, to judge without the standard of final cause. Aristotle's account of human action is in terms of final cause or happiness: all men, whether they know it or not, always act for the sake of happiness, which is the final and self-sufficient good. If all of one's actions are directed to the same end, then human actions should be consistent. But consistency is an extremely rare achievement. Thus, Aristotle's account of human action in terms of final cause or happiness cannot really explain the actions of most men who are merely tossed about by desires, circumstances, passions, and so forth. Montaigne says: "I do not recognize in Aristotle most of my ordinary actions: they have been covered and dressed up in another robe for the use of the school" (VS874, F666). Montaigne concludes "Of the Inconsistency of Our Actions" with the admonition that we must not judge men simply by their outward actions but must probe the inside to find the springs of action (VS338, F244). To see and understand human action as it is, not as it ought to be, means to judge it in its beginnings and implies, therefore, an acceptance of imperfection and incompleteness.

This understanding of judgment is thus, at the same time, the overcoming of the traditional hierarchy. Action is not the actualization of a potentiality. Instead, Montaigne replaces potentiality by possibility, and that is why invention is indispensable for judgment. Judging "what is" requires openness to the possible: "We must not judge what is possible and what is not, according to what is credible and incredible to our sense" (VS725, F548). This is especially true of human actions: while it is easy to judge the limits of what the body can do, it is very difficult to know the limits of the soul (VS723, F546). Judging as determining "what is" means judging by the standard, or the limits, of the possible.

The mind "represents" to itself both what is and what is not, the true and the false, as well as what it wants to possess. Since representation gives us no way of separating the true from the false, judgment is the only way to determine what is, or what is true. Whereas for Aristotle we can know the truth about what something is only in the light of what it ought to be, for Montaigne determining what is true is inseparable from inventing the possible. Montaigne's conscience allows him to accept or to borrow testimony and stories: "I refer the stories that I borrow to the conscience of those from whom I take them." And he is free to alter the details of the stories he borrows, to omit and replace the explanations offered by the historians, and to fill in details that are not given in the histories because the historians are themselves inventing. "My conscience does not falsify one iota; my knowledge, I don't know." This sets him apart from the philosophers and theologians who are closed to testimony. The philosophers and theologians are people of "exquisite and exact conscience" who would not be willing to testify concerning even what happens right before their eyes or to accept the testimony of others because they would not stake their fidelity on the fidelity of a common man (VS105–6, F75–76).

Montaigne does not judge others by the standard of the perfection of final cause; but neither does he judge others by the standard of himself, as most men do. He judges each man as he is in himself. "Of Cato the Younger" begins with a statement of Montaigne's practice of judgment: "I do not share that common error of judging another by myself. I easily believe that another man may have qualities different from mine. Because I feel myself tied down to one form, I do not oblige everybody to espouse it, as all others do. I believe in and conceive a thousand contrary ways of life, and in contrast with the common run of men, I more easily admit difference than resemblance between us. I am as ready as you please to acquit another man from sharing my conditions and principles. I consider him simply in himself, without relation to others; I mold him to his own model. I do not fail, just because I am not continent, to acknowledge sincerely the continence of the Feuillants and the Capuchins, and to admire the manner of their life. I can very well insinuate myself by imagination into their place, and I love and honor them all the more because they are different from me. I have a singular desire that we should each be judged in ourselves apart, and that I may not be measured in conformity with the common examples" (VS229, F169).

Montaigne's judgment is unique. Most men judge others according to the measure of themselves: "It seems to each man that the ruling pattern of nature is in him; to this he refers all other forms as to a touchstone. The ways that do not square with his are counterfeit and artificial. What brutish stupidity!" (VS725, F548). Montaigne does not share that "common error" for, "in contrast with the common run of men," he judges by a standard that is not biased. "My weakness in no way alters my necessarily high regard for the strength and vigor of those who deserve it. 'There are men who praise nothing except what they are confident they can imitate' [Cicero]. Crawling in the slime of the earth, I do not fail to observe, even in the clouds, the inimitable loftiness of certain heroic souls" (VS229, F169).

In the case of Cato, for example, he indicates his disgust with those who insist on attributing base motives to great men: these detractors "play at ingenuity" clumsily and crudely. "The same pains that they take to detract from these great names, and the same license, I would willingly take to lend them a shoulder to raise them higher. These rare figures, whom the consensus of the wise has selected as examples to the world, I shall not hesitate to restore to their places of honor, as far as my ingenuity [*invention*] allows me to interpret them in a favorable light" (VS231, F170). Montaigne says that "to judge of great and lofty things we need a soul of the same caliber; otherwise we attribute to them the vice that is our own" (VS67, F46). Although Montaigne's deeds are lowly, his soul is of the same caliber as Cato's because his judgment is true and good. Since he does not judge others in relation to himself, his esteem is not based on his own lowliness and weakness but on his strong and free judgment.

How is it possible for an individual to judge each man as he is in himself, "without relation to others"? Judgment would seem to require a universal standard against which individuals can be measured and compared with each other. Yet, Montaigne says: "I mold him to his own model." It appears, then, that he judges each man according to that man's own standard, according to that man's own conscience or judgment. At the same time, however, Montaigne is not a moral relativist nor does he claim that the good is simply what it appears to be for each man. He does condemn vices and vicious actions, but he condemns the action, not the man; he hates the vice, not the man. He weighs both the good and the bad in order to arrive at an assessment of the individual. Judgment is "weighing" or "assaying." Weighing or assaying implies a standard against which the action or the man is measured, and that standard must be the good. Because he does not judge according to the standard of the perfection of form, he accepts imperfection and is able to see the good in the imperfect. He sees how men *are*. That is, indeed, our experience of other men. In fact, the social requires the acceptance of imperfection.

Montaigne uses imagination and invention to enter into the conscience of the other and to judge that other from his own perspective. Montaigne insinuates himself by his imagination into the place of those whose way of life is entirely different from his own: "Thinking about the poor beggar at my door . . . I put myself in his place, I try to fit my mind to his bias" (VS243, F179). Montaigne's judgment of other men can be described as generous, for the tendency of his judgments is toward esteem for others. "I find it a rough task to judge a man in whom the bad qualities exceed the good" (VS1077, F825). He loves and admires Cato the Stoic, the Epicureans, the Skeptics, Plato, Socrates, the Capuchins, and countless others who pursue the good in very different ways.

Montaigne judges each man as he is in himself, without relation to others, and yet he also ranks men. These two actions seem mutually exclusive: the first kind of judgment rejects a universal standard, while the act of ranking appears to require it. How is it possible for Montaigne to escape the charge that he is contradicting himself? The answer lies in the locus of his standards: he judges not by outward actions—by the standard of final cause—but by the internal springs of action. Montaigne judges each man according to that man's own conscience, and he ranks men according to the purity of their consciences. That is how it is possible for Montaigne to rank incommensurables.

Montaigne's ranking can be seen especially clearly in "Of the Most Outstanding Men." Epaminondas is ranked as the most outstanding man, surpassing Alexander the Great, Caesar, and even Socrates because his conscience is innocent. The valor of Epaminondas is as great as that of Alexander and Caesar, "but as for his character and conscience, he very far surpassed all those who have undertaken to manage affairs. For in this respect, *which must principally be considered, which alone truly marks what we are, and which I weigh alone against all the others together,* he yields to no philosopher, not even to Socrates. In this man, innocence is a key quality, sovereign, constant, uniform, incorruptible" (VS756, F573, emphasis added). The standard by which Montaigne judges is the standard of innocence or goodness: the "extreme goodness" of Epaminondas (VS757, F573). Innocence and goodness are "so close to weakness and imperfection" that it is difficult to distinguish them: judgment must get beyond the appearance of the first sense.

In his act of judging "what is" in its imperfection, we can understand the way in which Montaigne's judgment accomplishes the many "reversals" that occur throughout the *Essays,* including the reversals of high and low, strong and weak. The weak is stronger than the strong, the low is higher than the high. When the traditional hierarchy is undermined, these oppositions collapse. Yet, Montaigne must use the language of the hierarchy in order to undermine it. Truth is in these reversals.

Montaigne's judgment overcomes the three conditions of error and falsehood from which thought begins. He is able to sift the true from the false by returning to his first opinions, to the truth that was always there, and by subjecting reason to the good. He goes beyond the appearance of the first sense through the overcoming of the traditional hierarchy. And he gets rid of the violent prejudice of custom by bringing the new out of the old and replacing the weak with the good.

Judgment Reformed

Montaigne criticizes those who seek to reform morals through new opinions. "Oh what an easy and applauded route those superficial men take, compared with ours!" (VS888, F677). Montaigne's own reform is the deepest possible, because he seeks to effect the purification of judgment, the reform of conscience itself, the reform of the will. Judgment is conscience, and conscience is determined by the will.[26] Neither contemplation nor prudence admits an act of the will.

In his description of the act of judgment, Montaigne points to the role of the will in judgment and to the possibility of the uncorrupted will: "It is a great deal for me to have my judgment regulated, if my actions [*les effects*] cannot be, and to maintain this sovereign part free from corruption. It is something to have my will good when my legs fail me" (VS229–30, F169). The will can be "good" and uncorrupted, even if one's actions are weak and unregulated.

In "Of Prognostications" Montaigne says that his task is "to give some authority" to "the prompt, vehement, and accidental" opinions that sometimes come to us. These are impulsions of the will or "inclinations," and in a purified soul, such as Socrates's, they are important and worthy of being followed. Montaigne himself has experienced such stirrings, which were "as weak in reason as violent in persuasiveness" and "by which I let myself be carried away so usefully and fortunately that they might be judged to have in them something of divine inspiration" (VS44, F30). Such is perhaps the desire that "seized" him to tell his ways of being in public, the desire that is the beginning of the *Essays*. These impulsions of the will are "weak in reason"; the good is irrational, and it is the will, not reason, that gives rise to these accidental opinions. The *Essays*, then, must be seen as Montaigne's attempt to "give some authority" to the impulsions of the pure will.

Montaigne produces his thoughts out of himself, and that is why they are his own. But the decisive act, the act that makes them entirely and precisely his own, is the removal of the self. Reason, representation, and judgment are all purified of his self. It seems that the more the *Essays* are his own, the less of himself is present in them. The act of judgment does include the will, but purity of judgment means eliminating the self-assertion of the particular will. The self, then, appears as pride, self-assertion, and the desire to dominate. The self-ordered soul can be left to go its own way, beyond the common opinions, in the freedom of its judgments, because its will is purified of self.

In the "Apology" Montaigne says that "our first and original malady" is presumption (VS452, F330) and that presumption is the first tyranny of the evil spirit (VS449, F328), implying that presumption is original sin. Presumption, then, must be essential to that "unruliness of thought" that is said to distinguish man from the other animals. When Montaigne describes himself as "innocent" he is pointing to the way in which he escapes our first and original malady.

In "Of Presumption" Montaigne says that the only thing he esteems himself for is just what every man esteems himself for: "My recommendation is vulgar, common, and popular, for who ever thought he lacked sense?" We recognize the superiority of others in courage, strength, and beauty, "but an advantage in judgment we yield to no one" (VS656, F498). This is the presumption that is universal. Montaigne, then, is just like every other man. But here he does offer a way in which he can justify the uniqueness and the soundness of his opinions: "I think my opinions are good and sound; but who does not think as much of his? One of the best proofs I have of mine is the little esteem I have for myself; for if these opinions had not been very firm, they would easily have let themselves be fooled by the singular affection I have for myself" (VS657, F499). His lack of self-esteem is the best proof of the truth of his opinions. This is a new sense of proof: not the proof of demonstration, but proof based on the removal of the bias of self-esteem, the proof of reason.

But the *Essays* are all about himself. How, then, can his self be eliminated? Montaigne represents a particular, "very ill-formed." By the standard of the traditional hierarchy, he is imperfect. His representation of himself is without self-esteem. The removal of self-esteem from Montaigne's representation, reason, and judgment is the condition for his transcendence of the traditional hierarchy, the hierarchy that establishes the superiority of the philosopher to all men, of masters over slaves and strong over weak. In removing his self-esteem, he eliminates the identification of himself with the philosopher's perfection of the human form. At the same time, he affirms his imperfection: he is "ill-formed." In other words, the new type that emerges against the background of the traditional hierarchy transcends that hierarchy but also incorporates within itself the imperfection that it has in relation to that hierarchy.

Montaigne does not judge others by the measure of himself, pulling others down to the level of his own lowly deeds. His judgment is uncorrupted. "Judgment holds in me a magisterial seat, at least it carefully tries to. It lets my feelings go their way, both hatred and friendship, even the friendship I bear myself, without being changed and corrupted by them. If it cannot reform the other parts according to itself, at least it does not let itself be deformed to match them; it plays its game apart" (VS1074, F823).

From the perspective of the purified judgment, then, ancient philosophy never sees itself for what it is. It never purifies itself of the self of the philosopher in spite of the fact that it goes beyond the self to the eternal and divine. That is why it sees being as hierarchical. The reason that justifies the traditional hierarchy of master and subject is merely private reason, biased and self-interested. Reason becomes inflexible, impassive, and able to transcend the hierarchy when it is purified of "private interest." It becomes public when it is purified of the self of the philosopher. Purging the will of self-interest and self-esteem eliminates the pride of the philosopher and the desire for mastery. Montaigne's own judgment is superior, but his elimination of self-esteem from his judgment is the renunciation of any claim to superiority and mastery: the purified judgment subjects pride and mastery itself. Montaigne thus achieves a public reason and a public will.

Reason inflexible and impassive requires the self-effacement of the philosopher in an act of extreme generosity. The requirement of the self-effacement of the philosopher helps us to make sense of what has to be one of the strangest statements in the *Essays*. In his discussion of the motives for suicide, Montaigne mentions first the desire to escape the evils of this world. But, as usual, he offers another possible cause: "men also sometimes desire death in the hope of a greater good." Then, as he frequently does, he points to a Christian and a pagan example: "I desire," says Saint Paul, "to be dissolved, to be with Jesus Christ." And Cleombrotus of Ambracia threw himself into the sea because his reading of Plato's *Phaedo* had given him such a strong desire for the life to come. Montaigne, again, is a third type: "Whence it appears how improperly we call 'despair' that voluntary dissolution to which we are often borne by the ardor of hope, and often by a tranquil and settled inclination of our judgment" (VS360, F260). This is an inclination *of judgment,* no longer a mere natural inclination of sympathy: it is an act of the will made constant and consistent. Voluntary dissolution means that the will is purified of the self; the will is good. This third type of voluntary dissolution of the self, this tranquil and deliberate inclination of judgment, refers, I believe, to Montaigne's own self-effacement, the self-effacement of the philosopher for a greater good.

The philosopher must become a new figure: an unpremeditated and accidental philosopher. He subjects ancient philosophy to himself, disappearing behind the face of the tradition while doing something radically new. In the same act through which he effaces himself, he refounds philosophy. He refounds *because* he effaces himself. This is the separation of the man from the philosopher.

Chapter Four

✦

The Philosophical Act (II): Ending in Experience

Montaigne's unpremeditated and accidental philosophy is the reformation of philosophy because it separates the man from the philosopher and thus humanizes him. The philosopher, in the tradition, believes that he alone bears "the entire form of the human condition." In accordance with the traditional hierarchy, the philosopher alone is the complete actualization of the human form because he participates in the divine activity of contemplation. This identification of the philosopher with the human as such, that is, the human at its highest, in fact dehumanizes the philosopher because it separates him from all other men. Montaigne, however, is only accidentally a philosopher. His thoughts are born with him and "without a model," but when he brings them out into the public, he finds that they resemble the teachings of ancient philosophy. His mores are natural and weak, for he has not called in the help of any discipline to build them. Yet, he discovers, to his astonishment, that his thoughts and mores are conformed by accident to many different philosophical teachings. Because ancient philosophy has not formed him, however, there is only an accidental similarity—not a sameness of essence—between his thoughts and mores and the teachings of ancient philosophy.

Philosophy, as understood by Aristotle, dehumanizes the philosopher also because it destroys sympathy. The philosopher sees himself as divine and loses the sense of his common humanity. In "Of Cruelty" Montaigne identifies sympathy with the good. If the philosopher loses the capacity for sympathy, he does not possess the good. He may *contemplate* the good, but he does not *possess* it. The good, according to Montaigne, is a property, a possession, not an object of contemplation.

A third way in which the tradition dehumanizes the philosopher (and the theologian) is in the attempt to separate the soul from the body in order to attain the divine and the eternal; this is a kind of violence to the man. Montaigne repeatedly shows that any attempt to rise above our humanity, to attain the divine or the angelic, makes us inhuman, not more fully human. Reflecting on those who despise the bodily pleasures of "that brattish rabble of men that we are," Montaigne says: "These are two things that I have always observed to be in singular accord: supercelestial thoughts and subterranean conduct. . . . They want to get out of themselves and escape from the man. That is madness: instead of changing into angels, they change into beasts; instead of raising themselves, they lower themselves. These transcendental humors frighten me" (VS1115, F856).

The unpremeditated and accidental philosopher, in contrast, is the self-ordered soul who is free in his judgments to go beyond common—or traditional—opinions. It is, however, very difficult to impose order and measure on the unruly mind. Most of those who possess some rare excellence of mind are "incontinent in the license of their opinions and conduct [*mœurs*]." Therefore, "it is a miracle if you find a sedate and sociable one" (VS559, F419). Excellent minds, then, are inclined to be solitary, unsociable, immoderate, and dangerous. The miracle is the self-ordered soul that is sociable. That is why philosophy itself must be refounded and reformed, why Montaigne becomes the new figure of the philosopher. To paraphrase Hume: Montaigne is a philosopher but, in the midst of all his philosophy, he is still a man.[1]

Inventing the Essay, Inventing Society

Montaigne invents society as a new form of human association and he invents the essay as a new form of philosophy. It might be said that he invents society by inventing the essay. David Hume, in his essay "Of Essay-Writing," argues that this form brings together what he calls the learned and the conversible worlds: "The separation of the learned from the conversible world," he says, "seems to have been the great defect of the last age, and must have had a very bad influence both on books and company." The social world suffers because, without the influence of philosophy, conversation is reduced to stories and gossip. But philosophy itself also suffers from this separation. Cut off from the world, philosophy becomes barbarous because it lacks "that liberty and facility of thought and expression which can only be acquired by conversation." Philosophy, Hume says, "went to wrack by this moaping recluse method of study, and became as chimerical in her conclusions as she was unintelligible in her stile and manner of delivery." In becoming social, in "descending" into the social, philosophy is freed from philosophical presumption and self-esteem. Further, philosophy suffers when practiced in isolation, because experience, upon which philosophy rests, is to be found only "in common life and conversation."[2]

Thus, Pascal describes Montaigne's style as "totally composed of thoughts born out of the ordinary conversations of life."[3] That is why the Socrates of Montaigne's invention is not the Socrates who ascends to the Forms but rather the Socrates who descends to the most lowly opinions of the most ordinary men. At the same time, as Auerbach claims, Montaigne was the first author who wrote for the non-specialized but educated reader: "By the success of the *Essays* the educated public first revealed its existence."[4] That is, Montaigne actually brings this public into existence by revealing it. The *Essays,* then, include all men—the learned and the simple—in the conversation that they initiate.

Michael Oakeshott sees the *Essays* as the clearest example of what he calls "the conversation of mankind." This conversation, he says, "is not only the greatest but also the most hardly sustained of all the accomplishments of mankind. Men have never been wanting who have had this understanding of human activity and intercourse, but few have embraced it without reserve and without misgiving, and on this account it is proper to mention the most notable of those who have done so: Michel de Montaigne."[5] That Montaigne embraced this activity "without reserve and without misgiving" is a manifestation of his generous sociability.

The Essay Form

T. S. Eliot describes the *Essays* as "apparently formless and disconnected, but subtly unified."[6] The appearance of formlessness is the perfect form of unpremeditated and accidental philosophy because the essay form is the submission of reason to experience. I will consider five features of the essay form in order to bring out the ways in which it produces this effect.

Quotation

Montaigne's learning is present in the *Essays* as direct quotations, usually in the original Latin (or rarely, Greek) of the author. The practice of quotation allows him to distance himself from the philosopher in question by showing that he is using him as the occasion allows. Ancient philosophy has not made him what he is, has not formed him. He tells us that he has studied the opinions of others "not at all to form my opinions, but certainly to assist, second, and serve those which I formed long ago" (VS666, F505). In "Of Presumption" he says that ancient philosophy has given him only a more secure and complete possession of his own original opinions and has helped him to make his judgments more his own (VS658, F499). He uses ancient philosophy, in fragments, to say what he himself wants to say. "I do not speak the minds of others except to express myself better" (VS148, F108).

Robert Sokolowski's analysis of the phenomenon of quotation helps us to account for Montaigne's stance toward ancient philosophy: "I can be . . . related to things either on my own cognitive authority or refractedly, through the authority of another speaker. When I quote someone, I have the quoted state of affairs as proposed by someone else; but in principle it is always possible for me to go on to possess the state of affairs by myself without an intermediary, to register the situation on my own. . . . When, after having quoted, I thus see for myself, I do not just register the situation; I register it as confirming or disconfirming what someone else has said. . . . The immediacy of my own cognitive possession of a situation becomes itself a qualified immediacy because I now know that I can be cognitively related to it not only by myself but also through another. *By myself* takes on a deeper hue."[7] In this way, Montaigne brings the philosophers into conversation through his expression of himself: he makes ancient philosophy his own.

In "Of the Education of Children" Montaigne says of the young man who is to be educated: "Truth and reason are common to everyone, and no more belong to the man who first spoke them than to the man who says them later. It is no more according to Plato than according to me, since he and I understand and see it in the same way. The bees plunder the flowers here and there, but afterward they make of them honey, which is all theirs; it is no longer thyme or marjoram." The student will do the same with the pieces borrowed from others: "he will transform and blend them to make a work that is all his own, to wit, his judgment" (VS152, F111).

By his practice of quotation, in fragments and as the occasion allows, Montaigne is forcing the philosophers into ordinary conversation, submitting them to the practice of everyday life. At the same time, he also brings common opinions out into the open through the "they say," or *on dit,* one of the most frequently used expressions in the *Essays*. The *on dit* is the way in which he takes the stance of quotation toward common opinion. Thus, he brings the learned and the common into conversation with each other.

Sokolowski says that there are two types of people who do not understand the stance of quotation. First, the gullible person simply takes over what others say, repeating it without making it his own. Second, the obstinate person is so convinced of his own opinion that he can only see what others say as either confirming his own views or as foolish fancies not to be taken seriously.[8] Montaigne presents these same two types in terms of the learned and the simple. He escapes both the presumption of the learned, who cannot accept what they have not themselves experienced, and the presumption of the simple, who are under the power of common opinion.

The Language of the Streets, Markets, and Taverns

Like Socrates, who brought philosophy down from the heavens and into the cities of men, Montaigne brings philosophy down from the heavens and into the streets and markets and taverns of France. The *Essays* are written in French, rather than Latin (the language of the learned). Montaigne's first language was Latin. His father, who had formed certain unusual ideas about education, hired a tutor who spoke nothing but Latin with the young boy. In fact, the entire household joined in this project, so that Montaigne heard and spoke only Latin until he was six years old. As a young man, he was sent to the Collège de Guyenne in Bordeaux where he excelled in the study of Latin literature. Yet, Montaigne chose to write the *Essays* in French, giving only his quotations from the ancient philosophers and poets in their original Latin. French, he says, is a "weaker idiom" than Latin (VS440, F320).[9]

Not only does he choose the weaker idiom, but Montaigne also insists that he simply follows common usage in his writing (VS796, F604). He makes no attempt to dress up his thoughts in the manner of those who want to seek the world's favor. "In language," he says, "the search for novel phrases and little-known words comes from a childish and pedantic disposition. Would that I might use only those that are used in the markets of Paris!" (VS172, F127). He tells us that he does not avoid any of those words that are used in the streets of France (VS875, F667). And he asks: "Do we witness more of a jumble in the chatter of fishwives than in the public disputations of the professional logicians? I would rather have my son learn to speak in the taverns than in the schools of talk" (VS926–27, F707). The *Essays* are written in the language of the markets, the streets, and the taverns of France, not in the language of the schools or the courts. Montaigne writes in the ordinary everyday language of the people, *the language which forms the social bond.*

Impropriety

Montaigne sometimes goes beyond the bounds of propriety in speaking about the parts and functions of the body and about sexual matters. And he defends what he calls his "excessive license" and his "immoderation" in speaking about the sexual (VS845, F642). He asks: "What has the sexual act, so natural, so necessary, and so just, done to mankind, for us not to dare to talk about it without shame and for us to exclude it from serious and decent conversations?" (VS847, F644). He disdains "those petty, feigned, customary, provincial rules" of propriety and ceremony that would keep him from presenting a complete portrait of himself to the public. And so, he concludes that "whoever would wean man of the folly of such a scrupulous verbal superstition would do the world no great harm" (VS888, F677).

Montaigne's violation of the norms of propriety with respect to speaking about the body is intended to bring the philosopher down from the heights of disembodied contemplation to the lowest, most common bodily functions which he shares with all men.[10] So he imagines the philosopher in the sexual act: "The most contemplative and wisest of men, when I imagine him in that position [of making love] seems to me an impostor to put on wise and contemplative airs; here are the peacock's feet that humble his pride: 'Against truth said in laughing/Is there a law?'" [Horace] (VS877, F669). He makes the philosopher look ridiculous and shameful: "Kings and philosophers shit, and so do ladies" (VS1085, F831). Philosophers and kings need to be reminded that they are just human beings: "I love to see these leading souls unable to shake off our common lot. Perfect men as they are, still they are men, and most heavily so" (VS835, F634). It is "thanks to our sickly, kill-joy mind" that we are disgusted with the ordinary pleasures of life. Montaigne says "I, who operate only close to the ground, hate that inhuman wisdom that would make us disdainful enemies of the cultivation of the body" (VS1106, F849).

Montaigne also therefore rejects any philosophical understanding of the human that would separate soul from body: "Plato fears our hard bondage to pain and pleasure, since it obligates and attaches the soul too much to the body; I, on the contrary, because it detaches and unbinds it" (VS58, F39). This is the basis for his moderation of pleasure, to keep the soul attached to the body, not to master the appetites. His body and soul are one: "my two ruling parts, of their own volition, live in peace and good accord" (VS1059, F811).

Therefore, Montaigne rejects both Stoic imperturbability and Epicurean apathy. He feels the passions and suffers the evils and accidents of human life. Unlike the Epicureans, he wants to feel even the evils of life: "Crantor was quite right to combat the apathy of Epicurus, if it was built so deep that even the approach and birth of evils were lacking. I have no praise for the insensibility that is neither possible nor desirable. I am glad not to be sick; but if I am, I want to know I am; and if they cauterize or incise me, I want to feel it. In truth, he who would eradicate the knowledge of good and evil would at the same time extirpate the knowledge of pleasure, and in fine would annihilate man" (VS493, F364).

Montaigne says: "I am no philosopher. Evils crush me according to their weight" (VS950, F725). Yet, he also says that he is a new figure of the philosopher. This apparent contradiction—that he is not a philosopher and that he is a philosopher—helps us to see that his reformation of philosophy involves the humanization of the philosopher. The unpremeditated and accidental philosopher does not escape the human condition.

In the tradition, it is the body that the philosopher regards as most shameful. Nevertheless, the body is what makes us present to each other. Montaigne is overcoming the shame of the body by bringing its lowliest actions into the light of the public. He makes philosophy look ridiculous and shameful by exposing the pride and pretensions of the philosopher. Thus, he makes the philosophical mind ashamed, not of the body, but of itself.

Testimony and Stories

The sociability of the essay form can be seen in the stance that Montaigne takes toward testimony and also in the central role he gives to stories and examples in the expression of his thought. In "It Is Folly to Judge the True and the False by Our Own Capacity" Montaigne confesses that he used to pity the simple who claimed to have witnessed all kinds of supernatural events. He had been guilty of the presumption of the learned, who cannot accept anything as true which they themselves have not experienced. Now, however, he is open to the testimony of the simple because he has recognized that the limits of the possible are not determined by his own limited experience.

In "Of the Power of the Imagination" he tells us that fabulous testimony is just as useful to him as true testimony, for his task is to tell not what has happened but what can happen. Throughout the *Essays*, Montaigne displays this openness to the testimony of others, an attitude that reflects his openness to the possible. He takes neither the attitude of the learned, who refuse to testify concerning actions that have happened right before their eyes and who will not stake their belief on the belief of a common man, nor the attitude of the simple, who think they see what is not there (VS106, F76).

David Hume, accounting for the fact that men are so unequal in the degree of understanding they achieve, says that: "After we have acquired a confidence in human testimony, books and conversation enlarge much more the sphere of one man's experience and thought than those of another."[11] By not rejecting out of hand the testimony of others, Montaigne enlarges his own experience; his experience is no longer limited to what has happened to him, but now expands to include a kind of philosophical attitude toward his own experience. That is, he does not experience what happens to him in a presumptuous way: he overcomes both the presumption of the learned and the presumption of the simple. Experience itself is changed for him.

Montaigne's openness to testimony is especially evident in the stories that fill the pages of the *Essays*. Although he says the work is to be only about himself, the stories that he recounts are in fact almost exclusively about other men. In "Of the Disadvantage of Greatness" Montaigne says that the disadvantage of greatness is the inability of the great to "essay" themselves against other men, causing them to miss one of the most important of all human pleasures, the playful testing of one's strength in struggle with others (VS918, F701). In order to experience this essaying of himself, the great man must "step down" from the heights of power (VS916, F699).

Montaigne essays himself against philosophers, poets, historians, princes, and common people. The stories of other men are forms of experience, of what is possible, and of the limits of the human soul. Montaigne is not testing himself against the standard of the universal, but measuring himself against other individuals. Thus, to essay himself is essentially a social act.

The Order of Shepherds and Shopboys

It must be acknowledged that the *Essays* look unphilosophical. There are no arguments, no syllogisms, and no conclusions. Neither does Montaigne seem concerned to arrive at universals or essences. As the title *essais* suggests, he weighs opinions, looking at many sides of a given topic. His topics themselves are generally unphilosophical—thumbs, smells, coaches, drunkenness—and appear trivial; they are not the weighty and essential topics of philosophy. His topics present themselves in an accidental way: "I take the first subject that chance offers. They are all equally good to me" (VS302, F219). These are the topics of everyday life which come into conversation in a haphazard way.

Montaigne's mind seems to move in a world of accidental similarities rather than a world of forms and essences. Thus, the *Essays* seem to be without any rational order: they move from accident to accident. Yet, he says that there is an order, albeit a very strange one: "it is the only book in the world of its kind, a book with a wild and eccentric plan" (VS385, F278). Indeed, it is order that he most concerned with: "the order that we see everyday in the altercations of shepherds and shopboys, never among us [the learned]. . . . at least they understand one another" (VS925, F706). Because the *Essays* descend below and behind the most common opinions to the level at which everyone can understand them, they do not follow the order of philosophical argument. Rather, the order of the *Essays* is the order of shepherds and shopboys, the order of everyday life.

Once again, the Socrates of Montaigne's invention can help us to see what Montaigne himself is doing. Montaigne re-forms Socrates, affirming and elevating him, yet at the same time lowering him, transforming him, and subjecting him to Montaigne's own purposes. The Socrates of the *Essays* does not ascend to the knowledge of the Forms; instead, he descends to the most lowly opinions of the most common men. Socrates "makes his soul move with a natural and common motion. So says a peasant, so says a woman. His mouth is full of nothing but carters, joiners, cobblers and masons. His are inductions and similes drawn from the commonest and best-known actions of men; everyone understands him. . . . By these vulgar and natural motives, by these ordinary and common ideas, without excitement or fuss, he constructed not only the best regulated but the loftiest and most vigorous beliefs, actions, and morals that ever were. It is he who brought human wisdom back down from heaven" (VS1038, F793). To those who think that the discourse of Socrates is far above common opinions, Montaigne responds: "I judge otherwise, and hold that it is a speech which in its naturalness ranks far behind and below common opinions. In an unstudied and artless boldness and a childlike assurance it represents the pure and primary impression and ignorance of Nature" (VS1054, F807). Indeed, it is possible to see in the *Essays* themselves much of what Montaigne describes as the lowliness of Socrates. The strength of the philosopher is in descending, not in ascending. This is the new kind of strength of the self-ordered soul, which is strong "in itself." The self-ordered soul orders his thought to the lowest and most common. The order of the *Essays,* then, is not the order of the syllogism. Rather, it is the order of a new logic of possibility which looks very much like the haphazard order of the conversations of ordinary human beings.[12]

Although Montaigne is not concerned with universals or essences, he does point to a capacity that belongs to all human beings: the capacity for communication, for making oneself understood. In the course of setting out the context for his claim that he is an unpremeditated philosopher, Montaigne tells us: "In Italy I advised a man who was at pains to speak Italian, that provided he sought only to make himself understood, without wishing to excel at it otherwise, he should simply use the first words that came to his mouth, Latin, French, Spanish, or Gascon; and that by adding the Italian ending, he would never fail to hit some dialect of the country. . . . I say the same thing about philosophy; it has so many faces and so much variety, and has said so much, that all our dreams or reveries are found in it" (VS546, F408). Using "the first words that come to his mouth" points to the spontaneity of everyday communication and the way in which philosophy can make him understood, accommodating itself to the immediacy of the occasion.

One of the first characteristics of men and animals that Montaigne discusses in the "Apology for Raymond Sebond" is the ability to communicate and, in particular, the ability of men to communicate not simply by words but also by gestures.[13] "Our mutes dispute, argue, and tell stories by signs. I have seen some as supple and versed in this, that in truth they lacked nothing of perfection in being able to make themselves understood." He then goes through a long list of gestures of the hands, head, eyebrows, and shoulders by which we communicate our desires and passions. "There is no movement that does not speak both a language intelligible without instruction, and a public language; which means, seeing the variety and particular use of other languages, that this one must rather be judged the one proper to human nature" (VS454, F332). The ability to communicate, whether by words or gestures, belongs to all men regardless of their differences and inequalities of intellect. The universal ability to communicate is the basis of society. The *Essays* are the perfect instantiation of that ability to communicate.[14]

Montaigne's Generous Gesture and Great Deed

There are, however, two instances in the *Essays* where neither philosophical nor everyday language can express precisely what Montaigne wants to convey. The first instance concerns his intended audience, "souls regulated and strong in themselves," which is an audience so sparse that it has "neither name nor rank among us" (VS657, F498). It has no name because it has no rank. In pointing to this lack of rank, Montaigne implies that his project involves a transcendence of the traditional hierarchy, the traditional order of high and low, strong and weak.

The second instance in which Montaigne finds both philosophical and everyday language insufficient concerns the confusion in both types of language, the confusion of goodness and innocence with imperfection and weakness. These conditions look so much alike that it is difficult to distinguish them. That is why "the very names of innocence and goodness are for this reason to some extent terms of contempt" (VS426, F310). Montaigne, then, must overcome this confusion and articulate his overcoming of the traditional hierarchy while using only the everyday language that is thoroughly imbued with that hierarchy. He continues to use the language of perfection and imperfection, high and low, strong and weak; he must also, however, find a way to convey the radical changes in the meaning of those terms effected by his own philosophical project. Since language fails him in these two decisive instances, he cannot communicate by words alone but only by a gesture or great deed.

Still, Montaigne insists that he has no great deeds to tell, so that he must come into the public with only words. That is what makes his emergence into the public potentially shameful and it is why his self-revelation is always enacted against the background of the accusation of weakness and the possibility of ridicule. He is bringing the private and common into the public where, until now, only great deeds justified such acts of self-revelation. It seems, then, that his self-communication could only be idle, frivolous, and ineffective.

The central action, the great deed, of the *Essays,* however, is the invention of society. We look through the various essays for arguments and conclusions in vain, because judgment is not an argument but an act. Montaigne's judgment is not expressed in propositions but in the very act of bringing the private into the public, the act of reordering the mind to the common and lowly, of reversing the traditional hierarchy, and finally of subordinating the high to the low. This is the generous gesture of the philosopher in and through which he reveals and communicates himself; it is the action by which he reveals the meaning of the self-ordered soul and the strength of goodness. Montaigne's generous gesture is the great deed which does justify his emergence into the public.

Reordering and Reversing

When the desire to tell his weak mores seizes him, Montaigne calls upon the help of philosophy to express them so that he might go out a bit more decently in public. He is a common, private man who claims no great learning or great deeds but who nevertheless emerges into the public wearing the fig leaf of ancient philosophy. This emergence of the private man into the public is the defining action of the *Essays* for it is the bringing into existence of the new realm of the social.

In the tradition, the private is the hidden and shameful, hidden because it is shameful. The actions of private life are the actions that are merely necessary, that is, unfree or servile, for they are associated with mere life.[15] The deeds of great men, on the contrary, are great because they show contempt for mere life, a contempt that manifests itself most clearly in risking life in the face of imminent and violent death. The great philosophers, too, show contempt for mere life. This philosophical contempt manifests itself in several ways: in the view that philosophy is the separation of the soul from the body; in the contempt that the philosopher has for the pleasures of the body; in the claim that philosophy is the highest activity of leisure which is freed from the servility of labor and work; in the philosopher's escape from the temporal and from this world to the eternal and celestial realm.

But here is Montaigne, a common, private, and weak man, presuming to bring out into public view everything that the philosophers and the great actors of history despise. By bringing the private out into the public, into visibility, Montaigne is overcoming its shame. He makes his mind ashamed of itself for its attempt to be divine, and by bringing the body and its everyday needs into the public, he overcomes the shame of the human. Thus, he initiates a reform of the great and of the philosophers.

Without great deeds or learning, the particular is anonymous, and yet Montaigne emerges into the public as a particular. The *Essays* are *The Essays of Michel de Montaigne*. He emerges out of the anonymity of the common in his concrete particularity. Thus, he overcomes the anonymity and invisibility of the individual who is merely an undifferentiated part of the common herd. He presents himself, the particular, as weak: his mores have not been formed by philosophy. It is the accidental conformity of his weak mores to the teachings and examples of philosophy that astonishes him. Philosophy allows him to see the weak, the private, and the shameful in a new light. Unpremeditated and accidental philosophy is the subordination of ancient philosophy to his desire for self-revelation, and the subordination of philosophy itself to the social.

The very first words of the *Essays* assert the primary significance of this emergence of the private into the public: Montaigne's end is merely domestic and private. This is the reversal of the Aristotelian order. Once again, he presents himself as too weak for the lofty goals of glory or public service. He simply wants to present himself in his "simple, natural, ordinary form, without striving." Thus, he concludes his address to the reader: "you would not be rational to spend your leisure on such a frivolous and vain subject" (VS3, F2). He is presenting his particularity, his weak and defective particularity, as it is in the realm of the domestic and private, not in the studied posture of the learned or of one seeking the favor of the world. To say that his end is domestic and private is to say that his end is the social, for the social is the domestic and private brought into the public. The reader would not be "rational" to study Montaigne's self-revelations, because the traditional notion of reason makes his reversal of the hierarchy look irrational. Thus, the generous gesture that brings the private into the public, which is a free act of the will, looks like a mere caprice.

Montaigne describes his decision to study only himself as a lowering of his mind: "Other men study themselves in order to elevate their minds and hoist them up tight; I to lower it and lay it to rest" (VS821, F623). He supports this claim with a quotation from Horace's *Odes* that illustrates the turn from the glorious enterprise of war to merely domestic concerns: "You sing of Aeacus' line and the wars beneath the sacred walls of Ilium: but you do not say how much I must pay for a jar of Chian wine, or who will heat my water on his fire, where I shall find shelter and when I shall escape from the cold of the Pelignian mountains" (Horace, *Odes,* 3.19, 3–8). But this lowering to the domestic and private actually turns out to be a new kind of perfection, for the bringing into existence of the social—his end—is the good.

Montaigne reorders philosophy to the human, rather than to the divine; to the lowest, rather than the highest; to the weak, rather than the strong; to the imperfect, rather than the perfect; to what is, rather than what ought to be; to the particular, rather than the universal; to the domestic and private, rather than the political; to the ordinary, rather than the extraordinary. In the terms of the traditional hierarchy, this reordering looks like a mere "lowering" of the mind. However, Montaigne's overcoming of the hierarchy is in fact a new kind of freedom, the freedom of the mind to order itself and to order the world. The order of the great and the everyday, the extraordinary and the ordinary is reversed: the lowest is higher than the highest. This reversal is very difficult to express, because ordinary language is imbued with the traditional hierarchy, confusing goodness and innocence with weakness and imperfection. Montaigne's subordination of the great to the everyday shows that we already possess the good, in the domestic and private. Enjoyment is possession. The good is not an end that we must strive for. It is already our own, "without striving," in the everyday. Thus, Montaigne's project is not simply the lowering of the high but rather the reversal of high and low and finally the subordination of the high to the low.

In pursuit of this project, Montaigne reorders the mind, and thus philosophy itself, to the familiar and the everyday, thereby overcoming the natural tendency of the mind to prefer the strange and extraordinary. Through the movement of Montaigne's thought in the *Essays,* the ordinary becomes extraordinary, the familiar becomes astonishing. From the most ordinary, common, and familiar things, if we could put them in their proper light, the greatest miracles of nature and the most marvelous examples would appear, especially on the subject of human actions (VS1081, F829).

Considering "the things that are right in our hands, it is rather familiarity than knowledge that takes away their strangeness." If these now familiar things were presented to us for the first time, we would be surprised by them and find them incredible (VS179, F132–33). The everyday is marvelous and miraculous because it subjects the extraordinary, rare, and strange to itself. Philosophy allows him to see the everyday—to put the everyday—in a new light. This is Montaigne's transformation of experience. The experience in which he ends is not the same as the experience in which he began, that is, experience formed by inherited philosophical opinion, for it is now freed from philosophical presumption.

Ending in Experience

"Of Experience" is the last of the essays. Montaigne literally, then, ends in experience. Experience, he says, is "weaker" than reason (VS1065, F815), yet reason must submit to experience. The first sentence of "Of Experience"—"There is no desire more natural than the desire for knowledge"—echoes the first sentence of Aristotle's *Metaphysics*—"All men by nature desire to have knowledge."[16] Aristotle begins in experience and ends in knowledge. In the first book of the *Metaphysics,* he sets out the ascent of the mind to the first causes of all things, the subject matter of "first philosophy." From sensation the mind ascends to memory. Memory is higher than sensation because it does not require the actual presence of the object: memory recalls the object to mind. Experience is "many memories of the same thing" (*Meta.* 1.1, 980b25–981a1). Thus, experience is the first level at which the mind unifies, bringing together many memories into one experience. Experience, however, knows only "that" something is the case but not "why" it is the way it is. From experience, then, the mind ascends to art, which is higher than experience because it involves the knowledge of causes. Finally, the mind ascends to knowledge and to the first science, which is most comprehensive because it deals with being as such and the first causes of all things. Thus, metaphysics is the highest of the sciences. In "Of Experience" Montaigne says: "I study myself more than any other subject. That is my metaphysics, that is my physics" (VS1072, F821). At the conclusion of that essay, he writes: "Of our sciences, those seem to me most terrestrial and low which have risen the highest" (VS1115, F856).

Aristotle's description of experience—many memories of the *same* thing—reveals the way in which the mind draws the particulars into a unity: the particular is seen from the start as an instance of form. Montaigne's understanding of experience, on the other hand, might be described in terms of the invention or imagination of the accidental similarities of particulars. Thus he is able to articulate the weak through accidental similarity to the strong, the lowest through accidental similarity to the highest. Whereas Aristotle's experience leads to form, Montaigne's experience leads to astonishing new particulars which, by virtue of their particularity, are "deformed."[17]

Montaigne reverses the Aristotelian order: he begins in knowledge and ends in experience. The knowledge in which he begins is the knowledge that comes from familiarity. Montaigne ends in experience, but this is not Aristotle's notion of experience, that is, many memories of the same thing, for Montaigne's memory is "monstrously deficient" (VS34, F21). Indeed, experience for Montaigne requires "the science of forgetfulness" (VS494, F365). The experience in which he ends is what I would call "astonished familiarity." He begins in familiarity and ends in astonished familiarity: unpremeditated and accidental philosophy is just this movement of thought. When he wants to tell his thoughts and mores in public, to tell what is most familiar to him and thus what he already knows, he calls on the help of philosophy to express himself and then is astonished to find that his mere caprices and his weak mores conform, by accident, to so many of the teachings and examples of ancient philosophy.

In "Of Cripples" he writes: "I have seen no more evident monstrosity and miracle in the world than myself. We become habituated to anything strange by use and time; but the more I frequent myself and know myself, the more my deformity astonishes me, and the less I understand myself" (VS1029, F787). He has not experienced the miracles that the simple have seen. Rather, the most familiar, himself, is astonishing to him. The more he is familiar with himself the more he knows himself. But this knowledge, this familiarity, has not accustomed him to his own strangeness. And the more he knows himself, the less he understands himself: he does not know why he is the way he is. This is a kind of Socratic ignorance, "a certain strong and generous ignorance that concedes nothing to knowledge in honor and courage, an ignorance that requires no less knowledge to conceive it than does knowledge" (VS1030, F788).[18] This strong and generous ignorance destroys knowledge and replaces knowledge with wonder. Montaigne's "master-form" is ignorance (VS302, F219) because he remains in this condition of astonished familiarity.[19]

The knowledge that is unastonished familiarity might be described as presumptuous knowledge or custom. Thus it could be said that Montaigne begins in presumptuous knowledge or custom and ends in philosophical experience or astonished familiarity. Custom, he says, is the tyrant, the master of thought. "The violent prejudice of custom" is the traditional hierarchy of high and low, strong and weak, in which the familiar and common are despised. Philosophy, understood as astonished familiarity, overcomes the violent prejudice of custom which dulls the mind and makes it so difficult to recognize the possible and the new. The new is just the most familiar seen in its proper light. The familiar itself, then, is transformed. That is how Montaigne both brings out the familiar into the light and, at the same time, introduces the new: the familiar is new. Philosophy, then, is just experience, but it is experience without presumption.[20] Experience, stripped of all presumption and arrogance, becomes philosophical. Philosophy, then, does not begin in wonder. Rather, the philosopher effects wonder.

But why is the most familiar astonishing? How are the most common human actions miracles of nature? What is the "proper light" in which they appear as astonishing miracles? The domestic and private realm is the place of the most common human actions, which are undifferentiated from man to man. It would be only in great deeds that men distinguish themselves and appear as individuals, while the most common human actions display what the individual has in common with all other men, that is, subjection to the necessities of life and the possession of "life itself." The individual disappears into the common, and the common therefore seems to lack any possibility of provoking astonishment.

For Aristotle, then, freedom is freedom from work and labor, from the need to labor and work for the necessities of life, in order to devote oneself to the "higher" activities of politics and philosophy, activities which are free because they are not instrumental but are "ends in themselves." Therefore, the life of the polis, to which leisure is essential, is made possible by the institution of slavery.

Once again, Montaigne reverses Aristotle: the most common human actions are not servile but free. How is this possible? The Aristotelian lives of politics and of philosophy are the striving for immortality. Thus, what at first appears to be contempt for death is really the attempt to escape death: the prince by achieving immortal glory and the philosopher by attaining the eternal causes of all things. The prince and the philosopher both want to escape our mortality and our temporality. The unpremeditated and accidental philosopher is content to live "in the moment." One way to describe what is presented in the *Essays,* then, is as the picture of human life when the striving for immortality—insofar as it is attainable by human power—has been given up.

In their "proper light" the most common and familiar human actions show themselves to be non-instrumental. Society is "for its own sake." Society is the practice of everyday life freed from the shame of servility. In effect, then, Montaigne frees the slaves.

Further, the most familiar and common human actions are astonishing because in them the violence of great deeds is subordinated to the domestic and private. "When I see both Caesar and Alexander, in the thick of their great tasks, so fully enjoying natural and therefore necessary and just pleasures, I do not say that that is relaxing their souls, I say that it is toughening them, subordinating these violent occupations and laborious thoughts, by the vigor of their spirits, to the practice of everyday life: wise men, had they believed that this [the violent] was their ordinary occupation, the other [the everyday] the extraordinary" (VS1108, F850). In their submission to the body's constant demands for food, digestion, sleep, and sexual pleasure, Alexander and Caesar are "toughening" their souls: the good is not weak but strong because it subjects the strong and violent to itself.

If the "proper light" is Montaigne's view of the human condition—in which the violent becomes ordinary and the everyday extraordinary—then the human condition must be the condition of war, of violence, and of the natural conflict between masters and slaves. The most common human actions are astonishing miracles because they overcome that natural condition of war. When the violent prejudice of custom is stripped away, when our most common impressions of weakness and strength are called into question, the weak reveals itself as stronger than the strong.

For Montaigne, the philosophical attitude or stance is neither contemplative nor practical for it is the stance of judgment, the attitude of possession and enjoyment. Judgment makes the object of contemplation—"the thing-itself"—one's own. The subjection of the thing itself to judgment is, at the same time, an ordering to the lowest. Thus, Socrates "brings down" the thing itself to his own "original level." In "Of Experience" Montaigne says that pleasure and pain, love and hate are the "first things" that a child feels (VS1111, F853). Judgment subjects the thing itself to these first things: for example, Montaigne "cruelly *hates* cruelty."

For Aristotle, these first things—pleasure and pain—originate at the lowest level of animal life, the level at which animals are distinguished from plants. It is to this lowest level that Montaigne returns in the philosophical act of judgment.

In the single philosophical act of making the familiar astonishing, Montaigne both reforms philosophy and frees the servile realm of the domestic and private from its bondage to the violent. By that single action, philosophy transcends the Aristotelian distinction between the theoretical and the practical. That is, the philosophical act itself refounds human association.

Unlike the ecstatic beholding of the thing itself, which the Aristotelian philosopher experiences in those few moments of his life when he escapes to the eternal and participates in the divine activity of contemplation, experience is simply the here and now, fully present to the unpremeditated and accidental philosopher. When the familiar is seen in its proper light, the light of the purified judgment of the philosopher, the divine reveals itself as the good of the everyday. That is why the ordinary is miraculous. The new is just the most familiar, what was there all along, but hidden. The act of reversing the most familiar and the most extraordinary, then, is a kind of revelation, bringing the divine out of its hiddenness. Truth is just this astonishing revelation.[21]

Thus, philosophical experience is not Aristotelian contemplation, but neither is it immersion in the temporal realm of practice or dissipation in the immediacy of the moment; that is, philosophy is neither theoretical nor practical. The astonishment of "astonished familiarity" suggests a kind of contemplative attitude directed toward the temporal realm of human life and action, but it is not a contemplative attitude that disdains the fleeting temporal as nothing. It is not a subjection of the temporal to the eternal but rather a subjection of the philosopher's stance toward the eternal to the merely temporal. In this way, Montaigne's philosophical attitude brings the eternal into the temporal and makes the eternal his own in time. Tzvetan Todorov captures this sense of Montaigne's stance toward the everyday in his explication of Montaigne's admonition that "the practice of everyday life should be an aim unto itself" (VS1051–52, F805). Todorov writes: "The sage will try to achieve this intransitive state, *the rejection of instrumentalization,* in each of his actions."[22] The actions of "mere life" become the philosophical experience of life "for its own sake."

Thus, leisure for Montaigne is not the condition for the philosopher's escape to the eternal and divine. His sense of leisure appears especially clearly in "Of Experience." Here, he disapproves of Socrates's contemplative ecstasies, of the theologian's "transcendental humors," and of the philosopher's attempt to escape from the man. But he approves wholeheartedly of the Socrates "who never refused to play cobnut with children or to ride a hobbyhorse with them" (VS1110, F852), as well as of the legendary "theological drinking and feasting" at the Sorbonne (VS1108, F851). Montaigne clearly hates to be told that we must keep our minds in the clouds while our bodies are at table. He is, he says, "intellectually sensual, sensually intellectual" (VS1107, F850).

Experience, understood as astonished familiarity, is the source of the philosopher's constant joy, for experience is ever present to the whole man, body and soul. "The surest sign of wisdom is constant joy" (VS161, F119). Philosophy is constantly joyful because the philosopher actually possesses the good in this world and in this life. The philosopher is not transported to the "other world," but rather experiences "this world" in a new way.

"Of Experience" begins with Aristotle's claim that all men desire knowledge and it ends with Montaigne's claim that the absolute perfection of knowing how to enjoy our own being rightly is "gay and *sociable* wisdom" (VS1116, F857). In "Of Experience" leisure is philosophical drinking and feasting, the bringing together of philosophy and society. Philosophy thereby becomes merely unpremeditated and accidental, and the philosopher is separated from the man. This joining with his fellow human beings in their astonishing particularity is the free act, the generous gesture, of the philosopher in which he rediscovers his own humanity. Montaigne himself is the miracle of the self-ordered soul that is sociable.

Part Two

✦

The Invention of Society

Chapter Five

✦

Overcoming Natural Mastery

Unpremeditated and accidental philosophy is both the separation of the man from the philosopher and also the humanization of the philosopher through the submission of philosophy to the social. In the same way, the overcoming of natural mastery is both the separation of the man from the prince and also the humanization of the prince through the submission of the political to the social. Montaigne refounds human association by introducing a new kind of rule, one which eliminates the master-slave relationship. The new foundation replaces the old foundation of "the common good," which Montaigne sees as the pretext for the mastery of the strong over the weak.[1]

Montaigne's Project of Refounding

In "Of Vanity" Montaigne makes what is perhaps his strongest statement against innovation in human association: "Nothing presses a state hard except innovation; change alone gives form to injustice and tyranny. When some part is dislocated, we can prop it up; we can fight against letting the alteration and corruption natural to all things carry us too far from our beginnings and principles. But to undertake to refound so great a mass, to change the foundations of so great a structure, that is a job for those who wipe out a picture in order to clean it, who want to reform defects of detail by universal confusion and cure illnesses by death, 'who desire not so much to change as to overthrow everything' [Cicero]" (VS958, F731).

This opposition to innovation entails rejecting the classical notion of perfection, that is, "the best cities" of Plato and Aristotle. Even the worst forms of political association "have nevertheless maintained their bodily health and long life as well as those of Plato and Aristotle could do. And indeed all those descriptions of a government imagined by art prove ridiculous and unfit to put into practice. These great, lengthy altercations about the best form of society and the rules most suitable to bind us, are altercations fit only for the exercise of our minds. . . . Such a description of a government would be applicable in a new world, but we take men already bound and formed to certain customs; we do not create them, like Pyrrha or Cadmus. By whatever means we may have the power to correct and reform them, we can hardly twist them out of their accustomed bent without breaking up everything" (VS956–57, F730). However, this opponent of innovation makes the surprising statement that "it is always a gain to change a bad state to an uncertain one" (VS972, F743). But the man who seeks to introduce change "must be very sure that he sees the weakness of what he is casting out and the goodness of what he is bringing in" (VS121, F88).

Montaigne reforms without destroying because he replaces the weak with the good. The weak foundation in the politics of the tradition is the presumed strength of natural mastery. The good foundation, in Montaigne's re-formed politics, is the presumed weakness of submission.

If the prince believes himself to be the natural master, he justifiably identifies himself with his unlimited power; thus, his power is in the service of his interest and his passions. He sees himself as superior to all other men and perhaps even as a god among men. Montaigne, however, separates the man from the prince, an act effected by the attainment of reason inflexible and impassive. Only reason inflexible and impassive can settle the conflict between masters and slaves. This separation seems to bring about the dehumanization of the prince, taking his very self out of his exercise of rule; Montaigne, however, effects this separation through the submission of the prince to the social. Thus, he in fact humanizes the prince.

Montaigne begins the *Essays* in "To the Reader" with the statement of his purpose: his book was written in good faith. He warns us from the outset that he has set himself merely a domestic and private end (VS3, F2). This, as we have seen, is the reversal of the Aristotelian order: for Aristotle, the domestic and private is not the end but the beginning. The domestic and private finds its completion in the city, the political association, and the end of political association is the common good. The standard of the common good is Aristotle's answer to the claim that all rule is really the rule of masters over slaves. In other words, for Aristotle, genuine political rule is not the rule of masters over slaves: whereas the master rules in his own interest, the ruler who acts for the common good rules for the good of the ruled (*Pol.* 3. 6–7). In the tradition, Aristotle's principle of the common good is the standard of moral virtue, especially justice. It is a very high standard and it is rarely, if ever, achieved in practice.

Montaigne, however, rejects the standard of the common good for he sees it as the justification for natural mastery. Given the fact of natural inequality, the pursuit of a common good requires the rule of the superior, wiser men. Hobbes characterizes this Aristotelian view that natural inequality justifies the rule of one man over another: "I know that Aristotle in the first booke of his Politiques, for a foundation of his doctrine, maketh men by Nature, some more worthy to Command, meaning the wiser sort (such as he thought himselfe to be for his Philosophy;) others to Serve, (meaning those that had strong bodies, but were not Philosophers as he;) as if Master and Servant were not introduced by consent of men, but by difference of Wit."[2] Hobbes, then, like Montaigne, sees natural superiority as the foundation of Aristotle's political philosophy.

Montaigne's rejection of the common good is ultimately grounded in his rejection of the idea of a single, common human form. Since philosophy has not been able to find a way to the good that is common, "let each one seek it in his particularity" (VS622, F471). The individual must be free to pursue the good in his own way. Therefore, any attempt to enforce a standard of the common good would require an illegitimate use of force. The common good justifies coercion and force.

For Montaigne, the idea of the common good is simply the "pretext of reason" for the actions of vicious men (VS802, F609–10). The political realm is not rule for the sake of the common good but the rule of masters over slaves. Virtue itself betrays this origin of political association: "It is probable that the first virtue that manifested itself among men and gave some advantage over others was this one, by which the strongest and most courageous made themselves masters of the weaker" (VS384, F277). If rule is to overcome the distinction between masters and slaves, then natural inequality cannot justify the domination of one man over another.

Montaigne's project of refounding is the resolution of the conflict between masters and subjects through the introduction of a new kind of rule and a new kind of freedom based on the overcoming of natural mastery. In "Of Custom" he writes: "Peoples brought up to liberty and to ruling themselves consider any other form of government monstrous and contrary to nature. Those who are accustomed to monarchy do the same. And whatever easy chance fortune offers them to change, even when with great difficulties they have rid themselves of the importunity of one master, they run to supplant him with a new one, with similar difficulties, because they cannot make up their minds to hate mastery itself" (VS116, F83–84).

Peoples must hate mastery *itself,* not simply this or that master. The admonition to "hate mastery itself" suggests that all of the old forms of rule are essentially the same: they are all forms of domination or mastery.[3] This is a radical break with the Aristotelian tradition for which regimes are judged to be either good or bad, just or unjust, depending upon the criterion of the common good: regimes that pursue the common good are just; those that pursue only the interests of the rulers are unjust. Regimes that do not pursue the common good are all versions of the master-slave relationship.[4]

Rousseau says in the *Discourse on the Origin and Foundation of Inequality:* "It is very difficult to reduce to obedience one who does not seek command."[5] In order to be free, in order not to be a slave, one must first renounce the desire to be a master. The desire to rule and the willingness to serve are two sides of the same coin. The master-slave is within each man. Freedom just is the condition of being "neither master nor slave." Montaigne's love of freedom expresses itself in his hatred of "every sort of tyranny, both in words and acts" (VS931, F711). When he says: "I am disgusted with mastery both active and passive," he explains what he means through a story. Otanes, who had the right to pretend to the throne of Persia, abandoned that right to his companions provided that he and his family be allowed to live in the empire "outside of all subjection and mastery" except to that of the ancient laws. He could not support either commanding or being commanded. Montaigne says that Otanes took the course of action that Montaigne himself would willingly have taken (VS917, F700).

But how can the condition of "neither master nor slave" become the principle of political association, since the political is necessarily the relation of ruler and ruled, of masters and subjects? Montaigne answers with a distinction that brings out the nature of princely power: he separates private will and public power. "The souls of emperors and cobblers are cast in the same mold. Considering the importance of the actions of princes and their weightiness, we persuade ourselves that they are produced by some causes equally weighty and important. We are wrong: they are led to and fro in their movements by the same springs as we are in ours. . . . Their will is as frivolous as ours, but their power is greater" (VS476, F350). If the souls of emperors and cobblers are cast in the same mold, then there are no natural princes, no natural masters: the emperor is essentially a private man. If the only difference between the will of the emperor and the will of the cobbler is the power of the emperor, then the will of the emperor is only a private will and therefore merely as frivolous as that of the cobbler.

Montaigne says that "the judgment of an emperor should be above his imperial power, and see and consider it as an extraneous accident;

and he should know how to find pleasure in himself apart, and to reveal himself like any Jack or Peter, at least to himself" (VS1012, F774). Judgment reveals that princely power is only an extraneous accident: the man is not essentially a prince. This is the separation of the man from the prince. Whereas for Aristotle, rule is justified by the natural superiority of the prince, for Montaigne there is no natural prince. All men are equally and essentially private men. If there is no natural prince, then overcoming natural mastery requires separating the man from the prince so that the power of the prince is no longer in the service of the man.

Speaking of his own exercise of rule, Montaigne says that "the Mayor and Montaigne have always been two, with a very clear separation" (VS1012, F774). Montaigne here introduces something like a public will, or rule that is not merely private will; it is rule as will or power without the self. The rejection of the common good rests on the claim that rule by the standard of the common good is really and simply the imposition of a private will on other men.

Montaigne's refounding replaces force—the domination of the strong over the weak—with consent. "As I do not like to take a hand in legitimate actions against people who resent them, so, to tell the truth, I am not scrupulous enough [*je ne fas pas assez de conscience*] to refrain from taking a hand in illegitimate actions against people who consent to them" (VS1063, F814). Consent, not superior wit, legitimizes rule.

Montaigne's refounding thus institutes a new kind of freedom. He praises the Theban general Epaminondas because he fought for "the inestimable good of restoring liberty to his country" (VS801, F609). This reference to "the inestimable good" is, I believe, the only instance in the *Essays* where Montaigne points to something like a highest or greatest good. The language that he uses is the language of restoration, of regaining or returning to something that had been lost. He uses this language because he is going back to the origins of political association and replacing them. The freedom that he institutes cannot be precisely the natural freedom of pre-civilized peoples who live under the "sweet freedom of nature's first laws" (VS3, F2). But it is also not simply a return to the ancient understanding of freedom, for there are two notions of freedom that are thematic in the *Essays:* the freedom of self-determination of a political entity and the freedom of the individual.

In his essay "The Liberty of the Ancients Compared with That of the Moderns," Benjamin Constant maintains that the liberty of the ancients consisted "in exercising collectively, but directly, several parts of the complete sovereignty." This included deliberating in the public square, forming alliances with foreign governments, voting, judging, and so on.

"But if this was what the ancients called liberty, they admitted as compatible with this collective freedom the complete subjection of the individual to the authority of the community."[6] Constant refers to this ancient liberty as "political" liberty. Modern liberty, on the contrary, is "personal" liberty, expressed in terms of certain rights of the individual. Personal freedom is the rejection of the Aristotelian notion of the common good. In "Of Glory" Montaigne writes: "All the glory that I aspire to in my life is to have lived it tranquilly: tranquilly not according to Metrodorus, or Arcesilas, or Aristippus, but according to me. Since philosophy has not been able to find any way to tranquility which is good in common, let each one seek it in his particularity!" (VS622, F471).

Montaigne's "restoration" is the reconciliation of these two notions of liberty. He expresses the first, ancient notion of liberty in his hatred of domination itself and the second, modern notion in his "end" which is "domestic and private." Bringing the domestic and private into the public means freeing the domestic and private from the domination of the political, and thus inventing society as a free mode of human association.

Reconciling these two kinds of freedom amounts to nothing less than a radically new understanding of rule itself. If rule is to be compatible with freedom, and if freedom is the condition of "neither master nor slave," then rule must become representation. Constant says that the bringing together of these two kinds of freedom is a modern invention. Representative government is a "discovery of the moderns"[7] that allows the individual to participate in sovereignty by electing representatives and, at the same time, allows him the freedom to pursue his own personal goals, to seek the good in his particularity.

According to Francis Slade, "rule detached from its natural embodiment is the core of modern political philosophy."[8] Thus, "the principle of ancient constitutions is the regime; that of modern, representation."[9] Whereas "a regime is rule embodied in those who rule,"[10] representation is "the separation of rule from human beings."[11] Representation is the separation of the man from the prince, for the representative is not a natural prince.

We see this notion of representation in Hobbes: "A person is he whose words or actions are considered, either as his own, or as representing the words or actions of an other man, or of any other thing to whom they are attributed, whether Truly or by Fiction. When they are considered as his owne, then he is called a Naturall Person: And when they are considered as representing the words and actions of an other, then he is a Feigned or Artificiall person." Rule is, then, representation of the will of every man: "A Multitude of men, are made One Person, when they are by one man, or one Person, Represented; so that it be done with the consent of every one of that Multitude in particular."[12]

Although Montaigne does not discuss the idea of representative government, his epistemological notion of representation provides the basis for this possibility. The mind represents not only what is and what is not but also "what we want." Therefore, the will can be represented.[13] Representation is not the apprehension of form, of a universal essence. Rather, Montaigne represents "a particular, very ill-formed." Representation is of particulars, particular and diverse wills. As Hobbes says, the consent of each is united in the words and actions of the one person who represents the multitude.

Montaigne says that "mastery, of itself, breeds contempt of what we hold and rule" (VS634, F480). If natural inequality is not justification for mastery, then those who believe themselves superior must be brought into unity with the common herd which they naturally hold in contempt. Only the magnanimous act of the proud can make possible the resolution of the conflict between master and slaves. The proud must renounce the right to rule. This is an act of the will which looks irrational—like a mere whim or caprice—because it is uncalculated. And, because it is uncalculated, it is entirely free. Yet, the will is in accord with reason inflexible and impassive, because this public reason is the renunciation of self-interest and self-esteem.[14]

We find in Montaigne, then, a kind of "moralization of pride" similar to what Oakeshott sees in Hobbes's political philosophy. Hobbes relies on the fact that the greatest fear that most men experience is the fear of death. This fear drives them out of the state of nature and into the contract that is the commonwealth. But Hobbes recognizes that not all men can be ruled by the fear of death. The proud man would rather die than submit, would rather die than be forced to accept equality with the common men who do submit out of fear. In fact, according to Oakeshott, Hobbes actually needs such proud men because they are more likely to make the first gesture toward peace. They are the ones who must be counted on to risk their lives by laying down their arms while the others retain theirs. This gesture comes not from fear but from a certain kind of generosity that can belong only to the proud. The proud achieve through courage what others achieve through rational calculation inspired by fear.

Oakeshott's depiction of the generous man's character is worth quoting in full because it describes so precisely Montaigne's character. The man whose pride has been moralized is "a man whose disposition is to overcome fear not by reason (that is, by seeking a secure condition of external human circumstances) but by his own courage; a man not at all without imperfections and not deceived about himself, but who is proud enough to be spared the sorrow of his imperfections and the illusions of his achievements; not exactly a hero, too negligent for that, but perhaps with a touch of careless heroism about him; a man, in short, who (in Montaigne's phrase) 'knows how to belong to himself,' and who, if fortune turned out so, would feel no shame in the epitaph: '*Par delicatesse/ J'ai perdu ma vie.*' "[15]

Montaigne's essay "Of the Disadvantage of Greatness" actually begins with a discussion of the *advantage* of greatness: "In general greatness has this evident advantage, that it can step down whenever it pleases, and that it almost has the choice of both conditions" (VS916, F699). Greatness "almost" has the choice of both conditions only because, when it steps down to the condition of lowliness, greatness still differs from lowliness in that its lowliness is freely chosen. To choose lowliness means the disappearance of the great into the anonymity of the common. Illustrious, shining deeds are swallowed up in the darkness of privacy. The noble man who chooses this condition does not assert his superiority, does not claim what is his by right, but acts on an "inclination" of his judgment to disappear into the anonymity of the common.

In order to effect the condition of "neither master nor slave," the institution of true freedom, the noble man must step down. Greatness must lower itself; pride must become generosity; and the desire to rule must become the gift of equality and freedom. "Giving belongs to rule and mastery" (VS1026, F785). In his *Travel Journal,* Montaigne records that in a house in Pisa he saw a representation of King Charles VIII on his knees before the Madonna who appears to be giving him counsel. "The inscription says that when the said king was supping in this house it came into his mind to give the Pisans their ancient freedom, whereby he surpassed the greatness of Alexander. . . . The words concerning that matter of the granting of freedom have been purposely disfigured and half effaced."[16]

The condition of "neither master nor slave" is the condition of "voluntary servitude," to use the expression of Montaigne's friend La Boétie. The old foundation of political association rests on the justification of the mastery of the naturally strong over the weak. In contrast, voluntary servitude is the transformation of the natural relationship of masters and slaves into the free, non-natural association of equals. Voluntary servitude does not assume the superiority or perfection of the master. On the contrary, it is voluntary because the master's rule cannot be justified by his superiority. Montaigne says: "Let us make this concession to the political order: to suffer [princes] patiently if they are unworthy. . . . But, our dealings over, it is not right to deny to justice and to our liberty the expression of our true feelings, and especially to deny good subjects the glory of having reverently and faithfully served a master whose imperfections were so well known to them" (VS16, F9).

So also, the motives for entering into the condition of voluntary servitude do not matter. In a passage that anticipates Hobbes, Montaigne writes of false and lax rules in philosophy: "Robbers have seized you; they have set you free again after extracting from you an oath to pay a certain sum. People are wrong to say that an honest man will be quit of his word without paying, once he is out of their hands. Nothing of the sort. What fear has once made me will, I am bound still to will when without fear. . . . Otherwise we shall come by degrees to overthrow all the rights that a third person obtains from our promises and oaths. *As if force can be brought to bear on a brave man* [Cicero]. In this alone does private interest have the right to excuse us for failing our promise, if we have promised something wicked and unjust in itself; for the rights of virtue must prevail over the rights of our obligation" (VS801, F608). For Montaigne, the promise as the expression of and the binding of the will is the social bond. "Since mutual understanding is brought about solely by way of the word, he who falsifies it betrays human society. It is the only instrument by means of which our wills and thoughts communicate, it is the interpreter of our soul. If it fails us, we have no more hold on each other, no more knowledge of each other. If it deceives us, it breaks up all our relations and dissolves all the bonds of our society" (VS666, F505). Lying is such a destructive vice because "we are men and hold together only by our word" (VS36, F23).

Although, as Oakeshott maintains, Hobbes must presume upon the generosity of the proud, he constructs his commonwealth on the foundation of the fear of death that is characteristic of the weak. That is, the proud or spirited, who play such an important role in the state of nature, disappear from his commonwealth, apparently dismissed by the ninth law of nature. "If Nature therefore have made men equall, that equalitie is to be acknowledged: or if Nature have made men unequall; yet because men that think themselves equall, will not enter into conditions of Peace, but upon Equall termes, such equalitie must be admitted. And therefore for the ninth law of Nature, I put this, *That every man acknowledge [every] other for his Equall by Nature.* The breach of this Precept is *Pride.*"[17]

In Montaigne, however, the moralization of pride, which is presumed but not accounted for by Hobbes, is made explicit, for, unlike Hobbes, Montaigne wants to preserve the spiritedness of the proud in the form of resistance to mastery. Freedom is central for Montaigne in a way that it is not for Hobbes. Montaigne wants to overcome mastery but, at the same time, preserve spiritedness. In other words, he wants to remove the desire for mastery from the proud without destroying the love of freedom. The moralization of pride is just this combination of the renunciation of the desire for mastery with the love of freedom. Being the first to lay down one's arms looks like surrender and submission. The hero, however, does not care that he might look weak and cowardly. He knows that his willingness to take the risk is his freedom, for he risks his life and is ready to lay down his life, not for the sake of his honor, but rather for the sake of a good greater than either life or honor. The good worthy of his risk is twofold: the freedom he exhibits in his choice to lower himself and the freedom he thereby wins for his fellow citizens.

How, then, does Montaigne effect his refounding? How does the philosopher, who effaces himself and has no great deeds to tell, exercise power over the minds and hearts of men?

Essaying: Producing the Marvelous

The invisible power of the *Essays* is exercised through the production of the marvelous. In his *Reflections on the Revolution in France,* Edmund Burke reports on an observation made by Rousseau to Hume: "Mr. Hume told me that he had from Rousseau himself the secret of his principles of composition. That acute though eccentric observer had perceived, that to strike and interest the public, the marvelous must be produced; that the marvelous of the heathen mythology had long since lost its effect; that giants, magicians, fairies, and heroes of romance which succeeded, had exhausted the portion of credulity which belonged to their age; that now nothing was left to the writer but that species of the marvelous which might still be produced, and with as great effect as ever, though in another way; that is, the marvelous in life, in manners, in characters, and in extraordinary situations, giving rise to new and unlooked-for strokes in politics and morals."[18]

In Baconian terms, the essay is a new logic, a logic of discovery, which replaces the old logic of the syllogism. Through particulars and accidental similarities, rather than universals and essences, the new logic discovers or invents new particulars, new possibilities. In "Of the Disadvantage of Greatness" Montaigne's thought moves from the *advantage* of greatness—the ability to step down and thus to have the choice of both conditions—to the disadvantage of greatness: "There is perhaps nothing more pleasant in association with men than the trials [*essais*] of strength we have with one another, in rivalry of honor and worth, whether in exercises of the body or of the mind; and in these sovereigns have no real share" (VS918, F701). The prince can only essay himself if he steps down. There is a sense of essaying, then, that means trying oneself out against other men, and this conveys the sense of spiritedness, struggle, and striving to assert and display one's superior strength. Essaying can only occur in a condition in which the master gives up his conventional and customary power in order to depend upon only his natural abilities. The activity of essaying, then, combines "stepping down," that is, renouncing mastery, and the spiritedness of trying out one's strength in rivalry with other men. Montaigne invents this form and essays himself against princes, philosophers, historians, and poets. He emerges from his rivalry as an astonishing new possibility.

By Diverse Means

The very first essay, "By Diverse Means We Arrive at the Same End," will serve as my example of Montaigne's activity of essaying as the production of the marvelous and as a structure for presenting a more complete account of his project. I will first give a brief summary of this essay and then offer a thematic interpretation.

Montaigne begins with the distinction between the common and the extraordinary: "The most common way of softening the hearts of those we have offended, when, vengeance in hand, they hold us at their mercy, is by submission to move them to commiseration and pity. However, audacity and steadfastness—entirely contrary means—have sometimes served to produce the same effect." This observation is illustrated with three stories of avenging princes who were not moved to compassion by the submission of the common people but who were moved by esteem for the valiant defiance of a few. Immediately after the first stories of these three princes, Montaigne writes: "Either one of these two ways would easily move me. For I am marvelously weak in the direction of mercy and gentleness. As a matter of fact, I believe I should be more likely to surrender more naturally to compassion than to esteem. Yet to the Stoics, pity is a vicious passion; they want us to succor the afflicted, but not to unbend and sympathize with them" (VS8, F4).

On the basis of the examples of the three princes, a possible explanation is offered of why some men are moved by compassion and others by esteem: "It might be said that to subdue your heart to commiseration is the act of easygoing indulgence and softness, which is why the weaker natures, such as those of women, children, and the common herd, are the most subject to it; but that, having disdained tears and prayers, to surrender simply to reverence for the sacred image of virtue is the act of a strong and inflexible soul which holds in affection and honor a masculine and obstinate vigor" (VS8, F4). This first plausible explanation is given in the terms of the hierarchy of strong and weak, a hierarchy said to be according to nature: virtue is associated with strength and identified with the divine ("the sacred image of virtue"). But this explanation does not hold up, for Montaigne brings in other examples to show that "in less generous souls, astonishment and admiration can engender a like effect" (VS8, F4). Two stories of "the people," the common herd, illustrate the way in which an entire assembly and an entire army can be so astonished at the spectacle of extraordinary valor that it turns from its pursuit of vengeance to admiration and mercy. Epaminondas, for example, addresses the Theban assembly in a haughty and arrogant manner, refusing to ask for mercy, and the people are so astonished that they walk out without casting their ballots against him. In the second story, the tyrant Dionysius decides to make the captain Phyto an example of his extreme vengeance, but when Phyto is dragged through the town to be led to execution, he keeps calling out the honorable and glorious cause of his death, that he refused to surrender his country to the tyrant. The rank and file of the army are so astonished that they turn against the tyrant and are on the verge of mutiny.

At this point in the essay, Montaigne makes his first assertion about the diversity—the marvelous diversity—of human beings: "Truly man is a marvelously vain, diverse, and undulating object. It is hard to found any constant and uniform judgment on him" (VS9, F5). The examples of Pompey and Sulla, in their very different responses to heroic self-sacrifice, illustrate this diversity of character. Pompey pardoned the entire city of the Mamertines on account of the valor and magnanimity of one citizen, Stheno, who took upon himself the fault of the people and asked to bear their punishment; Sulla, however, refused to pardon the city of Praeneste when his host asked to take on himself the punishment of the city.

Now Montaigne turns to Alexander as his example of another prince who was not moved to mercy at the spectacle of valor. Alexander is "directly contrary" to the first three princes whom Montaigne has cited. Montaigne does say that Alexander was "the bravest of men and one very gracious to the vanquished" (VS9, F5), thus implying that these two instances of cruelty are unusual and out of character. He then goes on to tell two stories of Alexander's cruelty: his encounter with and monstrous treatment of the Persian governor Betis after the siege of Gaza;

and the story of the desolation of Thebes in which 6,000 Theban soldiers were slaughtered and the old men, women, and children were taken as slaves.

"Neither Master nor Slave": Princes and People

Montaigne's first essay thus presents us with the fundamental situation of mastery and subjection in its most extreme form: the defeated are entirely at the mercy of the avenging conqueror. That, in fact, is the defining situation, the setting, of the *Essays*. "By diverse means we arrive at the same end" becomes "by diverse means we produce the same effect." The most obvious sense of "the same effect" is the softening of the heart of the avenging conqueror, that is, the humanization of the prince. The effect that is being manifested in this first essay is the transformation of the master-slave relationship: rule as mastery is replaced with a new form of rule that transcends mastery and subjection and is, therefore, humanized.

The first plausible explanation of the fact that the princes are moved to mercy by esteem but not by compassion is that strong natures can revere only "the sacred image of virtue," whereas weak natures sympathize with those who are like themselves. Montaigne here goes beyond the appearance of the first sense, the explanations offered by the tradition. This first explanation is based on the classical hierarchy of weak and strong, but it does not entirely hold up: the two stories of "the people," the common herd, show that, in "less generous souls," astonishment can have the same effect as esteem.

The three stories of the princes and the two stories of the people have in common the element of surprise. The princes are bent on vengeance, relentlessly pursuing conquest and revenge, indifferent to the cries of women and children. Suddenly, they are brought up short by the spectacle of heroic action. A possibility is offered to the prince so suddenly that he has the chance of not acting according to habit. The man separates himself from his power. In these three cases, the prince goes beyond habit, recognizes the equality or even superiority of the defiant, his esteem softens his heart and, in the cases of two of these princes, mercy expands to the entire city. The stories of the people present a similar phenomenon. In both cases, the people are moved by astonishment at heroic virtue and are deterred from their course of revenge. The first words of the essay are "the most common": submission is the most common way to soften the heart of the avenging prince. The last word of the essay is "slaves": after the slaughter of 6,000 Theban soldiers, Alexander takes 30,000 Thebans—old men, women, and children—as slaves. But the stories Montaigne tells of the people display the desire to escape such slavery and gain freedom. The Thebans regained their freedom from Sparta under the leadership of Epaminondas. When he is charged with the crime of having held onto the position of leader beyond the legal limit, he reminds them of the fact that they are free on account of him, that it was he who led them to defeat the invincible Spartans. In the story of the rank and file of the army of Dionysius, we are shown the possibility of rebellion. At the same time that the crowd is astonished at the heroic virtue of Phyto, they reach the point of mutiny against the tyrant. This account challenges the view that the common herd is weak and submits on account of fear. Even though Dionysius is making an example of Phyto, using him to demonstrate the extreme to which his vengeance will take him, the crowd is ready to rebel. The people are not *naturally* slaves.

How is it possible that an entire people, an entire assembly or army, can be astonished? How is this response communicated? In both the story of Phyto and the story of Epaminondas, the people are moved by words. Phyto not only acts with incredible fortitude while being whipped through the streets on his way to execution, he keeps calling out in a loud voice the reason for his condemnation: he resisted the tyrant. Epaminondas likewise reminds the Thebans in a proud and haughty manner of what he had done for them. Whereas the three princes are not moved by speech, the people are moved and are united by speech. The explanation that might be offered is that the people show their desire for freedom because they realize that there is strength in numbers, while individually they are weak and cowardly. But this reasoning neglects the fact that their reaction is spontaneous, not calculated. Further, as we see in the last story of this essay, the Theban soldiers are in fact extremely brave as individuals.

When the princes are taken by surprise, they are moved beyond mastery by esteem, and that transcendence of mastery has the effect of mercy. Esteem is the way in which the "natural envy" of masters is overcome, for esteem is the recognition of the equality or even superiority of the defiant. When the people are taken by surprise, they are moved beyond subjection to both mercy and freedom: like the princes, they recognize something of themselves in the defiant. The similarity of the people to the princes is Montaigne's rejection of the idea of natural mastery and natural slavery.

Stheno and the Anonymous Man: Representing the People

The contrasting stories of Pompey and Sulla are taken from Plutarch's "Precepts of Statecraft," in which Plutarch discusses the characteristics of the true statesman who "even though he had no part in the wrongdoing of the people, [takes] dangers upon himself in their behalf. For this is noble; and besides being noble, one man's excellence and wisdom by arousing admiration has often mitigated anger which has been aroused against the whole people and has dissipated the threatened terror and bitterness" (815e). When Pompey was going to punish the Mamertines for revolting, "Sthenno [*sic*] told him that he would be doing wrong if he should destroy many innocent men for the fault of one; for, he said, it was he himself who had caused the city to revolt by persuading his friends and compelling his enemies. This so affected Pompey that he let the city go unpunished and also treated Sthenno kindly." But when Sulla was going to slaughter the citizens of Praeneste, his guest-friend, an unnamed man to whom he had a private duty, could not produce the same effect. Sulla offered to let this anonymous man go on account of his guest-friendship. But that noble man "declared that he would not be indebted for his life to the slayer of his fatherland, and then mingled with his fellow-citizens and was cut down with them" (815f–816a).[19]

Both Stheno and the anonymous man unite their cities in themselves by taking on the guilt of the entire city and by standing in the stead of all the citizens. It could be said that they represent the people before the conquering prince. In these stories we are presented with an instance in which the same means produces diverse effects. Pompey accepts the single individual as standing in for the entire city and his response is forgiveness, whereas Sulla does not accept the single individual as standing in for the city. The magnanimous gesture is a risk taken in desperate circumstances. Sulla would have spared his guest-friend, but that man disappears into the anonymity of the crowd in an act of unity with the people and voluntary dissolution of the self.

The Power of Homer and the Weakness of Aristotle: Alexander and Betis

Betis was the governor of the city of Gaza at the time of Alexander's invasion. He fought valiantly, but when the siege was near its end, was abandoned by his men and fought on alone although badly wounded. Alexander had also been wounded twice in the course of the battle. When Betis was finally captured, Alexander confronted him with threats of torment, but Betis remained silent: his look was "not only confident but insolent and haughty." At that point, Montaigne says, Alexander turned his anger into rage. "He ordered Betis' heels to be pierced through and had him thus dragged alive, torn, and dismembered, behind a cart" until dead (VS9, F5).

Montaigne's source for this story is the *History of Alexander* by Quintus Curtius. When his recounting of this story is compared with this source, his invention becomes evident.[20] He both omits crucial elements of Curtius's account and changes one of the details of Betis's death.[21] Concerning the manner of Betis's execution, Curtius claims that Alexander "boasted that in taking vengeance on an enemy he had imitated Achilles, from whom he derived his race."[22] Montaigne omits this entirely, a striking omission since he himself provides three possible motives for Alexander's action, none of them involving the deliberate imitation of Achilles. The detail that Montaigne changes has to do with the way Betis was fastened to the chariot. Quintus Curtius says that "thongs were passed round his ankles" and "he was bound to the king's chariot."[23] Montaigne says that Alexander "commanded that his heels be pierced." This change of detail is important, because in Homer's description of the way Achilles bound the body of Hector to his chariot, it is specified that Achilles pierced the feet of Hector (*Iliad,* bk.22, 468–70). By altering this detail from Curtius's version, Montaigne shows quite clearly that he is thinking of Homer, of Achilles's treatment of Hector's body, and thus of Alexander's boasting that he was imitating Achilles, just as Curtius reports. Thus, Montaigne's omission concerning Alexander's own statement of his motive is both deliberate and meant to be noticed.

Montaigne is silent concerning the role of Homer and Alexander's desire for immortality through his family origins. Instead, he offers three other possible motives or "springs" for Alexander's action: "Could it be that hardihood was so common to Alexander that, not marveling at it, he respected it the less? Or did he consider it so peculiarly his own that he could not bear to see it at this height in another without passionately envious spite? Or was the natural impetuosity of his anger incapable of brooking opposition?"

These three possible motives display the contempt and envy that mastery has for subjection. The first—that bravery was so common to him that he could not admire it—manifests the contempt that the ruler has for what he holds and rules. The second—that he could not stand to see bravery at such a height in another man—manifests the "natural envy" between masters and subjects, the envy that the master feels in the presence of an equal or superior. The third—the natural impetuosity of Alexander's anger—is not assigned a possible cause by Montaigne, but Quintus Curtius attributes his anger to the fact that in the battle for Gaza, Alexander was wounded twice.[24] Montaigne may, in fact, favor this third spring of action since he goes on to say: "In truth, if [his anger] could have been bridled, it is probable that it would have been in the capture and desolation of the city of Thebes" (VS9–10, F5).

Could it be that he, who was descended from the gods, suddenly, in being wounded, faced the possibility of his mortality and that this caused his uncharacteristic rage and cruelty? Montaigne does not mention this possibility. Could it be, then, that Alexander deliberately produced the spectacle of Betis's punishment in order to display his divinity and his immortality, as Dionysius deliberately produced the spectacle of extreme vengeance? Indeed, Alexander goes beyond Achilles's treatment of the body of Hector, for Betis is alive when he is fastened to the chariot. In "Cowardice, Mother of Cruelty" Montaigne says that anything beyond simple death in the executions of justice is "pure cruelty" (VS700, F530).

Alexander's anger turns to rage and cruelty because Betis will not submit. Betis was "alone, abandoned by his men," wounded and covered with blood. He is silent before Alexander and will not beg for mercy. His look is insolent and haughty. It is clear that Alexander wants him to speak, to acknowledge his submission by words or gestures. Alexander calls out: "Has he bent a knee? Has any suppliant cry escaped him? I'll conquer your muteness yet; and if I cannot wring a word from it, at least I'll wring a groan." Montaigne does not mention a possible cause for Betis's silence: Quintus Curtius tells us that silence was one of the most important traits instilled into the Persian captains.[25] Betis, then, was the subject of a despot and remains fiercely obedient to him even in the most dire circumstances when he is alone and cannot be protected and saved by his prince. Quintus Curtius describes Betis as "a man of exceptional loyalty to his king."[26] Indeed, he is not only loyal to his prince, but he also displays defiance, haughtiness, and insolence to Alexander who has him entirely in his power. He refuses to submit. Betis may be one of those men who, even though he is brought up under tyranny, has the desire for freedom.[27]

Alexander's encounter with Betis, as invented by Montaigne, displays two fundamental features of mastery: domination which of itself breeds contempt for what is dominated, and the natural envy between masters and subjects. It also, silently, points to the enchantment of the origins: Alexander is bound to Achilles, his divine and immortal ancestor, for he is held by the power of Homer. The divinity of Alexander, which silently marks his first appearance in the *Essays,* is mentioned explicitly in his last appearance at the very end of the last essay. "I find nothing so humble and so mortal in the life of Alexander as his fancies about his immortalization" (VS1115, F856–57).

Montaigne is entirely silent about the role of Homer in Alexander's actions toward Betis. He is breaking the enchantment of Homer and thus breaking the power of Alexander's belief in his divine origins. Montaigne reduces Alexander's action from participation in the divine (through his ancestor Achilles) to the infinite desire to be and to appear superior to and stronger than all other men. By replacing the divine with the human he shows that the desire to participate in the divine is the vain desire to be and to appear superior to all other men.

Montaigne breaks the enchantment of Homer because he is replacing Homer. As Homer is the poet of Alexander—Alexander carried his *Iliad* everywhere in his drive to conquer the world—Montaigne is the poet of Epaminondas, who fought for the inestimable good of restoring freedom to his country. In his essay "Of the Most Outstanding Men" Montaigne discusses Homer, Alexander, and Epaminondas. Epaminondas is the most outstanding of all.

Although Montaigne does not mention Aristotle in this first essay, Aristotle is nevertheless present as the teacher of Alexander. It would seem that the two stories of Alexander's cruelty are intended to manifest, in particular, the failure of Aristotle's teachings to moderate the infinite desires and passions of Alexander and, in general, the ineffectiveness of Aristotle's restraints on the power of the natural master. For Aristotle, philosophy, not rule, is man's participation in the divine. Philosophy, then, ought to have a moderating effect on the prince's aspirations to divinity. But the power of Homer is greater: Montaigne is the poet of Epaminondas, but he is also replacing the impotent Aristotle with his own invisible power to moderate the prince.

Separating the Man from the Prince: Epaminondas and Thebes

Epaminondas, who, as we have already seen, figures prominently in the *Essays,* was the commander who led the Thebans to victory over the Spartans and freed Thebes from the domination of Sparta at the battle of Leuctra in 371 BC. Plutarch's life of Epaminondas has not survived and even though Cicero refers to him as "the first man of Greece," very little remains of the writings about him.[28]

Given the sparseness of the ancient sources available to us, Victor Davis Hanson, in *The Soul of Battle: From Ancient Times to the Present Day, How Three Great Liberators Vanquished Tyranny,* provides an unusually detailed portrait. Epaminondas was a Pythagorean, a philosopher, and "may have been the best educated man of action in the ancient world."[29] Two features of the character of Epaminondas stand out in Hanson's portrait. First, "the entire Epaminondan laudatory tradition is rooted in contemporary observations of his zeal . . . to free the unfree."[30] He felt great repugnance for Spartan helotage, and his goal was to liberate both serfs and free men from the autocracy of Sparta.[31] His disdain for tyrants caused him to fight in order to give democracy to his fellow Boeotians, autonomy to the cities of the Peleponnese, and freedom to the helots of Messenia.[32]

Second, Hanson notes, the character of Epaminondas was "selfless."[33] The liberation of Thebes, of the cities of the Peloponnese, and of the helots of Messenia was accomplished "all without gratuitous killing, personal lucre for himself, or political exploitation by his Boeotians."[34] According to Plutarch, Epaminondas never executed any person of a captured city, nor ever sold any Greek captive into slavery.[35] Remarkably, in spite of his great military victories, Epaminondas was himself indifferent to domination. He fought to bring freedom, not to conquer and rule.[36]

In Montaigne's first essay, Epaminondas appears before the Theban assembly on trial for having kept his command of the troops for four months longer than the people had directed. Cornelius Nepos explains that Epaminondas did this because he was convinced that the new commanders appointed by the people were inexperienced and would bring about the destruction of the army: "Epaminondas did all of this under the shadow of the Theban law which punished with death all who kept their command longer than the prescribed period. Since he recognized that this law was enacted to preserve the state, and since he did not want the same law to ruin the state," he held onto the command, violating the letter of the law.[37] Montaigne presents him as defiant in his speech before the assembly. Epaminondas reminds the people of the fact that under his leadership, they had been set free from the yoke of Spartan domination, and they are so astonished that they cannot proceed against him. He is the only prince profiled in the first essay who speaks to the people.

The last story Montaigne includes in "By Diverse Means" also concerns Thebes: here, he recounts Alexander's destruction of the city. Alexander has all of the soldiers slaughtered and then takes the rest of the inhabitants as slaves. The 6,000 Theban soldiers are described by Montaigne as "lost and without any further means of common defense." It is clear from his account of the battle that the soldiers were dispersed, silent, alone, each on his own, seeking out the enemy. Not one of them attempted to flee and not one asked for mercy. What we see here is the same Theban army that, under the leadership of Epaminondas, had defeated the Spartans thirty years earlier.[38] The essay ends, then, with the display of the valor of the individual, anonymous Theban soldiers. As David Quint says: "In this case, valor really has become 'common,' since it is displayed in the entire adult male population of the doomed city. These are, ironically, the same Thebans who . . . had shown themselves capable of reverencing—and sparing—their valorous fellow citizen Epaminondas."[39]

The individuals who make up the "rank and file," the common herd, display as much valor as any of the noblemen of the first stories, even as much as Alexander himself. However, without Epaminondas, they are defeated, and their country is enslaved. Without Epaminondas, they are not united. Montaigne concludes his portrait of Epaminondas in "Of the Most Outstanding Men" with the observation that "the prosperity of his country died, as it was born, with him" (VS757, F574).

That the freedom and prosperity of Thebes depended entirely on the character and ability of Epaminondas is a fact noted by the ancient historians as well. As Epaminondas lay dying, he ordered the Thebans to make peace because they had no one left to lead them.[40] Cornelius Nepos concludes his life of Epaminondas with a "comment about his character and life, a comment no one can dispute. Before Epaminondas was born and after he died Thebes was the satellite of a foreign power. But while he directed the state, Thebes was the leader of the most powerful city in Greece. From this fact anyone can see that Epaminondas as an individual was mightier than the whole state."[41]

What had happened to Thebes in the thirty years between the death of Epaminondas and its destruction by Alexander? In the *Discourses on Livy,* Machiavelli tells us that "after the death of Epaminondas, Philip of Macedon was made captain of their troops by the Thebans; and after his victory he took their liberty from them."[42] In other words, the Thebans submitted themselves to a master—to Alexander's father—when they no longer had Epaminondas to unite them.

Montaigne's portrait of Epaminondas is consistent with the ancient sources, but he also "probes the inside" and invents the "springs of action" in his interpretation of the histories. Epaminondas, Montaigne says, was a great and fearless warrior. He has not nearly as much glory as Alexander or Caesar, but "of resolution and valor, not that which is sharpened by ambition, but that which wisdom and reason may implant in a well-ordered soul, he had all that can be imagined. As for proof of this virtue of his, he has given as much, in my opinion, as Alexander himself and as Caesar." In spite of the fact that Epaminondas has not nearly as much glory as Alexander or Caesar, Montaigne regards him as a more outstanding man than either. What is it, then, that makes the Theban commander superior in Montaigne's eyes? The resolution and valor of Epaminondas are not, according to Montaigne's judgment, due to ambition, the vice that ruined Caesar. The resolution and valor of Epaminondas are due to wisdom and reason: his was a "well-ordered" soul. His soul is ordered to freedom, not to mastery.

The resolution and valor, the "virtue," of Epaminondas is equal to that of Alexander and Caesar, but his character (*mœurs*) and conscience far surpassed all those who have ever undertaken to manage affairs. "For in this respect, which must be principally considered, which alone truly marks what we are, and which I weigh alone against all the others together, he yields to no philosopher, not even to Socrates." The character and conscience of Epaminondas are marked especially by goodness and innocence. Innocence is, in him, "a key quality, sovereign, constant, uniform, incorruptible," whereas in Alexander it appears as "subordinate, uncertain, streaky, soft, and accidental."

Montaigne gives several examples of the "exceeding goodness" of Epaminondas. Epominondas said that the sweetest contentment he had in all his life was the pleasure he gave his mother and father by his victory over the Spartans at Leuctra. "It says a lot that he preferred their pleasure to his own." Here Montaigne is pointing to the primacy that Epaminondas accords to his private duty to his parents. Also, Epaminondas "did not think it was permissible, even to recover the freedom of his country, to kill a man without full knowledge of the case. . . . He also held that in battle a man should avoid encountering a friend who was on the opposite side, and spare him." He showed humanity even toward enemy forces. (VS756–57, F571–74). Montaigne invents the innocence of Epaminondas. That is, he interprets his actions in a way that distinguishes between his virtue and his innocence or goodness.

The goodness and innocence of Epaminondas, which make him superior to Alexander, are seen most clearly in his refusal to put aside his "private duty" even at the risk of failing in his greatest enterprises: "To what a height did he raise consideration for his private duty, he who never killed a man he had vanquished, who even for the inestimable good of restoring liberty to his country scrupled to kill a tyrant or his accomplices without due form of justice, and who judged anyone a wicked man, however good a citizen he was, who among his enemies and in battle did not spare his friend and his host. . . . Terrible with blood and iron, he goes breaking and shattering a nation invincible against anyone but himself, and turns aside in the middle of such a melee on meeting his host and his friend. Truly that man was in command of war itself, who made it endure the curb of benignity at the point of its greatest heat, all inflamed as it was and foaming with frenzy and slaughter. It is a miracle to be able to mingle some semblance of justice with such actions; but it belongs only to the strength of Epaminondas to be able to mingle with them the sweetness and ease of the gentlest ways, and pure innocence" (VS801–2, F608–9). The goodness and innocence of Epaminondas are manifested in the fact that he did not seek his own good in power. He preferred his private duty to the pursuit of glory. His strength is exercised in declining mastery.[43]

In this choice to decline mastery, Epaminondas separated the man from the prince. Therefore, he was able to combine the ferocity of the prince in battle with the gentleness of the man. Montaigne's emphasis on Epaminondas's preference for his private duty is his way of humanizing the prince: Epaminondas submits his ferocity to the social. "There is a soul of rich composition. To the roughest and most violent of human actions he wedded goodness and humanity, indeed the most delicate that can be found in the school of philosophy" (VS801–2, F608–9).

In the *Discourses,* Machiavelli provides his own account of Epaminondas's virtue in turning the Theban peasants into a fierce army and of the reason for the decline of Thebes after the death of Epaminondas: "After the Thebans Pelopidas and Epaminondas had freed Thebes and had brought it out of the servitude of the Spartan empire, though they found themselves in a city used to serving and in the midst of effeminate peoples, they did not hesitate—so much was their virtue—to put them under arms, and to go with them to meet the Spartan armies in the field, and to conquer them."[44] In Machiavelli's terms, the "matter" was corrupt, for the city was accustomed to servitude, and the people were effeminate, probably because of the idleness of the oligarchs. Therefore, Thebes could not maintain itself as a republic without the virtue of Epaminondas: "Where the matter is not corrupt, tumults and other scandals do not hurt; where it is corrupt, well-ordered laws do not help unless indeed they have been put in motion by one individual who with an extreme force ensures their observance so that the matter becomes good. I do not know whether this has ever occurred or whether it is possible." A corrupt city can only rise through the virtue of one man, but "as soon as such a one is dead, it returns to its early habit, as occurred in Thebes, which could hold the forms of a republic and its empire through the virtue of Epaminondas while he lived, but returned to its first disorders when he was dead." This is because the virtuous man cannot live long enough to transform a city from bad to good. His city "is ruined, unless indeed he makes it to be reborn with many dangers and much blood. For such corruption and slight aptitude for free life arise from an inequality that is in that city; and if one wishes to make it equal, it is necessary to use the greatest extraordinary means, which few know how or wish to use."[45]

The extraordinary means to which Machiavelli refers is the elimination of the idle and rich oligarchs. "Those are called gentlemen who live idly in abundance from the returns of their possessions without having any care either for cultivation or for other necessary trouble in living. Such as these are pernicious in every republic and in every province . . . in these provinces no republic or political way of life has ever emerged for such kinds of men are altogether hostile to every civilization." Machiavelli draws this conclusion: "that he who wishes to make a republic where there are very many gentlemen cannot do it unless he first eliminates all of them."[46] Given the gentleness of Epaminondas, and especially his manifest unwillingness to kill or do any harm to his fellow Thebans, it can be inferred that he would have refused to use the extraordinary means necessary to make the city's citizens equal. Epaminondas could not "learn to be able not to be good."

Montaigne concludes his portrait of Epaminondas in "Of the Useful and the Honorable" with the claim that Epaminondas is a "great preceptor" who teaches us that some things are illicit even against an enemy and that the common interest ought not to demand all things of all men against the private interest. "If it is greatness of heart and the effect of a rare and singular virtue to despise friendship, private obligations, our word, and kinship, for the common good [*le bien commun*] and obedience to the magistrate, truly it is enough to excuse us from this that it is a greatness that cannot lodge in the greatness of Epaminondas's heart" (VS802, F609–10).Montaigne wants to strip the pretext of reason from the actions of wicked men: "Let us take away from wicked, bloody, and treacherous natures this pretext of reason. Let us abandon this monstrous and deranged justice and stick to more human imitations" (VS802, F609–10).

Montaigne's praise of Epaminondas as the great preceptor who teaches us that the common good cannot require all things of all men has the most fundamental significance, for it presents the notion of "the common good"—the defining principle of classical and medieval political philosophy—as a pretext for cruelty. Appeals to the common good for justification of mastery, then, are in bad faith. Perhaps that is why the very first words of "To the Reader" are: "This book was written in good faith, reader," for they warn us that his end is merely domestic and private (VS3, F2).[47]

The separation of the man from the prince makes the prince inhuman, but in the example of Epaminondas, who never abandons his private duty, we are offered a "more human" imitation of rule. Montaigne's account of Epaminondas insists that, even for the sake of the inestimable good, and even in the midst of battle, Epaminondas would not put aside his private duty. His judgment as a man remains above his power as a prince: he does not see himself as a prince by nature, but accidentally. The priority of the domestic and private is the humanization of the prince and sets limits on the power of the prince.

Making Epaminondas Permanent

In those instances in which he prefers his private duty to glorious action, the goodness and innocence of Epaminondas appear to be at odds with his ferocity as the warrior who fights for "the inestimable good" of the freedom of his country. Consistency requires that this conflict be allowed to stand, for the innocence of Epaminondas is the very spring that pushes him to fight for the inestimable good of the freedom of his country. His innocence means that he does not want to dominate. Here we see the deep level at which the freedom of the individual and the freedom of one's country—Constant's "personal liberty" and "political liberty"—can come into conflict. Montaigne judges Epaminondas to be the most outstanding man, for the innocence of his conscience is unsurpassed. Montaigne must leave the conscience of the man uncorrupted in order to restore humanity to the prince.

The role of private duty in the humanization of the prince gives added significance to the stories of Pompey and Sulla in "By Diverse Means We Arrive at the Same End." Both are confronted with a friend who takes upon himself the guilt of an entire people. The "end" in this essay is to soften the heart of the avenging conqueror. In the case of Pompey, his forgiveness extends to the entire city. In the case of Sulla, his heart is not softened by his private duty.

In spite of Alexander's extreme cruelty toward Betis and his extreme vengeance in the destruction of Thebes, Montaigne includes Alexander among the three most outstanding men. The nature of Alexander was "excellently formed for goodness; and it was said of him, ingeniously, that he had his virtues from nature, his vices from fortune." He judges the character of Alexander to be almost above reproach for he weighs his outstanding virtues against certain individual actions which do merit criticism. "But it is impossible to conduct such great movements according to the rules of justice; such men require to be judged in gross, by the master end of their actions." Here he mentions the desolation of Thebes, the murder of Menander, and several other vicious actions that are "rather hard to excuse." He does not mention Alexander's cruelty toward Betis, perhaps implying that it is in fact entirely inexcusable. Alexander's "master-end" is glory. By using this expression, Montaigne points to Alexander's relationship to his teacher, Aristotle.

Two aspects of Montaigne's judgment of Alexander qualify the Macedonian commander to rank among men second only to Epaminondas. First, whereas the prosperity of Thebes ended with the death of Epaminondas, the conquests of Alexander remained under the control of even "ordinary captains" after the death of Alexander. Alexander "caused so many royal lines to spring from his soldiers, leaving the world divided after his death among four successors, ordinary captains of the army, whose descendants remained for so long in control of those great possessions" (VS754, F571). Second, Montaigne prefers Alexander to Caesar, whom he had also considered for this place among the most outstanding men. Caesar had many qualities equal to and even greater than Alexander's. But, although Caesar's ambition was more moderate in itself than Alexander's, "it is so unfortunate in having for its abominable object the ruin of his country" (VS755, F572). Montaigne's ultimate judgment of Caesar is that "this single vice . . . ruined in him the finest and richest nature that ever was, and has made his memory abominable to all good men, because he willed to seek his glory in the ruin of his country and the subversion of the most powerful and flourishing republic that the world will ever see" (VS733, F554).

These two aspects reveal what weighs so heavily in Montaigne's judgments of princes: the stability and the freedom of one's country. In Montaigne's judgment, the innocence of Epaminondas surpasses the virtue of Alexander. "I know no form or fortune of man that I regard with so much honor and love" (VS756, F573). Epaminondas is the better man but nevertheless he did not succeed in establishing the foundations for a permanent free society. The Theban general lacked ambition, which, for Montaigne, is a great vice. The valor of Epaminondas is "not sharpened by ambition," whereas the ambition of Alexander is unlimited. But the comparison of Alexander and Caesar allows us to see that even ambition is excusable if it does not have for its object the ruin of one's country and the destruction of its freedom, and if it does result in the permanence of one's foundations. Montaigne's own refounding, then, might be seen as surpassing both Epaminondas and Alexander by combining the innocence of Epaminondas—his indifference to mastery—with the permanence of Alexander's rule. Thus, Montaigne surpasses and replaces both the power of Homer and the weakness of Aristotle.

Montaigne: The Magnanimous Gesture

Montaigne appears in this first essay between the princes and the philosophers. "Either one of these two ways [submission and defiance] would easily win me, for I am marvelously weak in the direction of mercy and gentleness." Like the first three princes, he is moved by esteem, but, unlike them, he is also moved by compassion. "Yet to the Stoics pity is a vicious passion; they want us to succor the afflicted, but not to unbend and sympathize with them" (VS8, F4). Like the Stoics, he is merciful, but unlike them, he feels the passion of pity. Esteem unites him to the great, compassion unites him to the weak: he would always be merciful to all men. Unlike the princes who are surprised into mercy, Montaigne, like the Stoics, is consistently merciful. Surprise has been replaced by a settled inclination of judgment: both esteem and compassion would easily move him *because* he is already and always inclined to mercy and gentleness. Montaigne's mercy is beyond esteem and compassion, which are hierarchical dispositions.

Thus, Montaigne stands between the Stoics and the princes, neither of whom will bend with compassion. This is the submission of reason inflexible and impassive to sympathy, to the good. It is an irrational act for it is not the subjection of passion to reason, but rather the subjection of reason to passion. "Natural compassion," he says, has "infinite power" over him (VS1100, F844). Natural compassion has become in him a settled inclination of judgment, thus going beyond the natural. Reason inflexible and impassive cannot move without the will. This is why the *Essays* are not arguments: arguments do not move us. The generous gesture is the marvelous, and the marvelous is what moves men.

The opposite of esteem is not compassion but rather contempt. In the natural condition, displayed in the first three princes, esteem and contempt belong together in the same man: those who feel esteem do so toward those who are like themselves. Therefore, they at the same time feel contempt for those who are weak. Montaigne, however, shows no contempt for anyone, neither princes nor people. Through his esteem and compassion, he unites princes and people within himself. Since he does not judge others in relation to himself, his position with respect to the strong and the weak is not a position within the natural hierarchy. His esteem and compassion are instead due to his judgment, from which his own private will has been removed.

The overcoming of natural mastery is thus the transcendence of nature. The first plausible explanation for the fact that the first three princes are moved by esteem but not by compassion is based on nature: the princes are naturally strong and therefore can revere only "the sacred image of virtue" whereas the common people are weak; they are naturally slaves and therefore respond more readily to compassion. Montaigne, however, goes against that prejudice by showing that, when they are given a voice, the common people do recognize the loftiness of heroic virtue. In fact, they are moved to rebel against the tyrant for they are not simply moved by fear.

Montaigne here appears before us for the first time in terms of possibility: *if I were* the prince, I *would be* easily moved. Thus, he is the private man who deliberately emerges into the public as the prince and thereby transcends his origins as a private man. Montaigne is bringing the common man into the public, making him visible and giving him a voice. He unites the princes and the people in an act of forgiveness, and his marvelous weakness in the direction of mercy is the promise that his forgiveness is not an isolated act of caprice but rather demonstrates his constant will to forgive. Forgiveness is the act of refounding because it is the only way, apart from violence and force, to settle the natural contention between masters and subjects. Forgiveness is the only way to make a new beginning, to replace the origins. "Reason inflexible and impassive" requires the magnanimous gesture of forgiveness. Forgiveness allows us to erase the past and to start over again on a different footing. The promise makes the act of forgiveness permanent so that it is not simply a random and fleeting act. Surprise, which takes both princes and the people out of themselves, becomes a settled inclination of the will. In *The Human Condition,* Hannah Arendt discusses forgiveness and promise-keeping within the context of her account of human action. "The possible redemption from the predicament of irreversibility—of being unable to undo what one has done though one did not, and could not, have known what he was doing—is the faculty of forgiving. The remedy for unpredictability, for the chaotic uncertainty of the future, is contained in the faculty to make and keep promises. The two faculties belong together in so far as one of them, forgiving, serves to undo the deeds of the past, whose 'sins' hang like Damocles' sword over every new generation; and the other, binding oneself through promises, serves to set up in the ocean of uncertainty, which is the future by definition, islands of security without which not even continuity, let alone durability of any kind, would be possible in the relations between men."[48] Forgiveness makes it possible to refound, for refounding, in Montaigne's sense of restoring, conveys the sense of reversing the order of time.

Forgiving is a kind of action that, because it is spontaneous, reveals the character of action in an especially clear way, that is, as a beginning, not as actualization. Arendt says that "the act of forgiving can never be predicted; it is the only reaction that acts in an unexpected way and thus retains, though being a reaction, something of the original character of action."[49] Montaigne takes that spontaneous act, which in the first essay is always associated with surprise, and makes it permanent. Refounding means making forgiveness permanent, the firm ground for the possibility of action that is free. The promise is the representation of the will, and Montaigne's marvelous weakness "in the direction" of mercy is the constant inclination of his will to forgiveness.

Forgiveness as the foundation of society is necessary precisely on account of the presupposition of both human imperfection and human freedom. Indeed, the nature of freedom makes imperfection inevitable and, in a certain sense, acceptable. The freedom of particularity, to be a particular very ill-formed, is freedom from the perfection of form and final cause. Therefore, the unity through forgiveness that Montaigne effects between strong and weak is not the unity of the common good: forgiveness as the necessary condition for free society means that the unity of men in society is a unity of individuals who do not share a common form.

Montaigne says that one of the principal consolations that he has for his deficient memory is that he does not even remember injuries received (VS35, F23). Forgiveness—the constant will to forgiveness—is necessary because human freedom is such that men "trespass" against each other every day. "Trespassing is an everyday occurrence which is in the very nature of action's constant establishment of new relationships within a web of relations, and it needs forgiving, dismissing, in order to make it possible for life to go on by constantly releasing men from what they have done unknowingly. Only through this constant mutual release from what they do can men remain free agents, only by constant willingness to change their minds and start again can they be trusted with so great a power as that to begin something new."[50]

The introduction of forgiveness and promise-keeping as the new foundations of society brings with it a radical transformation of morality. Arendt argues that this new moral code is very different from the standards of domination and mastery of oneself and others. "Since these faculties correspond so closely to the human condition of plurality, their role in politics establishes a diametrically different set of guiding principles from the 'moral' standards inherent in the Platonic notion of rule," that is, domination of the self.[51] Montaigne's reformation of mores involves precisely this transformation of virtue from self-mastery and self-perfection to the virtues required for free society. The character necessary for forgiveness is the character necessary for unity in the absence of common form. If Machiavelli is correct—that Thebes could not remain a republic after the death of Epaminondas because Epaminondas would not or could not institute equality—then making Epaminondas permanent would have to involve the institution of equality. The Machiavellian reformation that Epaminondas could not or would not effect—the institution of equality by doing away with the idle and rich oligarchs—Montaigne seeks to effect by means of a radical transformation of mores.

By his silence about the role of Homer in the story of Alexander and Betis, Montaigne is silent about Alexander's desire for immortality, a desire that Alexander pursues by imitating his ancestor Achilles through whom he believed he was divine. Montaigne is silent about Homer because he himself replaces Homer and thus the notion of the divine and of heroic virtue that has its origins in Homer. The substitution of forgiveness for mastery points to the divinity of Christ. The silent presence that overshadows this first essay is the image of Christ before Pilate.

As Arendt says, "the discoverer of the role of forgiveness in the realm of human affairs was Jesus of Nazareth."[52] Forgiveness is "the exact opposite of vengeance," and "the freedom contained in Jesus' teaching of forgiveness is the freedom from vengeance."[53] It is Jesus who teaches that the power to forgive is not only divine but also human. "Forgive us our trespasses as we forgive those who trespass against us." Indeed, Jesus performs miracles to prove that he has the power to forgive. When the scribes accuse Jesus of blasphemy for telling the paralytic that his sins are forgiven, he says: "Now, which of these is easier: to say 'Your sins are forgiven,' or to say, 'Get up and walk'? But to prove to you that the Son of Man has authority on earth to forgive sins—he said to the paralytic—get up, and pick up your bed and go home" (Matthew 9:5–7). Arendt says, "It is his insistence on the 'power to forgive,' even more than his performance of miracles, that shocks the people."[54] Montaigne produces his effect through the production of the marvelous. The marvelous is the miracle of forgiveness.

"By Diverse Means" displays the fundamental philosophical movement of Montaigne's thought, the movement that begins in the most familiar and ends in astonishment at the most familiar. The essay begins with submission as the most common way to soften the heart of the avenging conqueror and ends with the submission of 30,000 common people to enslavement. What has happened in the development of this essay to cause our astonishment at submission?

Submission, which at first appears to be weakness and therefore worthy of contempt, is now seen in its "proper light." Montaigne's "marvelous weakness" is the surrender of his arms in the midst of violence and the submission of himself to the risk of death. Montaigne's generous gesture reveals the new possibility of the combination of the renunciation of mastery and the love of freedom, which is the effect he seeks to produce. The risk of his life in laying down his arms is both his freedom from fear of death and also his invention of a new form of society. This new society is freed from the power of the political and instead subjects the political to itself. Natural mastery is overcome, and the inestimable good is brought into being by this gesture that overcomes nature itself. Thus, while the most obvious effect produced "by diverse means" is the softening of the heart of the conquering prince, that is, the humanization of the prince, the deeper sense is Montaigne's own conquest of the temporal realm in his refounding and reordering of human life.

Limiting Violence

It must be acknowledged that the rejection of the common good as the standard of rule is dangerous for it seems to be the rejection of any moral foundation and of any restraint upon the power of the prince. Montaigne seeks to replace that foundation and to impose restraints through the separation of the man from the prince and through the invention of society as the limitation on the power of government. In another striking reversal of Aristotle, politics becomes the realm of necessity while the pre-political (society) becomes the realm of freedom.[55]

Only reason inflexible and impassive can settle the conflict between masters and slaves. The ascent to reason inflexible and impassive therefore requires the transcendence of experience, because experience cannot show us the possibility of a world without masters and slaves. It is a possibility that must be invented and brought into being by the philosophical act. But reason inflexible and impassive is inhuman. Reason must submit to experience. That is, we must take men as we find them with all of their passions and interests. Reason must submit to the imperfect.

To put it differently, if the standard of the common good is really the pretext for the prince's unlimited exercise of power in the attainment of that end, if it is really the pretext for his vicious actions, then the perfection of the common good must be abandoned as the goal of political life. Therefore, the new standard for the exercise of power must be the limitation of evil, rather than the pursuit of a good in common. Since consent is the basis for the legitimacy of rule, the limitation of evil is, for the most part, the limitation of force and violence.

In her reflections on liberty and the necessity of force, Simone Weil concludes that the formula of "the least evil" is the only one applicable in the political realm, provided it is applied with "the coldest lucidity." The struggle between those who command and those who obey is inevitable and even desirable, but it can only be suppressed by constraint. Therefore, the limitation of violence is the best that can be done by those who love liberty.[56]

In describing his role in the civil wars of his day and his loyalty to the Catholic side, Montaigne expresses his abhorrence of violence and force: "I do not know how to involve myself so deeply and so entirely. When my will gives me over to one party, it is not with so violent an obligation that my understanding is infected by it. . . . People adore everything that is on their side; as for me, I do not even excuse most of the things that I see on mine" (VS1012, F774). And in "Of Vain Subtleties," he distinguishes himself from those who are "extreme, injudicious, and unjust in the conduct of our cause, and stain it with infinite reproaches of violence" (VS313, F227).

Because the power of the prince is unmeasured and because the limitation of power depends upon the conscience of the prince, Montaigne recognizes the difficulty of judging the prince's actions. The conscience of the prince must be given the benefit of the doubt, and his actions must be excused or forgiven whenever possible. There is no one who would not be worse than the king if he were as continually spoiled by flatterers as the king is (VS1077–78, F825). "The toughest and most difficult occupation in the world, in my opinion, is to play the part of king worthily. I excuse more of their faults than people commonly do, in consideration of the dreadful weight of their burden, which dazes me. It is difficult for a power so immoderate to observe moderation" (VS917, F700).

Based on this understanding of the prince's predicament, Montaigne draws a distinction between vicious actions or effects and vicious means. "The weakness of our condition often pushes us to the necessity of using evil means to a good end. Lycurgus, the most perfect and virtuous lawmaker that ever was, hit upon this very unjust method of teaching his people temperance: to make the Helots, who were their slaves, forcibly drunk, so that the Spartans, seeing them thus lost and buried in wine, should hold the excess of this vice in horror" (VS684, F518). Even the most perfect and virtuous lawgiver judges that he must use force to produce his effect.

Montaigne recognizes the limitations that necessity places on the ruler's action: "The virtue assigned to the affairs of the world is a virtue with many bends, angles, and elbows, so as to join and adapt itself to human weakness; mixed and artificial, not straight, clean, constant, or purely innocent. . . 'Let him who would be pure from courts retire' [Lucan]." Montaigne says that he once tried to use in public dealings the pure and innocent opinions and rules that he uses in private matters, but, he says,

"I found them inept and dangerous" when applied to political matters (VS991, F758).

The imperfection of our condition is such that vices are actually necessary and useful in the public domain. "Whoever would remove the seeds of these qualities from man would destroy the fundamental conditions of our life." In every government there are necessary offices that are abject and vicious. Vices actually have a role in holding society together. "If they become excusable, inasmuch as we need them and the common necessity effaces their true quality, we still must let this part be played by the more vigorous and less fearful citizens, who sacrifice their honor and their conscience, as those ancients sacrificed their life, for the good of their country. We who are weaker, let us take parts that are both easier and less hazardous. The public welfare requires that a man betray and lie and massacre; let us resign this commission to more obedient and suppler people" (VS791, F600).

Individuals may escape the necessity of vice, but the prince cannot excuse himself from public affairs. "The prince, when some urgent circumstance or sudden and unexpected accident of state necessity makes him deviate from his word and his faith or otherwise forces him from his ordinary duty, should attribute this necessity to a blow from the divine rod. Vice it is not, for he has abandoned his own reason to a more universal and powerful reason; but it is certainly misfortune. So that to someone who asked me 'What remedy?' I replied: 'No remedy. If he was really racked between these two extremes . . . it had to be done. But if he did it without regret, if it did not grieve him to do it, it is a sign that his conscience is in a bad way.'" Montaigne will not call this "vice," because the prince has abandoned his own reason to a more universal and powerful reason. This is the difference between excusing the prince and giving him the pretext for wicked, self-interested, vicious actions. The prince whose conscience is troubled does not act in his own interest, according to his private reason, but on account of a more universal, public reason, that is, reason that becomes public through the elimination of self-interest.

Montaigne wants the conscience of the prince to be preserved in its purity even though his actions cannot be called honorable. The judgment of the prince should be above his own power. In other words, Montaigne wants the prince always to preserve the conscience of the man, judging the actions that he must perform as prince from a perspective outside of his position of power. "If there should be a prince with so tender a conscience that no cure seemed to him worth so onerous a remedy, I would not esteem him the less. He could not ruin himself more excusably or becomingly. . . . What is less possible for him to do than what he cannot do except at the expense of his faith and his honor, things which perhaps should be dearer to him than his own safety, yes, and even than the safety of his people?" (VS799, F607).

The conscience of the prince, then, should set the limits on his immeasurable power. He should be racked between his two choices: "We offer a good bargain to a man of conscience when we propose to him some difficulty as a counterpoise to vice. But when we shut him up between two vices, we put him to a rough choice" (VS846, F642–43). The use of vicious means such as breaking one's word should be the prince's last resort. "These are dangerous examples, rare and sickly exceptions to our natural rules. We must yield to them, but with great moderation and circumspection. No private utility is worthy of our doing this violence to our conscience; the public utility yes, when it is very apparent and very important" (VS800, F607).

The rejection of the common good on the grounds that it can serve as justification for vicious actions implies that the prince must not pursue his own private interests in public affairs. But the more difficult cases are those in which private duty (as distinguished from private interest) conflicts with public duty. The example of Timoleon brings this conflict into sharp relief. Timoleon killed the tyrant, but the tyrant was his own brother. He freed the Corinthians from slavery, and Montaigne says that "his end is excusable if any could be." Yet his conscience was troubled that "it had been necessary to purchase the public advantage at such a price in honorable conduct" (VS800, F607–8). There is no rule that can determine what is best in each case. This must be left to the judgment of the individual. The separation of the man from the prince allows the prince to bow to necessity while, at the same time, allowing his conscience as a man to limit the violence he must do.

Montaigne's Bold Stroke and Noble Risk

This brings us to the question of Montaigne's own effects and the manner in which they are produced. Montaigne's warnings against innovation are based on the risk of the greater harm and even destruction that usually results from attempts to change the foundations of the political structure. But "nothing noble is done without risk" (VS129, F94). Montaigne's refounding carries the greatest risk because it entails the overturning of the most fundamental moral basis of society: the standard of the common good and thus of classical virtue.

Montaigne's refounding is a bold and risky enterprise and his "new and unlooked-for strokes in politics and morals" require extraordinary means. As soon as he moves from his thoughts to the production of effects, as soon as he acts, it becomes impossible to avoid vicious means. These trouble his conscience, so he confesses them and makes them public. In these actions, we can trace the reformation of conscience that he is seeking to effect. I will consider four instances in which Montaigne confesses to the use of vicious means and the role that each plays in his refounding. Each of these instances of Montaigne's use of vicious means shows us something about the way he seeks to limit evil. In each case, he is willing to sacrifice a traditional or conventional virtue in order to produce his own effect.

First, in "By Diverse Means" Montaigne replaces the enchantment of Homer with his own production of the marvelous. The very notion of replacing one enchantment with another involves him in a kind of deception that troubles his conscience. In "Of the Power of Imagination" he tells the story of how he helped his friend on his friend's wedding night. His friend was fearful that the bride's former suitor had placed an enchantment on him that would cause him to be impotent. Belief in enchantments was widespread at the time, but Montaigne himself does not believe in such invisible powers. Nevertheless, he gives his friend a gold piece engraved with celestial figures sewn to a ribbon and tells him to put this ribbon on around his waist if he experiences any problems. The counter-enchantment works, and his friend's impotence is overcome. Montaigne introduces this as a story of how a "counterbattery of enchantments" was able to save someone from impotence. In conclusion, he says: "It was a sudden and curious whim that led me to such an action [*effect*], which was alien to my nature. I am an enemy of subtle and dissimulated acts and hate trickery in myself, not only for sport but also for someone's profit. If the action is not vicious, the road to it is" (VS101, F71). This sudden and curious whim is a "caprice" (VS103, F74). Montaigne's caprice is therefore an enchantment to take away the original enchantment of the invisible power of one man over another.

Second, in "By Diverse Means" Montaigne says that he would be moved by either esteem or compassion, but that compassion is more natural to him than esteem. He is the only prince who is moved by compassion for the people. Montaigne's compassion is extreme. He is not merely moved by compassion, but compassion also has "infinite power" over him (VS1100, F844) and makes him appear weak. According to the Stoics, compassion is a form of weakness and is therefore a vicious means to mercy.

Third, in "Of Diversion," Montaigne says that, in one actual case, in order to lead a young prince away from vengeance, "I did not tell him that we must turn our cheek to the man who has just struck the other one, for charity's sake, nor did I represent to him the tragic results that poetry attributes to this passion. I let the passion alone and applied myself to making him relish the beauty of a contrary image, the honor, favor, and good will he would acquire by clemency and kindness. I diverted him to ambition" (VS835, F634). Montaigne does regard ambition as a great vice, but it is a lesser vice than vengeance and the cruelty that accompanies revenge. He attempts to prevent the evil and the violence of vengeance by the lesser evil of ambition. He does what is possible, given the character of the prince, to direct the prince to forgiveness.

Fourth, in "On Some Verses of Virgil" he discusses the erotic and the sexual in a way that he admits goes beyond the limits of propriety. Then he clarifies the purpose of his open speaking: "God grant that this excessive license of mine may encourage our men to attain freedom, rising above these cowardly and hypocritical virtues born of our imperfections; that at the expense of my immoderation I may draw them on to the point of reason!" (VS845, F642). Immoderation is a vicious means but it is necessary in order to rise above cowardice and hypocrisy and to attain freedom.

The practice of making the private public goes beyond the sexual and extends to the *Essays* as a whole. Montaigne frankly and openly discusses a diversity of private matters in public, a practice that violates the very deep-seated prohibition against bringing the private into the public. Montaigne insists repeatedly that his project is the revelation of himself; it is, therefore, a new, strange, and even bizarre enterprise. Custom, however, has made speaking of oneself a vice because it assumes that speaking of oneself will always entail boasting, a vice opposed to the virtue of truth. But Montaigne finds more harm than good in this supposed cure for pride. "The supreme remedy to cure it is to do just the opposite of what those people prescribe who, by prohibiting talking about oneself, even more strongly prohibit thinking about oneself. The pride lies in the thought; the tongue can have only a very slight share in it" (VS379, F274). At the deepest level, then, he directs the *Essays* against the vice of pride, the remedy for which is another vice: speaking of oneself. This is the most fundamental sense in which he exploits vicious means, using one vice to limit another, worse vice, and it describes Montaigne's project as a whole.

Throughout Montaigne's discussions of the inescapability of evil and vicious means, the terms that are used most frequently are terms of confessing, compensating, limiting, and excusing. "If my heart is not great enough, it is compensatingly open, and it orders me boldly to publish its weakness" (VS917, F700). In his frank admission that his immoderate speech about the erotic is scandalous, he says: "I do not commend it, any more than I do any forms that are contrary to accepted practice; but I excuse it, and by particular and general circumstances I make the accusation lighter" (VS889, F678). Public confession, in particular, compensates and limits: "The worst of my actions and conditions does not seem to me so ugly as the cowardice of not daring to avow it. Everyone is discreet in confession; people should be so in action. Boldness in sinning is somewhat compensated and limited by boldness in confessing" (VS845, F642).

Open speech about oneself, the confession of one's imperfections and weakness, preserves purity of judgment: it makes it possible to keep one's judgment uncorrupted without justifying one's own actions. That is why Montaigne says that the judgment of the prince must be above his power and also that the prince must know how to communicate himself like any other man. Open judgment allows the man of conscience to participate in politics. As an advisor to princes, Montaigne always communicates his frank judgment to the prince, without fear and without self-interest. The role of the philosopher as advisor is to keep the judgment of the prince above the prince's power, that is, to separate the man from the prince. Thus, the philosopher will humanize the prince.

Public confession also assumes that forgiveness is the necessary condition for the kind of society in which open speaking and the expression of judgment are essential. By boldly publishing his own weakness, Montaigne makes that first, generous gesture that might possibly bring that kind of society into existence. This is his bold stroke and his noble risk.

Chapter Six

The Primacy of the Private and the Origins of a Free Society

Society is a new, modern form of association. As Francis Slade demonstrates, the distinction of having first invented society belongs to Machiavelli. Machiavelli "generates the distinction between State and Civil Society. The term itself, *civil principality,* is Machiavelli's invention."[1] According to Slade, "civil society is society from which what is political has been removed. . . . Depoliticized society and decontextualized rule are the great innovations effected by modern political philosophy."[2] This is precisely what we see in Montaigne, that is, the separation of the man from the prince and the separation of the social from the political.

While Machiavelli is the first modern philosopher to invent society, Montaigne is the first to give a full account of this new form of association and to actually bring it into existence through the publication of the *Essays*. The social is the domestic and private brought into the public. The separation of the man from the prince is the separation of society from politics, that is, it is the freedom of the social. Montaigne identifies the "social bond" as the free communication of our thoughts and wills. This is the bond that unites while at the same time allowing each human being to seek the good in his particularity.

The Emergence of the Private into the Public

Montaigne reorders the public and the private: his end is domestic and private. In "Of Repentance" he writes: "I set forth a humble and inglorious life; that does not matter. You can tie up all moral philosophy with a common and private life just as well as with a life of richer stuff. Each man bears the entire form of the human condition" (VS805, F611). A life of richer stuff is the life of politics. Whereas for Aristotle, human nature finds its ultimate fulfillment in the political community through the practice of moral virtue, Montaigne sees nothing superior in the public role of the prince. The traditional notion of human nature has been replaced by "the human condition," and in this condition each man is complete. The human condition is a private condition, and human perfection is now located in the private realm. "It is an absolute perfection and God-like to know how to enjoy our own being rightly." The sentences that follow tell us something about what our own being is. "We seek other conditions because we do not understand the use of our own, and go outside ourselves because we do not know what it is like inside. Yet there is no use our mounting on stilts, for on stilts we must still walk on our own legs. And on the loftiest throne in the world we are still sitting on our own rump" (VS115–16, F857). The prince is merely and essentially a private man, like every other man. As the *Essays* begin with his domestic and private end, so they end with the prince now become a private man.

Thus, "human condition" reduces all human beings to a private status, erasing the hierarchical distinctions implicit in the perfection of form, the perfection that is final cause. Each man bears the entire form of the human condition, not on account of a common end but on account of the "springs of action," that is, on account of beginnings that are not ends. "The souls of emperors and cobblers are cast in the same mold. . . . they are led to and fro in their movements by the same springs [*ressors*] as we are in ours" (VS476, F350). The will of the cobbler is equal to the will of the emperor. Equality is equality of the will.

Montaigne identifies three aspects under which a man might be judged: the way he appears in public, the way he is in the interior of his soul, and the way he behaves in the private, domestic setting. Any man can put on a good face in public, "but to be disciplined within, in his own bosom, where all is permissible, where all is concealed—that's the point. The next step to that is to be so in our own house, in our ordinary actions, for which we need render an account to no one, where nothing is studied or artificial" (VS808, F613). In "To the Reader" he presents the same three possibilities. Had he intended to seek the favor of "the world," he would have appeared in a studied posture. Had he been born in those nations that are said to still live under "the sweet freedom of nature's first laws," he would have shown himself wholly naked. Instead, since his end is domestic and private, he wants to be seen in his simple and "natural" form, without striving. The domestic and private, then, is still "natural." The private realm is where we act without being seen by others, where we are what we truly are. This is "our own being."

Montaigne wants to produce his effects on the hidden springs of action, to reform the will. When he studies the histories, therefore, he is more interested in the private actions and lives of the great: "Every movement reveals us. That same mind of Caesar's which shows itself in ordering and directing the battle of Pharsalia, shows itself also in arranging idle and amorous affairs" (VS302, F219). Montaigne would rather know the conversation that Brutus had with his friends in his tent than the speech Brutus made to his army; he would rather expose what Brutus was doing in his study and his chamber than what he did in the public square and the Senate. That is why biographies are so interesting to him: they focus more on "what comes from within than on what happens without" (VS415–16, F302–3). "It takes a keen and select judgment to perceive the order in these humble, private actions" (VS809, F614). Judging the men of his day, he finds that "the real condemnation" is that even their private lives are corrupted (VS811, F615–16).

Montaigne shines the light of publicity on the private and thereby brings it into the public. To make it appear is to make it public. The private can now emerge into the public view without shame, and this emergence radically changes the public realm.

Judgment Restored

How, then, does Montaigne bring about this reordering of public and private and this radical reformation of the public sphere? In "Of Custom" he tells us that, at one time, he had found himself in the position of having to justify an authoritative customary observance. He wanted to establish this custom, not simply by the force of the laws and examples, but by tracing it back to its origin. But in doing so, he discovered that its "foundation" was "so weak" that he, who was supposed to justify it to others, instead became "almost disgusted" by this practice (VS116–17, F84).

Where, then, does he stand with respect to the authority, the foundational status, of custom? When the mask of custom is torn off, it exposes an authority based on nothing but time and usage; and when Montaigne subsequently measures custom by the standard of truth and reason, his judgment is "all upset" but "nevertheless restored to a much surer status" (VS117, F84–85). How can his judgment be "restored" once he has seen the weak origin of custom?

The examples he uses to show what happens to him in his attempt to rid himself of the prejudice of custom illustrate the strangeness and even barbarity of French laws: they illustrate the way that judgment is upset when one refers custom to truth and reason. What could be more strange, he asks, than to see a people governed by laws it does not understand, that is, laws written and published in Latin, which therefore require paid interpreters? It is "monstrous" that reason, law, and justice must be bought and sold. What could be more barbarous than the simultaneous existence of two codes of conduct: the code of arms, which binds the nobility by the standard of honor, and the civil code, which forbids the avenging of insults? "There are two sets of laws, those of honor and those of justice, in many matters quite opposed. The former condemn as rigorously a man's enduring being given the lie as the latter condemn his avenging it." He asks, "what could be more barbarous" than the condition in which a man is degraded from honor and nobility if he endures an insult without avenging himself and incurs capital punishment if he does avenge himself? (VS117–18, F85)

Immediately after the discussion of these strange and barbarous customs, he turns to consider more "indifferent things," such as clothing. Just as there are monstrous laws, so also there are monstrous fashions in clothing, monstrous because they do not serve the needs and comfort of the body "on which depend their original grace and fitness." It is possible, then, that someone would "want to restore them to their true end" (VS118, F85). By turning to indifferent things, Montaigne suggests that in a similar way custom and the laws might also be restored to their true end.

Further, within the discussion of strange and monstrous laws, there are suggestions of other possibilities. With respect to the burdens imposed by the Latin laws, which bind the people in all of their domestic affairs and which must be interpreted by paid lawyers, Montaigne mentions the "ingenious opinion" of Isocrates who advised the king "to make the trades and negotiations of his subjects free, gratuitous, and lucrative, and their disputes and quarrels onerous." Montaigne also points to a time in their own history when the French were not governed under Latin laws: "I am grateful to fortune that, so our historians say, it was a Gascon gentleman, and from my part of the country, who first opposed Charlemagne when he wanted to give us Latin and imperial laws." By specifying that this unnamed man was from his part of the country, Montaigne associates himself with this Gascon gentleman who opposed Charlemagne's innovation.[3] In addition to the burdens forced on private life by the Latin laws, the result of their imposition is the barbarous but lawful custom of having to purchase justice and being denied justice if one cannot pay. Thus, Montaigne says, to the three "ancient" estates of Church, Nobility, and People, a fourth has been added, the estate of lawyers that has sovereign authority over life and property. Once again, Montaigne is recalling a time before the emergence of this fourth estate, the time of the three ancient estates.

In *Montaigne's Politics: Authority and Governance in the Essais*, Biancamaria Fontana describes the legal situation to which Montaigne refers: "An unfortunate combination of Roman law and feudal custom had produced in France an aberrant result, a judicial monstrosity, which subsequent interventions on the part of the crown had only succeeded in making more incoherent and unmanageable. . . . France had far too many laws. . . . Moreover, many of these laws were obsolete or redundant, some contradicted one another, and all were expressed in a characteristically cryptic jargon." French law "was distinguished by its remarkable obscurity: people were governed by codes that were not even written in their own language, and that they could neither read nor understand without the costly assistance of specialists." This resulted in what Montaigne calls the barbarous custom of having to pay for justice. Fontana says that "Montaigne was strongly opposed to the venality that characterized the French judicial system. To begin with, he disapproved of the fact that magistrates generally expected to be remunerated for their services by the parties involved in trials: payments ranged from simple fees, in themselves rather modest, to far more substantial benefits, such as pensions, appointments, or gratuities."[4] In 1584, Montaigne drafted comments on a project of judicial reform intended for Henry of Navarre in which he expressed "his belief that there should be 'one single justice,' and that consequently legal services should be free of charge and equally accessible to all, regardless of wealth and social position."[5]

Fontana's description explains the situation of the nobility that Montaigne finds monstrous as well as the existence of a fourth estate, which was so oppressive to the poor. "In France the magistracy represented a powerful caste, a 'Fourth Estate'; yet in practice only the lowest ranks of the population were subjected to their authority and to the prescriptions of the law. The nobility followed a code of honor of its own, which often clashed with ordinary legislation and was deemed superior to it; among the members of the Third Estate, the rich could pay to secure a favorable treatment from judges and tribunals, so that only the poor were exposed to the full rigor of the law."[6]

Montaigne says that "our French laws, by their irregularity and lack of form, rather lend a hand to the disorder and corruption that is seen in their administration and execution. Their commands are so confused and inconsistent that they are some excuse for both disobedience and faulty interpretation, administration, and observance" (VS1072, F821). As Fontana shows, Montaigne was involved in contemporary efforts to reform the French judicial system; but his reform also goes much deeper. By pointing back to an ancient condition, a time before the imposition of burdensome Latin laws, Montaigne is suggesting change that is really a "restoration" of a condition within the history of the French people, a possibility that he discovers within that history. Through introducing the "ingenious opinion" of Isocrates, he points to the desirability of freeing the private sphere from the control of the laws as much as possible: the trade and negotiations of the people should be free, gratuitous, and lucrative.[7] His restoration is not precisely a return to the past but the introduction of a new freedom.

The discussion of the barbarous situation of the nobility also points to a reform that is fundamental. In showing the contradictions between the laws of honor and the laws of justice, Montaigne refers to the dishonor incurred by enduring insult, specifically the insult of "being given the lie," that is, to be accused of lying. Montaigne devotes an entire essay to this subject, "Du démentir," or "Of Giving the Lie." He begins by describing his own project in writing the *Essays,* how he has taken himself as the subject of his book. So the question arises of how we can believe that a man would actually tell the truth about himself. At this point, the discussion turns to the custom concerning the gravity of the insult of being given the lie: why do the French regard this as the extreme of insult? "Our nation," he says, "has long been reproached for this vice" of lying. Salvianus of Massilia, who lived at the time of the Emperor Valentinian, says that "to the French lying and perjury are not a vice but a manner of speaking." Montaigne goes further: "If a man wanted to go this testimony one better, he could say that [lying] is now a virtue to them. Men form and fashion themselves for it as for an honorable practice; for dissimulation is among the most notable qualities of this century" (VS666, F505).

Given the French penchant for lying and also the honorable status of lying, Montaigne wonders "what could be the source of that custom, which we observe so religiously, of feeling more bitterly offended when reproached with this vice, which is so common among us, than with any other; and that it should be the worst insult that can be given us in words, to reproach us with lying." One possible cause is that it is natural to defend oneself most for the defects of which we are most guilty. Perhaps we try to unburden ourselves of guilt by becoming resentful of the accusation. We condemn it in appearance although we have it in fact. Once again, he makes the association between lying and cowardice: the reproach of lying is the accusation of cowardice and lack of courage. Indeed, there is no more obvious cowardice than to deny our own word and to deny what we know.

It is here that Montaigne sets out his understanding of the social bond and thus lays the new foundation of human association. Our word, he says, is the only instrument we have to communicate our thoughts and wills. "If it fails us, we have no more hold on each other, no more knowledge of each other. If it deceives us, it breaks up all our relations and dissolves all the bonds of society" (VS666–67, F505). In "Of Liars" he says, "Lying is an accursed vice. We are men, and hold together only by our word" (VS36, F23).

Montaigne concludes "Of Giving the Lie" with the observation that, among the ancient Greeks and Romans, giving the lie was not considered so great an insult and did not result in violence and revenge. This indifference of the ancients looks "novel and strange" to us. So he wonders how it came to pass that giving the lie has become the extreme insult: "As for the varied etiquette of giving the lie, and our laws of honor in that matter, and the changes they have undergone, I shall put off to another time telling what I know about that, and shall meanwhile learn, if I can, at what time the custom began of weighing and measuring words so exactly, and attaching our honor to them" (VS667, F506). In fact, he does not discuss this explicitly again in the *Essays*.

Montaigne's refounding consists in his discovery, his invention, of truth as the foundation of society. He does this by taking the custom concerning giving the lie and directing it to its true end. This entails the reformation of the nobility through a transformed notion of honor and courage. That is why he so strongly associates lying with cowardice. He turns the desire for honor, expressed in revenge for the insult of giving the lie, into the notion of honor as keeping one's word, telling the truth, and communicating one's thoughts and will.

While the philosophers either hide under the authority of custom or reject custom entirely on account of the weakness of its origins, Montaigne discovers or invents the possibilities already present in the tradition. There are two senses of the possible that must be addressed with respect to Montaigne's invention. The first is the sense of the possible as that which is "realistic," what can reasonably be expected to be accomplished. This meaning amounts to a rejection of the notion of perfection as unrealizable in practice and therefore involves a concomitant lowering of expectations based on the idea that to aim at perfection is futile and dangerous. Perfection, the attainment of the highest and the best state of affairs, is really impossible. It is this notion of the possible that seems to be Machiavelli's point in chapter 15 of *The Prince:* we must, he argues, turn to the "effectual truth" and away from the imagination of republics that have never actually existed. What has never actually existed is impossible. That Montaigne interprets Machiavelli in that way is suggested by his claim that Machiavelli's arguments are based on experience: since the imagined best has never actually occurred, it is not possible.

The second sense of the possible is that of what has never been seen before. According to this sense, the possible is distinguished both from the probable and from the actual. The fact that something has never existed in the past does not mean that it cannot ever exist, that it is impossible in principle. This is the openness to the possible that Montaigne has in mind when he says that his end is to tell not what has happened but what can happen.

Montaigne says that we must take men as we find them, already bound and formed to certain customs (VS957, F730). This attitude toward the givenness of the human condition is what makes the difference between change and overthrowing everything, between refounding and destroying. Both senses of the possible, then, are present here: the rejection of the hierarchical notion of perfection implied in his "taking men as we find them," and the introduction of a foundation of association that had never been seen before.

Michael Oakeshott describes this discovery of possibilities as the pursuit of "intimations." The amendment of traditional modes of behavior and of existing social arrangements is accomplished not by a process of making them conform to an ideology but "by exploring and pursuing what is intimated" in these traditional modes.[8] This is what preserves the continuity of a tradition: "authority is diffused between past, present and future; between the old, and new and what is to come."[9] This view of change and reform gives some assurance that "our mistakes of understanding will be less frequent and less disastrous."[10] Reform as the pursuit of intimations is in accord with Montaigne's criticism of reform undertaken by means of new opinions. That is why he can be disgusted with innovation and, at the same time, be the initiator of innovation. Montaigne's reform is reform through old opinions: his refounding is also a restoring. As Biancamaria Fontana puts it, recovery must come "from the hidden resources of French society itself, from the community's potential for self-regeneration."[11]

The Three Ancient Estates and the Origin of Society

The Reform of the Nobility: Pride and Shame

In *The Quality of Mercy*, David Quint argues that the *Essays* can be read as an extended commentary on "By Diverse Means We Arrive at the Same End," for this first essay reveals "Montaigne's shifting attitude toward a model of heroic selfhood."[12] The *Essays* are directed to his noble contemporaries, especially at the vice of cruelty which is so deeply associated with valor in combat. An ethical reform of his class is at the heart of his political project: "To be truly noble . . . is to forswear cruelty."[13] Quint argues persuasively that "by making clemency a form, indeed the supreme expression, of true valor, Montaigne here reveals the logic behind an argument that the *Essais* make elsewhere to *substitute* clemency *for* valor as the distinguishing sign of aristocratic identity."[14] Indeed, "the choice of pardon over revenge is the moral and political touchstone of the *Essais*."[15] In his chapter entitled "An Ethics of Yielding," Quint describes Montaigne's moral teaching as "an ethics of submission" that shows the nobility how to yield while retaining honor and integrity.[16] This is "an honorable kind of submission that is the result of free individual choice."[17]

As Hannah Arendt argues, the public sphere is radically changed by the emergence of the private into the public. Montaigne offers the possibility of the reform of the nobility through a new understanding of honor as the generous gesture of submitting their private selves to public scrutiny; thus, the nobility holds in itself the possibility of transforming the political through honorable submission. At the expense of his own immoderation, he wants to draw "our men" to freedom and reason. He is attempting to bring into being the character that is "neither master nor slave," the character that is necessary for the origin and the preservation of a free society. The nobility, who are born to rule, must learn to hate mastery. But spiritedness must not be crushed: it must be separated from the desire for domination. In other words, the noble man must be educated to hate both mastery and slavery.

For the proud, spirited man, shame has to do with the way he appears in public, before other men. Hence, the laws of honor that require him to risk his life rather than suffer the humiliation of enduring an insult. Shame is one of the few things that Montaigne says is unique to man. For the nobility, pride in one's family is pride in one's noble origins. The noble man sees himself as suited to rule by nature on account of his superior origins. Montaigne's open speaking about the sexual is intended to emphasize the point that all men share the same origins. It is in order "to make us all equal" that nature has made us this way (VS877, F668–69). Early in the *Essays,* Montaigne tells us that he is very susceptible to shame concerning the members and acts that custom orders us to cover up: "I, who am so bold-mouthed, am nevertheless by complexion affected by this shame" (VS18–19, F11). His speech, however, is excessively free with respect to the erotic and sexual. In "On Some Verses of Virgil" he discusses the erotic in a way that he admits goes beyond the limits of propriety. Then the purpose of his open speaking becomes clear: he intends his excessive license to encourage the nobility to attain freedom, by rising above the cowardly and hypocritical virtues born of their human imperfections; he writes as though he had no shame so that he might lead them on to the point of reason even at the expense of his immoderation (VS845, F642). Here he is addressing "our men," the nobility who are driven by the shame that belongs to spiritedness. Thus, his license in discussing the sexual is intended to effect a transformed sense of shame and of honor. By going against the instinctual shame associated with sex as the private and hidden, Montaigne is weakening the power of the shame associated with the private, overcoming one of the most deeply ingrained of all customs, or perhaps even of nature itself. He directs his license to the encouragement of freedom, the freedom of self-revelation.

Montaigne also intends his open speech about the sexual and about himself to bring words and deeds into harmony. We are not ashamed to do shameful things but we scruple to speak about them. "The words that men fear most are those that uncover them. We must tuck up this stupid rag that covers our conduct. They send their conscience to the brothel and keep their countenance in good order" (VS846, F643). Bringing words and deeds closer together, therefore, has the effect of limiting evil. Confession to some extent limits and compensates for sin. "Whoever would oblige himself to tell all, would oblige himself not to do anything about which we are constrained to keep silent" (VS845, F642).

Custom has made speaking about oneself a vice, but Montaigne sees this prohibition as one of those hypocritical and cowardly virtues that are obstacles to freedom. The vice of speaking about oneself is actually the cure for the greater vice of pride (VS379, F274). Self-revelation both overcomes pride and compensates for pride because it is a new way of showing oneself in public.

Dissimulation, on the other hand, or hiding oneself under a mask, testifies to cowardice and baseness of heart: "In that way our men train for perfidy; being accustomed to speak false words, they have no scruples about breaking their word. A generous heart should not belie its thoughts; it wants to reveal itself even to its inmost depths. There everything is good, or at least everything is human" (VS647, F491).

The new character of the noble man that Montaigne seeks to bring about combines the renunciation of mastery with spiritedness and courage; this is a character that is neither master nor slave. Therefore, Epaminondas is the new, "more human," figure of the prince. He was able to combine the ferocity of the prince in battle with the gentleness of the man. His was "a soul of rich composition," for he brought goodness and humanity to the roughest and most violent of human actions. Montaigne points to the possibility that the character of Epaminondas was not natural and could therefore be produced by education: "That heart, so great, full and obstinate against pain, death, and poverty—was it nature or art that had made it tender to the point of such an extreme gentleness and goodness in disposition?" (VS801–2, F608–9). It is possible, then, that the disposition of a man, the temperament that he is born with, his "nature," can actually be changed by art. Epaminondas achieved "the perfect reformation of mores" (VS1109, F851).[18]

"Of the Education of Children" is addressed to the widowed mother of a young nobleman. Montaigne advises her on how she should choose a tutor for her son and what the tutor should seek to effect. Above all, Montaigne says, the tutor must make it possible for the boy to form his judgment, which is a work that is "all his own." With respect to the boy's future role as a member of the prince's court, Montaigne writes: "If his tutor is of my disposition, he will form his will to be a very loyal, very affectionate, and very courageous servant of his prince; but he will cool in him any desire to attach himself to that prince otherwise than by a sense of public duty. Besides several other disadvantages which impair our freedom by these private obligations, the judgment of a man who is hired and bought is either less whole and less free, or tainted with imprudence and ingratitude. A courtier can have neither the right nor the will to speak and think otherwise than favorably of a master who among so many thousands of other subjects has chosen him to train and raise up with his own hand. This favor and advantage corrupt his freedom, not without some reason, and dazzle him" (VS155, F114). Therefore, the nobleman must resist the seduction of the court and maintain his freedom and independence at home: "In truth, our laws are free enough, and the weight of sovereignty scarcely touches a French nobleman twice in his life. The real and essential subjection is only for those among us who go seeking it and who like to gain honors and riches by his service; for anyone who wants to ensconce himself by his hearth, and who can manage his house without quarrels and lawsuits, is as free as the Doge of Venice: 'Slavery holds but few; many hold fast to slavery' [Seneca]" (F195, VS266). Slavery, then, is seeking one's own private good in the public realm. Freedom, in contrast, means a contentment with the domestic and private and a resultant detachment from any personal gain from political power or rule.

The reform that Montaigne wants to effect occurs, then, at the deepest level of action; it is a reform of the beginnings, the springs of action. "Those who in my time have tried to correct the world's mores by new opinions, reform the superficial vices; the essential ones they leave as they were." These "external, arbitrary reforms" cost little and bring public acclaim, leaving "the other natural, consubstantial, and internal vices" unaffected (VS811, F615). He criticizes those who concern themselves with the correction of trivial faults and "the vices of appearance" rather than the vices of reality. "Oh what an easy and applauded route those superficial men take, compared with ours!" (VS888, F677). Montaigne is not attempting to reform through new opinions. Rather he is attempting to reform judgment itself, and the reform of judgment entails a reordering of the will toward overcoming the desire for mastery.

Montaigne's project, then, is nothing less than a transformation of the moral life. The pride of the nobleman must no longer find its object in domination. Therefore, shame must be redirected, and honor understood, in a new way.

Reordering Virtues and Vices

"The Romans took the general term 'virtue' from their word for 'strength.' The proper, the only, the essential form of nobility in France is the military profession. It is probable that the first virtue that manifested itself among men and gave some advantage over others was this one, by which the strongest and most courageous made themselves masters of the weaker and acquired particular rank and reputation; whence it has retained this linguistic honor and dignity. Or else that these nations, being very warlike, gave the prize and the worthiest title to the one virtue which was most familiar to them" (VS384, F277). As he frequently does, Montaigne goes beyond the most common and familiar form of virtue, strength in war. He intends his new lesson to replace that familiar foundation of human strength with the foundation of goodness or innocence, a foundation that in the natural hierarchy appears weak.

This new foundation, however, gives rise to an entirely new ranking of the traditional virtues and vices. "Confusion about the order and measurement of sins is dangerous. . . . Even our teachers often rank sins badly, in my opinion" (VS340, F244–45). Montaigne's goodness leads him to the judgment that cruelty is the extreme of viciousness: "Among other vices, I cruelly hate cruelty, both by nature and by judgment, as the extreme of all vices" (VS429, F313). His hatred of cruelty verges on extreme "softness" and is therefore easily mistaken for weakness. Cruelty is the vice that would be most closely associated with the ferocity necessary for courage in war and with the willingness to fight for the freedom of one's country. Thus, the spirited would be most inclined to this vice.

Cruelty is, of course, regarded as a vice in the classical-Christian tradition, but it is not regarded as the extreme. By establishing cruelty as the worst of the vices, Montaigne changes the meaning of vice itself. Rather than ranking the virtues and vices according to the classical standard of self-perfection, he ranks them according to the requirements of the social. This reordering, announced in "Of Drunkenness," leads him to conclude: "I find [drunkenness] a loose and stupid vice, but less malicious and harmful than the others, which almost all clash more directly with society in general" (VS342, F247). The drunkard's lack of self-control does not threaten the social so deeply as the cruelty of a spirited ruler.

Together with cruelty, Montaigne ranks ambition as one of the worst vices. The valor of Epaminondas is "not sharpened by ambition": his was a "well-ordered soul" (VS756, F572–73). Montaigne himself had been tempted toward this vice, even seeing opportunities for satisfying ambition in the Reformation (VS320, F232). But he holds firm against these temptations (VS992, F759). As mayor of Bordeaux, he avoided all innovation that might have given him a glorious reputation but would at the same time have been harmful to the city (e.g., VS1021, F781). As we have seen, his most severe condemnation of ambition is reserved for his judgment of Caesar, because Caesar sought his glory in the ruin of his country and the subversion of the republic. However, ambition is still a lesser vice than revenge and cruelty. In fact, it is Caesar who shows that the vice of ambition is not necessarily accompanied by cruelty: Montaigne admires Caesar for his great clemency and sees in him many rare seeds of virtue (VS430, F314 and VS731, F552).

Ambition ranks so high on the list of vices because it entails the pursuit of glory and the desire to rule. The desire to rule, then, is not the legitimate and just assertion of one's superiority but rather the vice of wanting to assert one's right to mastery. Montaigne takes the honor out of ambition. He diverts the ambitious man to a different image of honor: "Since we will not do so out of conscience, at least out of ambition let us reject ambition. Let us disdain this base and beggarly hunger for renown and honor which makes us grovel for it before all sorts of people . . . abjectly and at no matter how vile a price" (VS1023, F783). Ambition is to seek one's own good in politics and is therefore a form of dependence upon one's master for one's own good. In this, it is servile and shameful.

Montaigne's treatment of ambition also brings out the way in which he understands and deals with the passions. In "Of Diversion," he tells how he led a young prince away from the passion of vengeance: "I let the passion alone" (VS835, F634). He does not try to persuade the prince to directly confront the passion of vengeance. Rather, Montaigne diverts him to ambition because ambition is a lesser vice than vengeance. Thus, the role of the passions is different for Montaigne than it is for Aristotle: Montaigne uses one passion to counter another more harmful one. He avoids the struggle between reason and passion, thereby minimizing the role of mastery in the practice of virtue. Further, he diverts the prince by means of an image of the honor and goodwill to be gained by mercy and kindness, thus affecting the prince's judgment of the true meaning of honor and leading him away from the customary view that honor is primarily a matter of avenging insults.

After cruelty and ambition, the vice that Montaigne hates most is lying. Truth is the "first and fundamental part of virtue" (VS647, F491). Indeed, "the first stage in the corruption of morals is the banishment of truth" (VS666, F505). Again, we see the connection of his ranking of vice and virtue with the social, for truth is the foundation of society. That is, truth is the first and fundamental part of virtue because it is the social bond.

Referring to the practices of the nobles at court (and apparently also to Machiavelli), Montaigne writes: "As for this new virtue of hypocrisy and dissimulation, which is so highly honored at present, I mortally hate it: and of all vices, I know none that testifies to so much cowardice and baseness of heart" (VS647, F491). Through his openness he wants to encourage the nobility to attain freedom by rising above cowardice and hypocrisy (VS845, F642). It requires courage to speak of oneself (VS664, F503), while "not to speak roundly of oneself shows some lack of heart" (VS942, F920). It is craven and servile to disguise and hide ourselves, and not to dare to show ourselves as we are. That is how "our men" train themselves for breaking their word. A "generous heart" does not belie its thoughts but rather wants to reveal itself entirely (VS647, F491). Montaigne is redirecting the virtue of courage to truthfulness rather than valor.[19]

But what action could initiate this reform of the nobility? What could make it possible for men of honor to lay down their arms and seek the conditions of society? Pride is transformed into generosity by open speech. Montaigne says: "My essential form is suited to communication and revelation. I am all in the open and in full view, born for society and friendship" (VS823, F625).

The *Essays* show us both a new notion of honor and a new notion of strength. Alexander and Caesar are not relaxing their souls, but "toughening" them by submitting their violent tasks to the practice of everyday life (VS1108, F850). Strength is not a matter of mastery over others but of "stepping down" and essaying oneself against other men using only what is all one's own in the freedom of social life.[20]

The emergence of the private into the public must entail an overcoming of the primitive instinct of shame that causes us to hide and cover up the private. Looked at in this way, the entire project of the *Essays* is the overcoming of shame. Montaigne uncovers himself, revealing the most private aspects of his life. This is the act of generosity that lies at the origin of society. Montaigne has made the first generous gesture.

The People

Like Hobbes, Montaigne insists on the legitimacy of fear as the motive for giving one's word. Whereas the noble man acts not out of fear but only out of a certain kind of pride, the common people are presumed to be reliably motivated by the fear of death. One of the most persistent themes of the *Essays,* however, is the way in which the common people, the weak, are accidentally similar to the strong. For example, in "By Diverse Means We Arrive at the Same End," the common people are moved to mercy through astonishment: astonishment produces the same effect in them as esteem produces in the princes. The story of the rank and file of Dionysius's army shows that the display of heroic virtue can elicit the response of rebellion against the tyrant. Astonishment brings out into the open what is hidden, what is present without our knowing that it is present, the hatred of mastery and the desire for freedom in the common people.

Furthermore, there are several stories in the *Essays* that illustrate the possibility of eliciting the trust of the common people: the confidence and trust of the great call forth trust in the many. That is what happens in the two stories that Montaigne tells in "Of Physiognomy." During the civil wars, a group of men arrived at his house, clearly with the intention of taking him and his house by surprise. It was Montaigne's practice always to keep his house open and undefended. The openness and trust that he demonstrated on this occasion caused the leader of the invaders to simply abandon his plan. Later, he often told Montaigne that his face and his frankness had disarmed the invaders. On another occasion, Montaigne was captured by a group of 15 or 20 armed men who demanded a large ransom. Montaigne refused to promise any ransom, and his captors began disputing over his life. Suddenly, a change came over them. Their leader returned to him all of his belongings and let him go free. One of these men took off his mask, told Montaigne his name, and explained to him that he owed his deliverance to his face and to the freedom and firmness of his speech. Montaigne tells these stories in order to illustrate his claim that his openness and trust often call forth a like trust (VS1060, F811–12). A similar incident occurs when there are rumors that some of the men on his side in the civil war are planning mutiny at a review of the troops. The other officers advise caution and scaling back the planned ceremonies, but Montaigne advises that they go out among the troops, heads held high, encouraging them to display their arms. This strategy succeeded because trust elicited trust (VS131, F96).

In "Of Various Outcomes of the Same Plan" Montaigne tells the story of a military governor of a great city who, in order to quell an incipient riot, went out into the mob and was brutally killed. Fontana cites this story as evidence of the importance of trust in Montaigne's political philosophy: "The current view—Montaigne explained—was that he was killed because he took a foolish risk; yet this was not quite true: his real mistake was not the choice of confronting the people in person, but the attitude he adopted in doing so, first surrounding himself with armed soldiers—showing his mistrust and his will to intimidate—then revealing his fear and his anxiety to win over the angry crowd. What was required instead to confront 'the frenzied populace' was an attitude of 'gracious severity . . . security and confidence,' which alone might have gained their respect."[21] Fontana notes the element of surprise—the surprise that can take us out of our accustomed modes of action—in this and other stories: "What interested [Montaigne] . . . was the precise nature of the feeling that led human beings, sometimes impulsively, to replace an instinctive response of fear and distrust with one of acceptance and cooperation. Thus his concern shifted from the conventional definition of an ideal moral posture to that decisive interaction between real people that so often determined the twists and turns of historical events. In the *Essais* this positive response to another human agent was identified as *fidelité, confiance, and fiance* (in English: fidelity, confidence, and trust) and gradually came to occupy a prominent place in Montaigne's analysis."[22]

"Of Various Outcomes of the Same Plan" begins with stories of princes who dealt with conspiracies by forgiveness, clemency, and trust rather than by revenge and suspicion. Montaigne's conclusion is that "those who preach to princes such an attentive distrust, under the guise of preaching them security, preach them their ruin and their shame. Nothing noble is done without risk" (VS129, F94). The strong assurance required for the show of trust "cannot be displayed truly entire and natural except by those who do not take fright at the imagination of death" (VS130, F95).[23]

Witness to his own strong assurance, Montaigne confidently places himself among "the dregs of the people" (VS1040, F795). He is unafraid to proclaim himself "only a man of the lowest form" (VS988, F755). Like the simple Christians, he sticks to the old ways, and in order to be like the peasants, he pulls back from learning as far as possible to the seat of ignorance. That is, he identifies himself with the people; he "steps down" by choice. The characteristic of Montaigne that comes through most forcefully on account of this moralization of pride is compassion. The first words that he says about himself in the first essay—"I am marvelously weak in the direction of mercy and gentleness. . . . I believe I should be likely to surrender more naturally to compassion than to esteem" (VS8, F4)—find an echo in the very last essay where he says that compassion has "infinite power" over him. Here he recalls the fact that his father had sent the infant Montaigne to the poorest village in his neighborhood to be nursed and had asked the lowliest villagers to hold his son over the baptismal font in order to attach and oblige the child to them. "His plan," Montaigne says, "succeeded not at all badly. I give myself willingly to the little people, whether because there is more glory in it, or through natural compassion, which has infinite power over me" (VS1100, F844). As is usual for him, he presents possibilities without concerning himself to identify one, true cause of his character: glory, natural compassion, and the grace of baptism are indistinguishable in him.

Montaigne acknowledges the need for the conventional distinctions made among men, distinctions of honor that are so coveted among the French nobility. But, he says, "I should be more at home in a country where these orders of precedence were either regulated or despised" (VS980, F749). With respect to the distinction between master and servant, he says: "It is inhuman and unjust to make so much of this accidental privilege of fortune. And the governments which admit the least disparity between servants and masters seem to me the most equitable" (VS821, F623).

In his *Travel Journal,* Montaigne writes: "Free nations do not have the same distinction between people's ranks as do the others; and even those of the lowest class have something lordly in their manner."[24] The elimination of such distinctions of rank, then, brings out the nobility of the common people. He also comments on the lost liberty of certain Italian cities and of the traces of the desire for freedom that he saw in their people. Of Pistoia he writes: "This poor town compensates for its lost liberty by a vain image of its ancient constitution." The citizens elect ceremonial functionaries who have no real power. Montaigne says: "I felt pity to see them feed on this monkey business; and meanwhile the grand duke has increased the taxes by ten times over what they formerly were."[25] He recounts that during his visit to Florence, the grand duke had opened the palace to the country people, who filled the place with dancing. "To these people I believe this is a kind of symbol of their lost liberty, which is refreshed at this main festival of the city."[26]

The greatest act of generosity to the people and trust in the people is the restoration of their freedom. In "Of Presumption" Montaigne says that every man presumes that his judgment is as good as anyone else's, that the simple productions of the understanding are within his power. That is why Montaigne's recommendation of himself is "vulgar, common, and popular" (VS656, F498). Founding on the lowly means founding on the presumption of the many. As a philosopher, he stands back and acknowledges the authority of the presumption of the common people. If you accept the presumption of every man, then you allow him to judge for himself. That is freedom, and that is how his refounding takes men as they are.

The Church

The role of the Church in Montaigne's invention of society was discussed at greater length in chapter 2. The spiritual power of the Church provides the basis for the social bond. In the custom of honor concerning "giving the lie," Montaigne invents a new intimation: truth as the social bond. He expresses the desire to find out what caused the shift from ancient notions of duty (which made little of accusations of dishonesty) to the central place that this insult to one's honor occupies in his own day. But he never explicitly returns to the search for the origin of that shift. I suggest that its origin is the foundational status of truth in the Christian religion. The ancient philosophers taught that religion is merely a human contrivance to bind society together; in contrast, Montaigne holds that "our sovereign creator" has "freed our belief" and "based it on the eternal foundation of his holy word" (VS579, F437). Christianity holds that its truth is accessible to all men, to the most simple peasant woman as to the most learned theologian.

In his *Montaigne and Religious Freedom: The Dawn of Pluralism,* Malcolm Smith argues that Montaigne's opposition to the Reformation and his views on religious toleration were similar, if not identical, to those of his friend Etienne de La Boétie and that the essay "It Is Folly to Measure the True and False by Our Own Capacity" (where Montaigne asserts the authority of the Church) was first written as an "introduction" to La Boétie's "Memorandum on Pacifying the Troubles."[27] La Boétie rejects persecution on the principle of freedom of conscience, but he also believes that tolerance will lead to a divided state. He rejects toleration on both political and theological grounds, arguing that "truth is one."[28]

Smith interprets Montaigne's remarks concerning the Church as a public and immutable institution to imply that society could not survive the very dangerous introduction of a variant form of Christianity.[29] The liturgy, Montaigne holds, is essentially public.[30] Smith argues that Montaigne rejects the idea of national religions[31] and may have been involved in attempts to reconvert Henry of Navarre to Catholicism.[32] Montaigne worried that, under the Reformers, the liberties of Catholics would be in jeopardy.[33]

But Montaigne also opposes the execution of heretics, a position that was very unusual in his day.[34] In the end, he bows to necessity and accepts the limits imposed by what is possible.[35] "Of Freedom of Conscience" concludes with reflections on the emperor Julian and their relevance for the situation in France. The emperor Julian used "to kindle the trouble of civil dissension, that same recipe of freedom of conscience that our kings have just been employing to extinguish it." On the one hand, it could be said that to give factions their freedom is to foster division. On the other hand, it could be said that civil unrest softens and relaxes the factions by taking away rarity, novelty, and difficulty. "And yet I prefer to think, for the reputation of our kings' piety, that having been unable to do what they would, they have pretended to will what they could" (VS671, F509).

Montaigne denounces the use of force and violence in religion.[36] In the "Apology for Sebond," especially in his reply to the first objection, Montaigne is highly critical of the conduct of those who call themselves Christians on both sides of the civil wars of his day. They use religion as a pretext for giving vent to their vicious passions, their ambition, hatred, and avarice. So also, in "Of Coaches" he describes the extreme cruelty of the Spanish conquerors toward the people of the New World and insists that cruelty and violence are means entirely contrary to the spread of Christian faith. Faith, he says, is not spread by conquest of territory but by "possession of men" (VS913, F697). Through his use of the spiritual power of the Church, Montaigne takes that possession and makes all men his own.

Chapter Seven

The Character of the Free Individual

Because society is the association of individuals that is free from the control of government, it therefore serves to limit the power of government. In the *Essays,* Montaigne reveals the new character of the free individual that is necessary for the existence of a free society. This is not to say that every member of society must or can exhibit this character, but without the presence of a sufficient number of such individuals, society cannot remain free. This character has already been described in previous chapters as "the self-ordered soul" that is also sociable; as the combination in one man of the renunciation of mastery and the love of freedom; and as the man who is neither master nor slave.

Individuality and the Human Condition

Michael Oakeshott locates Montaigne within the tradition of what he calls the politics of skepticism. "Montaigne," Oakeshott says, "has no illusions about human power."[1] He describes the changes that were taking place at the very origins of modernity: "During the late fifteenth and sixteenth centuries, governments all over Europe were, in varying degrees, acquiring a power to control the activities and destinies of their subjects such as their predecessors had never enjoyed." Now "the tireless, inquisitive, roving hand of government was beginning to be able to reach everywhere, accustoming the subject to the notion that nothing should be beyond its grasp." According to Oakeshott, "the most significant of all these changes was . . . the gradual disappearance of the intermediate authorities which had formerly stood between a then weak central government and the subjects, leaving them naked before a power which in its magnitude was becoming comparable to a force of nature."[2]

Not coincidentally, the fourteenth and fifteenth centuries saw "the emergence of the human individual in his modern idiom."[3] According to Oakeshott, the medieval condition of life was such that "relationships and allegiances normally sprang from status and rarely extricated themselves from the analogy of kinship. For the most part anonymity prevailed; individual human character was rarely observed because it was not there to be observed. What differentiated one man from another was insignificant when compared with what was enjoyed in common as members of a group of some sort."[4] The individual "became unmistakable when the habit appeared of engaging in activities identified as 'private': indeed, the appearance of 'privacy' in human conduct is the obverse of the desuetude of the communal arrangements from which modern individuality sprang."[5]

Oakeshott regards the emergence of this disposition to be an individual as "the pre-eminent event in modern European history."[6] Unsurprisingly, Montaigne is one of the exemplars of this disposition. "The disposition to regard a high degree of individuality in conduct and in belief as the condition proper to mankind and as the main ingredient of human 'happiness' had become one of the significant dispositions of modern European character. What Petrarch did for one century, Montaigne did for another."[7]

In *The Invention of Autonomy,* J. B. Schneewind argues that Montaigne was the first modern philosopher to attempt to articulate "a morality of self-governance."[8] Schneewind claims that this morality of self-governance is grounded in what he regards as Montaigne's moral skepticism: Montaigne's "moral skepticism was the starting point of modern moral philosophy."[9] The evidence that Schneewind finds for this moral skepticism includes Montaigne's rejection of universal natural laws and his acknowledgment of the variety of customs and beliefs among different cultures. He concludes that, like the classical Pyrrhonists, Montaigne's morality involves his adjustment of his beliefs to the demands of daily practice.

I would argue, however, that Montaigne's understanding of the freedom of the individual is not to be identified with the radical autonomy of contemporary notions of liberalism or postmodernism. True, Montaigne's character is that of the "self-ordered" individual, but he abhors vices and makes categorical moral judgments, for example, that cruelty is the extreme of all vice. Further, although Montaigne does often speak in terms of deferring to custom as the ancient skeptics did, he is also engaged in a project of reform, as we see in his reordering of the virtues and vices, and this reform implies a moral standard. In other words, there is a substantive good, the good of free association itself, that is at stake in Montaigne's reformation of the moral life. Thus, there are distinct virtues that the individual must cultivate if the substantive good of society is to be enjoyed. At the same time, there are also virtues that he must practice if society is to remain an association of free individuals.

What is at issue in the idea of the free individual can be expressed in terms of Constant's two kinds of freedom: political and personal. Montaigne clearly hates tyranny and wholeheartedly admires the ancients who willingly sacrificed their lives for the freedom of their country. On the other hand, he loves his own freedom and prefers private life to public occupations. These two freedoms are, at first glance, incompatible. The second seems to refer to a private life that turns people away from any common concerns and makes them indifferent to political freedom. If I can pursue my own economic goals in freedom, then what do I care whether I do so under a tyrannical or a democratic regime? The first seems to require a disregard for one's personal, private satisfaction for the good of the whole society. The compatibility of these two kinds of freedom is much more than a merely practical problem, for that compatibility implies a radical change both in the meaning of citizenship and in the set of virtues that are necessary for both personal goodness and life with other men. The reconciliation of personal with societal freedom requires a new character, one that is both necessary for the existence of a free society and suited for life in a free society. It is not enough to espouse the principles of liberalism, or even to place institutional limits on the power of the state and erect safeguards for the freedom of individuals. Only a certain kind of character, the formation of which depends on a reformation of human nature itself on the deepest level, makes freedom possible. Individuality is not simply given with "particularity" but must also be achieved: the individual is the self-ordered soul. Montaigne is unique among modern philosophers in presenting us with such a character.[10]

Montaigne's Marvelous Weakness

The *Essays* bring to light a new notion of strength, very different from the moral strength of ancient philosophy. Recall that Caesar and Alexander actually "toughen" their souls by submitting their violent occupations to the practice of everyday life; in the tradition, their strength would be shown in their freedom from and transcendence of the needs of everyday life. When Montaigne says that his end is domestic and private, he implies that the domestic and private is a lower or weaker goal than public service or his own glory: "my powers [*forces*] are inadequate for such a purpose." Although Montaigne is a self-ordered soul, strong in himself, he often describes himself as weak. He must use the vocabulary of weak and strong in order to capture what is new in his character. Weakness, therefore, is the way he expresses the fact that he acts "without striving," without any internal moral struggle. Weakness is the absence of mastery within the soul.

Montaigne comes into the public in order to reveal himself, but he reveals himself not as a powerful conqueror or great mind, but rather as weak. In doing so, he emerges into the public without pride. He is the possible prince without pride and without mastery. The first thing that Montaigne says about himself in the first essay is: "I am marvelously weak." His marvelous weakness is "in the direction of mercy and gentleness," and this, according to the standard of weak and strong, makes him resemble the common people who are moved by compassion because they are weak.

How can his weakness be marvelous? Weakness looks like a failure to attain the end or perfection of the human form. According to the Aristotelian hierarchy of the moral order, weakness ranks just above vice. Hints of this hierarchy, and Montaigne's assessment of it, come out especially in "Of Cruelty." Montaigne begins with the opinion that "virtue is something other and more noble than the inclinations toward goodness that are born in us" (VS422, F306). Virtue is "more noble" because it involves struggle and the difficulty of mastering the passions and appetites. The difficult and rare is more noble or higher than the ease of inclination. But Montaigne is brought up short by the images of Socrates and Cato: he cannot imagine any difficulty or struggle in their practice of virtue and, therefore, struggle and mastery cannot be essential to virtue. The two-place hierarchy of virtue and goodness has been superseded by the three-place hierarchy of perfect habitual virtue, ordinary virtue (virtue as moral strength), and the goodness or innocence that belongs to those who simply happen to be born with a good temperament and a distaste for vice (VS425–26, F310).

Montaigne locates himself at the lowest place in this three-place hierarchy: he is very far from that first and most perfect degree of excellence in which virtue becomes a habit, and he has given little evidence of the second degree of virtue or moral strength. Had he been born with a more unruly temperament, things would have gone pitifully with him, for he has not experienced much firmness in his soul to withstand passions: "I do not know how to foster quarrels and conflict within me" (VS427, F311). Comparing himself to Socrates and to Stilpo (both of whom are said to have corrected their natural inclinations to vice through discipline and study), Montaigne says that he, on the contrary, has whatever good is in him simply by the chance of his birth (VS427, F311). Montaigne does not or cannot imitate the loftiness of heroic virtue, and he does not strive for the perfection of virtue that would require the rule of reason in the soul. There seems to be no distance between what he is and what he should be.

By locating himself below the category of moral strength, Montaigne ranks himself in what looks like Aristotle's category of moral weakness. He calls attention to this by pointing out that the condition of goodness or innocence is "so close to imperfection and weakness" that it is difficult to distinguish them. Even the names "goodness" and "innocence" suggest a certain contempt (VS426, F310). Ordinary language lends itself to rank difficulty and mastery higher than goodness and innocence.

Montaigne's own goodness and innocence might be confused with moral weakness because in "Of Cruelty" he presents his goodness as "extreme softness." Since he attributes his goodness to his natural disposition, not to reason, it would be plausible to assume that extreme softness must be accompanied by cowardice.[11] So, an individual may have a natural inclination to one or another virtue, but not to all the virtues, because a natural disposition that inclines to one virtue also inclines to the contrary of another virtue. Therefore, a man who is naturally inclined to courage will also be naturally inclined to cruelty. Consistency of action requires the direction of the inclinations by reason to a single end. Looked at from the perspective of the tradition, Montaigne's goodness is just an impossible combination of natural inclinations.

But the picture of Montaigne's character that emerges in the *Essays* is not one of cowardice. On the contrary, he is not afraid of death. The gesture of laying down his arms is the risk of his life. In "Cowardice, Mother of Cruelty," he shows clearly that he hates cowardice and associates it with the character of the tyrant. His own openness, frankness, and honesty in dealing with the princes with whom he negotiates require courage, as he himself says. In "Of Physiognomy," the stories he relates about when he was captured and held for ransom and the threatened invasion of his house by enemy troops reveal a man whose openness is courageous. He hates especially the practice of dissimulation, because it originates in cowardice (VS647, F491).

Montaigne uses the traditional language of weakness and imperfection but displays a moral possibility that cannot be captured by the traditional moral categories. Goodness and innocence are "so close" to weakness and imperfection that even their names are "almost" terms of contempt. Montaigne has gone outside the ancient hierarchy to a position that, from the perspective of that hierarchy, looks like weakness. In fact, however, he is not holding himself accountable to that hierarchy but rather to an entirely new moral vision.

The distinction between classical virtue and Montaigne's notion of goodness can be seen in his description of Cato the Younger, one of his two exemplars of perfect virtue. Those who attribute Cato's death to ambition and the desire for glory are, he says, fools (VS231, F171). Rather, Cato acted for the nobility and beauty of the act itself and took great pleasure in it. Montaigne says: "I go so far in that belief that I begin to doubt whether he would have wanted to be deprived of the occasion for so fine an exploit. And if his goodness [*la bonté*], which made him embrace the public advantage [*les commoditez publiques*] more than his own, did not hold me in check, I should easily fall into this opinion, that he was grateful to fortune for having put his virtue to so beautiful a test and for having favored that brigand [Caesar] in treading underfoot the ancient liberty of his country" (VS424, F309). Montaigne here associates virtue with personal perfection, whereas he associates goodness with the public advantage, that is, the freedom of the country.

In "By Diverse Means We Arrive at the Same End" Montaigne presents himself as similar to the weak in that he is compassionate and easily moved. But he is also similar both to the strong princes on account of his capacity for esteem and to the Stoic philosophers on account of his consistency. His compassion is not due to fear for himself. He displays a character that includes both weak and strong but that is also not reducible to weak and strong. That is, his character transcends those traditional categories, for his character is not due to Aristotelian virtue but to his judgment. In terms of the traditional categories, his character is an impossible combination of compassion and courage for which the name is generosity. The emergence of goodness and innocence from their hiddenness into the public effects a new kind of virtue, a virtue without pride and mastery.

The Ease of Virtue

In "Of the Education of Children" Montaigne says that he has little to offer in the way of advice concerning this most difficult topic apart from "this new lesson," the ease of virtue (VS162, F120). The young man's tutor "will teach him this new lesson, that the value and the height of true virtue lies in the ease, utility, and pleasure of its practice, which is so far from being difficult that children can master it as well as men, the simple as well as the subtle. Virtue's tool is moderation [*le reglement*], not strength. Socrates, her prime favorite, *deliberately gives up his strength,* to slip into the naturalness and ease of her gait" (VS162, F120, emphasis added). Self-regulation, then, is not the same as self-mastery. Socrates deliberately gives up his strength so that his virtue is like the virtue of the simple; he does not, in other words, seek the virtue of the noble or the warrior. In this, Socrates demonstrates, for Montaigne, that the ease of virtue means there is no superior virtue of the nobility. Hence, "you can tie up all moral philosophy with a common and private life just as well as with a life of richer stuff" (VS805, F611).

The fact that Montaigne takes up his "new lesson" in this particular essay shows that the ease of virtue has to do with judgment, not with the rule of reason over the passions: the single goal of education, he says, is the formation of judgment. Socrates deliberately gives up his strength in order to slip into the ease of virtue: he *judges* the thing itself, *brings it down,* subjects it to himself, and makes it his own.

Why does Montaigne reject the classical idea of virtue as reason's mastery of the passions? As we saw in the discussion of "By Diverse Means we Arrive at the Same End," Aristotle's moral teaching proved to be ineffective for his pupil, Alexander the Great, at least with respect to the control of his anger and desire for revenge. Quintus Curtius reports that Alexander went into a "frenzy,"[12] and Montaigne tells us that Alexander's anger turned to rage in the confrontation with Betis so that Alexander treats his captive with extreme cruelty. This, I believe, is an instance of what Montaigne calls "the ravishment of reason."

In "Of Cruelty" Montaigne wanders into a "digression" immediately after his assertion that cruelty is the extreme of all vices. "Those who have to combat sensual pleasure like to use this argument to show that it is wholly vicious and unreasonable: that when it is at its greatest pitch it masters us to such an extent that reason can have no access. And they cite the experience of it that we feel in intercourse with women, . . . where it seems to them that the pleasure transports us so far beyond ourselves that our reason could not possibly then perform its function, being all crippled and ravished away in pleasure" (VS429–30, F313).[13] Montaigne, of course, does not simply accept this common judgment, for his own experience shows otherwise: "I know that it is possible to master the onset of this pleasure." It is possible to "cast our soul back to other thoughts at this very instant." In fact, his own experience leads him to say: "I do not take it for a miracle . . . or for an extremely difficult thing, to spend entire nights with every opportunity and in all freedom, with a long-desired mistress, keeping the faith one has pledged to her, to be content with kisses and simple contacts" (VS430, F313).

With respect to the ravishment of reason, Montaigne says: "I think the example of the chase would be more appropriate. Even as there is less pleasure in it, so there is more transport and surprise, whereby our reason, stunned, loses the leisure to prepare and brace itself against it, when after a long quest the beast starts up suddenly and appears in a place where perhaps we were least expecting it. This shock, and the ardor of the hue and cry, strike us so that it would be hard for those who love this sort of hunt to withdraw their thought elsewhere at that point" (VS430, F313–14). Montaigne himself does not love the hunt. "Natures that are bloodthirsty toward animals give proof of a natural propensity toward cruelty" (VS433, F316). Indeed, he cannot even bear to hear the scream of the hare in the teeth of his dogs. "The chase is a violent pleasure" (VS429, F313).

The civil wars of Montaigne's day have seen incredible examples of cruelty, unsurpassed even by those recorded in the ancient histories: "We experience this," he says, "every day. But that has not reconciled me to it at all. I could hardly be convinced, until I saw it, that there were souls so monstrous that they would commit murder for the mere pleasure of it . . . for the sole purpose of enjoying the pleasing spectacle of the pitiful gestures and movements, the lamentable groans and cries, of a man dying in anguish. For that is the uttermost point that cruelty can attain" (VS432, F315–16).

Reason is therefore unreliable and ineffective in ruling the passions because reason can be ravished away. Montaigne says that, while Plato fears pleasure and pain because they nail the soul to the body, he himself fears extreme pleasure and pain because they separate the soul from the body. Reason becomes "detached," and thus cruel and violent. In the example of the chase, reason is ravished away in the contemplation of the spectacle. The extreme of cruelty is the contemplative pleasure of the spectacle of the pain and despair of another human being who is entirely in our power. The ravishment of reason as it contemplates the suffering of another human being shows that this ecstatic beholding separates the soul from the body, dissociates us from our common humanity, and brings about the loss of all sympathy.

Montaigne would not have believed such extreme cruelty possible if he had not seen it with his own eyes, if he had not experienced it. It is experience, not reason, that instructs him in this. Although he has seen many examples of cruelty, he has not become accustomed to it: it always horrifies him. "I cruelly hate cruelty, both by nature and by judgment, as the extreme of all vices" (VS429, F313). That he *cruelly* hates cruelty shows that he has made it his own, not through the experience of being cruel, but through his judgment, which subjects reason to the good. Montaigne substitutes "a settled inclination of judgment" for the rule of reason in the soul.

In the examples of both his encounter with his mistress and the chase, Montaigne refers to "turning our thoughts elsewhere" or "back" at the instant of pleasure. He does not specify where thought is or should be directed. Turning one's thoughts elsewhere would seem to mean turning one's thoughts to the good. Reason, then, is not ravished away to the good; it is ravished away in the pleasure of mastery. In the encounter with his mistress, he mentions that he keeps faith with her: he keeps the promise he has made to her. He will not use force and violence to impose his will on her. The chase, he says, is more difficult: one's reason is ravished away by surprise, and the individual is caught up in the crowd. One "loses the leisure" to turn one's thoughts elsewhere. The chase is the mastery of the animal, not of another human being. But that is precisely, according to the tradition, what reason is supposed to do: master the animal within us. The example of the chase shows that the attempt to master the animal within us—that is, to master our passions—by force of reason lends itself to the ravishment of reason and the acceptability of cruelty, force, and violence.[14]

Montaigne does not separate the moral from the contemplative. Notice, the language that he uses to talk about the chase is associated with philosophy: surprise, leisure, the pleasure of the spectacle. Cruelty is a contemplative vice. Montaigne's reordering of the vices reflects his conviction that those which are more bodily are in fact less deadly than "the passions that are all in the soul" (VS729, F551). These more dangerous vices conflict more with society. Montaigne gives us two descriptions of the practice of his easy virtue: "unlearning evil" and "training the disposition." In "Of Cruelty" he explains his own natural goodness (as distinguished from virtue as struggle) in terms of Antisthenes's understanding of the best apprenticeship for virtue: "To unlearn evil" (VS428, F311). Throughout the *Essays,* he presents his own weak way of coming to terms with the accidents of life and with the occasions that force us to confront evil. In "Of Husbanding Your Will" he explains that his way involves avoiding such occasions whenever possible. Some philosophers have taken another way: they have not feared to seek out trials and test their powers of endurance in wrestling with misfortunes. But, Montaigne says, "Let us not tackle these examples; we would not come up to them. . . . For our common souls there is too much effort and harshness in that. . . . We little men must flee the storm from farther away; we must try to avoid feeling it, not try to endure it" (VS1015, F777). Later in the same essay, he writes: "Passions are as easy for me to avoid as they are hard for me to moderate. . . . He who cannot attain that noble impassibility of the Stoics, let him take refuge in the bosom of this plebeian stupidity of mine. What those men did by virtue, I train myself to do by disposition" (VS1019–20, F780).

Although training the disposition sounds much like the habituation to virtue described by Aristotle, Montaigne is here in fact distinguishing between the two: his reform deliberately adopts a disposition of "plebian stupidity" rather than struggling to master his passions in the manner of the strong. However, there are instances when he does speak in terms of a kind of mastery, for example, in his encounter with his mistress and also in his description of his temptations to ambition (VS992, F759). Yet he does not fit into Aristotle's categories of moral strength and moral weakness (*NE*. 7. 2–10, 1145b8–1152a35). For example, even though he presents himself as weak, he tells us in "Of Repentance" that he does not experience remorse as the morally weak man does. His description of mastery in the examples mentioned above seems to include no experience of struggle. Thus, training the disposition and attaining a settled inclination of judgment points to a standard of moral virtue that is different from Aristotle's.

"Unlearning evil" and "training the disposition" both show that naturalness can be deliberately acquired. So, for example, he asks whether the gentleness of Epaminondas's disposition is the result of nature or art. The disposition, for Montaigne, is the temperament one is born with; it is given by nature. Montaigne's reform is so difficult and so deep because it is the reform of nature itself. He *makes* his disposition natural: he reoriginates his disposition. (This is precisely what was discussed in chapter 3 concerning the way he judges natural inclinations, choosing the natural inclinations to which his judgment conforms.)

If virtue is not the mastery of the passions, how then does Montaigne propose to deal with the passions? Passions, he says, are easy for him to avoid. "Those who say that they have got the better of their vindictive passion or of some other kind of painful passion often tell the truth as things are, but not as they were. They speak to us when the causes of their error have been fostered and developed by themselves. But go back further, call these causes back to their beginning; there you will take them unprovided. Do they expect their fault to be lesser for being older, and the sequel of an unjust beginning to be just?" (VS1016, F777). Since the beginnings of all things are weak, he confronts the passions in their weak beginnings rather than test himself against them when they have reached their height. "If each man watched closely the effects and circumstances of the passions that dominate him, as I have done with the ones I have fallen prey to, he would see them coming and would check their impetuosity and course a bit. They do not always leap at our throats at a single bound; there are threats and degrees" (VS 1074, F822–23). Stopping the passion in its beginnings makes it possible to avoid the struggle between reason and passion.[15] Unlike the Stoics, Montaigne does feel the passions. His attitude toward them is not a matter of mastering them by the force of reason but of choosing the passions that he allows himself to feel and those that he wants to avoid.

Most of Montaigne's examples of passions to be avoided have to do with the violent passions associated with revenge. In fact, the first example of virtue as struggle and mastery in "Of Cruelty" concerns the overcoming of the desire for revenge. Comparing goodness to the more noble virtue, he writes: "He who through a natural mildness and easygoingness should despise injuries received would do a very fine and praiseworthy thing; but he who, outraged and stung to the quick by an injury, should arm himself with the arms of reason against this furious appetite for vengeance, and after a great conflict should finally master it, would without doubt do much more." The former should be called "good" and the latter "virtuous" (VS422, F307). This "natural" mildness and easygoingness—the good—can actually be deliberately acquired through training the disposition, that is, through deliberately giving up one's strength and becoming "marvelously weak."

Montaigne's new lesson, the ease of virtue, therefore amounts to a new understanding of what virtue is, a new ordering of the virtues and vices, and a transformation of classical virtue. The new foundation for the virtues is goodness rather than strength and truth rather than reason. Montaigne's new character—the self-ordered soul that is sociable, the combination of the renunciation of mastery and the love of freedom, the man who is neither master nor slave—is expressed in terms of the two virtues of generosity and integrity.

Generosity

In the sixteenth century, "generosity" referred to the virtue of the nobility and bore the connotations of valor and magnanimity belonging to that class. Generosity, then, was associated with "good birth": the word itself comes from the Latin *genus,* meaning "family." Montaigne uses the term that way in "By Diverse Means We Arrive at the Same End" when he says that, in the "less generous souls" of the people, astonishment can have the same effect that esteem has in the souls of the nobility. However, in accordance with his reformation of the nobility, the meaning of generosity is transformed and becomes a possibility for all men, because natural origins are not determinative.

The man who emerges from obscurity wants to be seen, to reveal himself, in his individuality and his superiority. He emerges in his pride and wants to be master. But Montaigne astonishes us. He removes the desire for mastery from his self-revelation. Instead, the desire that seizes him to reveal himself in public is generosity; and the *Essays* are that uncalculated gesture of generosity. Generosity is produced out of himself.

Montaigne says: "If my heart is not great enough, it is compensatingly open, and it orders me boldly to publish its weakness" (VS917, F700). Aristotelian magnanimity is greatness of soul (*NE.* 4.3, 1123a35–1125a35). Openness compensates for greatness: classical magnanimity has become generosity. "A generous heart should not belie its thoughts; it wants to reveal itself even to its inmost depths. There everything is good, or at least everything is human" (VS647, F491).[16] Generosity is the more human possibility. Montaigne's natural goodness becomes the virtue of generosity through judgment.

Descartes's treatment of generosity in the *Passions of the Soul* can help us to understand the distinction between magnanimity and generosity. "There is, it seems, no virtue so dependent on good birth as the virtue [generosity] which causes us to esteem ourselves in accordance with our true value, and it is easy to believe that the souls which God puts into our bodies are not all equally noble and strong (which is why, following the vernacular, I have called this virtue 'generosity' rather than 'magnanimity', a term used in the Schools, where this virtue is not well known). It is certain, however, that a good upbringing is a great help in correcting defects of birth." Descartes calls this virtue generosity rather than magnanimity *because* our souls are not all equally noble and strong by birth or by nature. He thereby suggests that anyone, whether naturally weak or strong, can acquire this virtue. Anyone can change his natural disposition by correcting the defects of his birth. But how can this change be brought about? "Moreover, if we occupy ourselves frequently in considering the nature of free will and the many advantages which proceed from a firm resolution to make good use of it—while also considering, on the other hand, the many vain and useless cares which trouble ambitious people—we may arouse the passion of generosity in ourselves and then acquire the virtue. Since this virtue is, as it were, the key to all the other virtues and a general remedy for every disorder of the passions, it seems to me that this consideration deserves serious attention."[17] In his discussion of "how generosity may be acquired," Descartes writes: "It should be noted that what we commonly call 'virtues' are habits in the soul which dispose it to have certain thoughts: though different from the thoughts, these habits can produce them and in turn can be produced by them." Habits can produce thoughts, and thoughts can produce habits. The virtues are thus "produced" in the soul by its thoughts. This is a very different account of how the virtues are acquired from Aristotle's account, which involves mastery and moderation of the passions and which depends upon the practice of performing virtuous actions by striving for perfection as the end.

Here, it seems, we have a picture of Montaigne's "weak way." We can acquire the virtue by arousing the passion in ourselves. We can "unlearn" the defects of birth and train the disposition by thinking about the nature of free will. Generosity has to do with judgment: classical, Aristotelian magnanimity becomes generosity on account of the generous man's judgment of and relation to the weak and the strong. Descartes's description of generosity fits well with Montaigne's practice of judgment. True generosity consists in the knowledge that nothing belongs to us but the freedom of the will and in the resolution to undertake and carry out whatever we judge to be best.[18]

Generosity, then, causes us to esteem ourselves in accordance with our true value but it also has to do with our judgment of others. The opposite of esteem is contempt, and Montaigne has contempt for no one precisely because generosity prevents us from having such contempt: "Those who possess this knowledge and this feeling about themselves readily come to believe that any other person can have the same knowledge and feeling about himself, *because this involves nothing which depends on someone else*. That is why such people never have contempt for anyone. Although they often see others do wrong in ways that show up their weakness, they are nevertheless more inclined to excuse than to blame them and to regard such wrong-doing as due rather to lack of knowledge than to lack of a virtuous will. . . . They suppose [a virtuous will] also to be present, or at least capable of being present, in every other person."[19] Montaigne has esteem for the strong and compassion, not contempt, for the weak. He has contempt and hatred for no man, but only for vice. Again, in Descartes's words: "we have contempt solely for vices."[20]

Magnanimity implies hierarchy, whereas generosity's openness suggests a disposition toward equality. The most explicit act of generosity is self-revelation, specifically the revelation of one's thoughts, not one's deeds. Unlike Aristotle's magnanimous man, Montaigne talks about himself but has no great deeds to tell.[21] Whereas Aristotle's magnanimous man is justifiably proud, Montaigne's self-revelation is the cure for pride. Generosity is thus the moralization of the desire for glory.

Generosity assumes and accepts the imperfection of our condition. As Oakeshott says of the generous man, he is "not at all without imperfections and is not deceived about himself" but is also proud enough to be spared the sorrow of his imperfections and the illusion of his achievements. This is a new kind of pride and a new kind of humility. Generosity assumes the need for forgiveness, for judging the actions of others in the most favorable light. It is not the worthiness or perfection of others that rationally justifies the good man's generosity, but rather the realization that no other human being is either higher or lower than himself.

This relationship of the generous man to imperfection begins to make sense of the fact that the same man is also "careless" or nonchalant. Oakeshott's generous man is "negligent . . . but perhaps with a touch of careless heroism about him." This description captures the freedom of generosity. To be wholly good is to be so "without law, without reason, without example." Nothing is calculated. The generous man seeks nothing for himself in his actions. Goodness, then, is a spontaneity of the will. In the case of Oakeshott's carelessly heroic man, generosity manifests itself in action that is free, for he does not act out of any need or lack of the good. This changes the meaning of human agency: it is not acting for an end, but producing out of itself.

Integrity

In his discussion of "the best city" Aristotle writes: "one ought not even consider that a citizen belongs to himself, but rather that all belong to the city; for each individual is a part of the city" (*Pol.* 8.1, 1337a27). Montaigne, on the other hand, says that "the greatest thing in the world is to know how to belong to oneself" (VS242, F178).

Knowing how to belong to oneself is what might be called "integrity," the character that is necessary for freedom of judgment. Integrity is about the free choice of possibilities rather than the direction of all of one's actions to a single end. Yet it is nevertheless a kind of consistency. Montaigne's consistency cannot be captured in the rules of any school of philosophy: it is a "natural movement . . . a picture of liberty and license so constant and inflexible" (VS795, F603). There is no notion of perfection, no common good, that can guide his choices.

Since the common good can serve as the pretext for the actions of wicked men, integrity is the virtue that is most necessary for a kind of association not defined by the common good: integrity, unlike the common good, is often about what one refuses to do.[22] It is the character that is proper to life in a free society. In *Enjoyment: The Moral Significance of Styles of Life,* John Kekes spells out the connection between integrity and independent judgment.[23] Integrity is a way of life "that reflects one's individuality."[24] It is the virtue of the "self-ordered soul" whose character is such that he can be left free in his judgments.

When Oakeshott portrays the character of the man whose pride has been "moralized" and who is willing to risk everything in the gesture of laying down his arms, he describes him as a man of careless heroism "who (in Montaigne's phrase) 'knows how to belong to himself,' and who, if fortune turned out so, would feel no shame in the epitaph: '*Par delicatesse/ J'ai perdu ma vie.*' "[25] If generosity is the transformation of Montaigne's natural goodness into virtue, integrity is the transformation of his natural innocence into virtue. In *The Morality of Pluralism,* Kekes distinguishes between pre-reflective and reflective innocence. Both are characterized by simplicity, spontaneity, and the absence of calculation.[26] Reflective innocence involves the realization that we may fail.[27] Thus, the careless heroism of the man who knows how to belong to himself is a carelessness about the success of his actions. He is without striving.

Belonging to oneself, or integrity, has the sense of wholeness and completeness. But this is a very different kind of completeness from the perfection of classical moral virtue. The good, for Montaigne, is not an end but a possession or property of the individual. He has made the good itself his own through judgment. He is what he ought to be. That is why he presents himself as nonchalant and "without striving." He does not need to look outside himself for the good. Therefore, the wholeness and completeness of the man of integrity is his independence from the city: he is not completed and perfected in relation to the common good but by his own judgment.

Limited and Conditional Allegiance: Separating the Man from the Citizen

The wholeness and completeness of the man of integrity, his independence from a common good, means that his allegiance to his country is not absolute but conditional and limited. For Aristotle, the domestic and private is incomplete and imperfect for it finds its perfection only in the political. Montaigne's end, however, is domestic and private. All of moral philosophy can be expressed in terms of a humble, private, and common life. Montaigne says: "Political philosophy may condemn, for all I care, the meanness and sterility of my occupation. . . . I am of the opinion that the most honorable occupation is to serve the public and to be useful to many. . . . For my part, I stay out of it; partly out of conscience, . . . partly out of laziness" (VS952, F727). That he stays out of politics on account of his conscience shows that he does not regard the political realm as the place for the exercise of moral excellence but rather as a threat to his innocence.

It is true, of course, that Montaigne did participate in political life: he served two terms as mayor of Bordeaux and acted as negotiator between the Catholic and Protestant princes during the civil wars. His accounts of this public service are given in terms of the principle that the judgment of the man must always be above his power as a ruler. That is, he always keeps the private man separate from the public role. Hence, the private retains its primacy.[28]

Montaigne contrasts his weakness with the strength of those like Cato whose country "possessed and commanded their entire will" (F777, VS1015). He counsels this weak way with respect to the performance of those vicious actions that are necessary for the survival of one's country. If such actions become "excusable" because of necessity, "we still must let this part be played by the more vigorous and less fearful citizens, who sacrifice their honor and their conscience, as those ancients sacrificed their life, for the good [*salut*] of their country" (VS791, F600; see also VS1015, F777). Montaigne's will, honor, and conscience, then, are not entirely bound to his country.

In "Of Husbanding Your Will" he gives an account of his service as mayor of Bordeaux, an office that he assumed only with reluctance, but which he must have fulfilled with great diligence since he was elected to a second term. Montaigne believes that he was elected because of the high regard in which his father was held for his service as mayor. Montaigne's father seems to have identified the theological virtue of charity with public service. But the son regards public service as a temptation to the vice of ambition and as a threat to his freedom: "By the little I have essayed myself in that profession, I am just that much disgusted with it. I sometimes feel rising in my soul the fumes of certain temptations toward ambition, but I stiffen and hold firm against them. . . . Freedom and laziness, which are my ruling qualities, are qualities diametrically opposite to that trade" (VS992, F759). Montaigne's weak way, then, is presented as a break with the classical tradition in which one's entire will belonged to one's country because the common good is the good of each.

Montaigne does not seek his own good in politics, for it is the realm of mastery and slavery and not of the common good. His freedom is the condition of being "neither master nor slave." In order to be a master, one must be willing to be a slave, because both involve seeking one's own good in rule. As Socrates points out in his portrait of the tyrant in the *Republic,* the tyrant cannot tolerate any man who is not servile.

Montaigne describes his non-servile attitude with respect to "the great, toward whom lack of submission is the ultimate offense, and who are rough on any righteousness that is aware of itself and does not feel itself to be abject, humble, and suppliant. I have often bumped myself on that pillar" (VS1045, F799). The man who seeks his good in politics "must live not so much according to himself as according to others, not according to what he proposes to himself but according to what others propose to him" (VS991, F758). According to Kekes, Montaigne "acknowledged the need to participate in public life, but set a limit beyond which he would not go. This formed his remarkably independent manner."[29] Montaigne's attitude toward politics is one of "detachment" and the absence of "enthusiasm."[30]

He is loyal to the ancient laws and to the side of the king and the Church in the civil wars, willing to risk his life and all his possessions, but Montaigne's allegiance to France is not absolute. "He who desires the good of his country as I do, without getting ulcers and growing thin over it, will be displeased, but not stunned, to see it threatened either with ruin or with conditions of survival no less ruinous" (VS1016, F777–78). He places his own freedom above his attachment to his country: "I am so sick for freedom, that if anyone should forbid me access to some corner of the Indies, I should live distinctly less comfortably. . . . If [the laws] that I serve threatened even the tip of my finger, I should instantly go and find others, wherever it might be" (VS1072, F820–21).

Montaigne's service as advisor to princes is not due to any private duty, or to anything that he owes to the prince or seeks to obtain from the prince. Therefore, he can describe his service as free: "I love a private life because it is by my own choice that I love it, not because of unfitness for public life, which is perhaps just as well suited to my nature. I serve my prince more gaily because I do so by the free choice of my judgment and my reason, without personal obligation, and because I am not thrown back on his service and constrained to it by being unacceptable and unwelcome to every other party" (VS988, F756). His will is free because he does not seek his own interest. "Moreover, I am not pressed by any passion either of hate or of love toward the great, nor is my will bound by personal injury or obligation. I look upon our kings simply with a legitimate and civic affection, which is neither moved nor removed by private interest" (VS792, F601).

In his account of his role as negotiator between princes, Montaigne says that he frankly tells the prince the limits of what he will do in his service. He will not lie, dissimulate, or betray any man. "This whole procedure of mine is just a bit dissonant from our ways. . . . Innocence itself could neither negotiate among us without dissimulation nor bargain without lying. And so public occupations are by no means my quarry; what my profession requires, I perform in the most private manner that I can" (VS795, F603).

Montaigne's service to the prince is also limited by the demands of his conscience. There are princes, he says, "who do not accept men halfway and scorn limited and conditional services. There is no remedy. I frankly tell them my limits. For a slave I must be only to reason, and even that I can scarcely manage. And they too are wrong to demand of a free man the same subjection and obligation to their service as they demand of a man whom they have made and bought, or whose fortune is particularly and expressly attached to theirs" (VS794, F603). He would not, he says, betray a private person for the prince (VS792, F600). He does "not want to be considered either so affectionate or so loyal a servant as to be found fit to betray anyone" (VS794, F603). Nor will he knowingly lie for the prince, so that if he is to serve as an instrument of deceit, "at least let it be with a clear conscience" (VS794, F603). The actions of those who betray and lie for the king are not only low, but "also prostitute [their] conscience" (VS799, F606).

Epaminondas held that a man cannot be a good man, however good a citizen he may be, if he does not spare his friend when confronted in battle. Integrity separates the man from the citizen. As the separation of the man from the prince is the separation of the man from mastery, so the separation of the man from the citizen is the separation of the man from servitude. In his account of the limits of what he will do for the prince, Montaigne places his private duty, his duty to private individuals, above his obligations to the prince. Generosity and integrity have something of the appearance of the irrational, the whimsical, or the capricious: they are uncalculating and careless of consequences. Oakeshott refers to the "negligence" and the "careless heroism" of the generous man. Generosity and integrity have this quality because they are the virtues of an imperfect human being in an imperfect world.

Thus, Montaigne lives in the world as it is given to him. Nietzsche takes note of this and says of Montaigne: "If my task were to make myself at home on this earth, it is to him that I would cleave."[31] In "Of Husbanding Your Will" Montaigne writes: "We must live in the world and make the most of it such as we find it" (VS1012, F774). He has no philosophical or religious contempt for this world. Of his negligence about his own affairs he writes: "This is not a philosophical scorn for transitory and mundane things; my taste is not so refined, and I value them at least at their worth" (VS953, F728). He is both attached to this world, valuing it for what it is worth, and detached from it because it is not all that there is: "Never did a man prepare to leave the world more utterly and completely, nor detach himself from it more universally, than I propose to do" (VS88–89, F61). What does it mean to judge the world as it is and to value transitory and mundane things for what they are worth? For Montaigne it means living in the attitude of nonchalance.[32] The attitude of nonchalance is the joyful acceptance of imperfection. The judgment that this world is not ultimate makes possible his carelessness about his own life: "I want a man to act, and to prolong the functions of life as long as he can; and I want death to find me planting my cabbages, but careless [*nonchalant*] of death, and still more of my unfinished [*imparfait*] garden" (VS89, F62). Nonchalance is therefore indistinguishable from hope.

Society as the Limit on the Power of the Prince

Friendship

Montaigne is one of the very few modern philosophers for whom friendship is a fundamental philosophical concern. Generosity and integrity coincide for him in the perfection of friendship. Although his essay on friendship refers to many classical tropes, Montaigne says that his unique friendship with La Boétie surpasses all of the ancient categories of friendship (VS184, F136). The discourses that antiquity has left on this subject seem weak to him when compared with his sentiments, and the facts "surpass even the precepts of philosophy" (VS192, F143). Their friendship is a "mystery" (VS189, F140) and a "miracle" (VS191, F142).

Montaigne's friendship with La Boétie surpasses the classical categories of friendship and the precepts of philosophy because it is due to the will: "Our free will has no product more properly its own than affection and friendship" (VS185, F137). Their friendship is the "complete fusion of [their] wills" (VS190, F141). Thus, "the springs of action" are "perfectly clean and true" (VS192, F142). The will *produces* friendship. In his *Divine and Poetic Freedom,* Ullrich Langer notices a strange impression that is conveyed in "Of Friendship." Montaigne, he says, sets out a conventional, classical view of friendship in describing his relationship with La Boétie. But then something else enters the picture: rather than depict their relationship as voluntary, Montaigne "removes any motivation."[33] Langer's observation here gives us an especially vivid example of the ease of Montaigne's action. It is "without striving" even when it is the most perfect act of the will. There is no calculation, no deliberation, no reason that can be given for their union: "If you press me to tell why I loved him,

I feel that this cannot be expressed, except by answering: Because it was he, because it was I" (VS188, F139).[34] Choice is not deliberation but judgment. Deliberation is directed to an end, in particular, to a naturally given end. Judgment is the free production of the will, and friendship shows that a man has the complete disposition of his will.

The spontaneous self-communication of friendship is the most perfect act of freedom. Friendship is "the perfection of society" (VS184, F136), and there is in it no element of mastery. But since this complete fusion of wills cannot be duplicated (VS191, F141), society can only ever be an imperfect form of friendship. Montaigne refers to "the acquaintanceships and familiarities formed by some chance or convenience, by means of which our souls are bound to each other" (VS188, F139). He also recognizes the demands of private obligation such as those between father and son. These too are kinds of friendship although they are less free: "the more they are friendships which law and natural obligation impose on us, the less of our choice and free will there is in them" (VS185, F137). If natural obligation is less free than perfect friendship, then perfect friendship is an expression of a kind of freedom that actually transcends the natural.

In "Of Friendship" many of the friendships of antiquity are presented as examples of opposition to tyranny. Tyrants have no friends and cannot tolerate the friendships of their subjects because they are always suspicious of conspiracies. Describing the friendship of Caius Blossius and Tiberius Gracchus, who were condemned for conspiracy by the Roman consuls, Montaigne says that "they were friends more than citizens, friends [to each other] more than friends or enemies of their country" (VS189, F140).

In *On Voluntary Servitude,* Etienne de La Boétie defends friendship against the tyrant's suspicions: "Indeed, it is certain that the tyrant is never loved, nor does he love. Friendship is a sacred word; it is a holy thing. It never occurs except between honorable people, and it arises only from mutual esteem. It maintains itself not so much by means of good turns as by a good life. What renders a friend assured of the other is the knowledge of his integrity. The guarantees he has from him are his good nature, faith, and constancy. There cannot be friendship where there is cruelty, where there is disloyalty, where there is injustice. Among the wicked when they assemble, there is a plot, not companionship. They do not provide for one another, but fear one another. They are not friends but accomplices. Yet even if it were not impossible to befriend a tyrant, it would still be hard to find in a tyrant a reliable love, because being above all [other people], and not having any peer, he is already beyond the bounds of friendship, which has its true foundation in equality."[35]

It is important to note that perfect friendship is not a relationship of dependence: it is not based on need but is entirely free. "In this noble relationship, services and benefits, on which other friendships feed, do not even deserve to be taken into account; the reason for this is the complete fusion of our wills . . . the union of such friends, being truly perfect, makes them lose the sense of such duties, and hate and banish from between them these words of separation and distinction: benefit, obligation, gratitude, request, thanks, and the like. Everything actually being in common between them—wills, thoughts, judgments, goods, wives, children, honor, and life. . . . they can neither lend nor give anything to each other" (VS190, F140–41).

Montaigne surpasses "all modern examples" in his independence from others. "Those who know me, both above and below me, know whether they have ever seen a man less demanding of others. If I surpass all modern examples in this respect, it is no great wonder, for so many parts of my character contribute to it," especially "my very favorite qualities, idleness and freedom" (VS969, F740–41). With respect to indebtedness to others, he says: "I see no one freer and less indebted than I am up to this point. . . . There is no one who is more absolutely clear of any others: *the gifts of princes are to me unknown* [adapted from Virgil]." He tries to have "no express need of anyone" (VS968, F739–40). He has conceived "a mortal hatred of being obliged either to another or by another than myself" (VS969, F741).

The idea of the common good in the tradition means that the members of the political association are dependent on each other for the good, because the good is such that it can only be attained in common. The good of all is the good of each. Thus, Montaigne's generosity and integrity are very different from Aristotelian virtue, because virtue is bound to the idea of the common good. If integrity means the possession of the good as a property, if it means completeness, then the man of integrity is not dependent on his city or country for his completeness. Montaigne does not seek his good in the dependent relationships of politics. His will belongs to him, not to his country. The common good is replaced by the inestimable good of freedom.

Education and Freedom

In "On the Education of Children" Montaigne says that "the greatest and most important difficulty in human knowledge" is the question of the upbringing and education of children (VS149, F109). The entire purpose of education is the formation of the judgment of the pupil, especially through the study of history and philosophy. Like his own upbringing, the education he proposes would teach the pupil to be "wholly incapable of submitting to force and violence" (VS176, F131).

C. S. Lewis takes Montaigne as his example of "the freeborn mind": "In adult life it is the man who needs, and asks, nothing of government who can criticize its acts and snap his fingers at its ideology. Read Montaigne; that's the voice of a man with his legs under his own table, eating the mutton and turnips raised on his own land. Who will talk like that when the State is everyone's schoolmaster and employer?"[36] Lewis is most concerned with the role of economic independence in providing an education not controlled by the state. Such an education is essential for freedom as well as for the knowledge that men must have of each other if they are to become and remain free. This is brought out forcefully in La Boétie's *Voluntary Servitude* where he discusses the importance of books and learning for men who, in spite of subjection, have the desire for freedom: "Always there live among them some who are better born than the others, who feel the weight of the yoke and who cannot refrain from shaking it off, people who never tame themselves into subjection. . . . It is truly these individuals who, having a clear understanding and a sharp mind, do not content themselves like the vulgar populace with looking at what is at their feet, but look both backward and forward, and moreover recall past events so as to judge about those of times to come, and in order to measure the present ones. They are those who, having their own heads well made, have also polished them through study and knowledge. Those, if ever liberty were entirely lost and wholly gone from the world, imagining it and feeling it in their minds, and still savoring it, would never find servitude to their taste, no matter how well it might be dressed up. The Great Turk having become well aware of this, that books and learning more than anything else give men the sense and understanding to know one another and to hate tyranny, I understand that he does not have in his lands any learned people, nor does he ask for them."[37] The education that Montaigne recommends for the nobleman includes the study of history so that the young man might form his independent judgment. The histories teach us to know men and recognize each in his individuality. Men who love freedom must be able to recognize each other. La Boétie describes the difficulties of this mutual recognition under conditions of tyranny: "But commonly, the good zeal and love of those who have preserved the devotion to freedom in spite of the times, no matter how large a number there may be of them, remain without effect because they do not recognize one another. The liberty of action and of speech, and almost of thought, is completely taken away from them under the tyrant. They live completely alone in their imaginings."[38]

Montaigne's account of his first meeting with La Boétie seems to be a description of just such mutual recognition: "We sought each other before we met because of the reports we heard of each other, which had more effect on our affection than such reports would reasonably have; I think it was by some ordinance of heaven. We embraced each other by our names. And at our first meeting, which by chance came at a great feast and gathering in the city, we found ourselves so taken with each other, so well acquainted, so bound together, that from that time on nothing was so close to us as each other. He wrote an excellent Latin satire, which is published, in which he excuses and explains the precipitancy of our mutual understanding, so promptly grown to its perfection" (VS188, F139).

Freedom of Speech

La Boétie says that the mutual recognition of freedom-loving men is made almost impossible under the tyrant because the tyrant prohibits freedom of speech. One of the most important aspects of Montaigne's character is the freedom of his speech. His manner of conducting himself in his role as negotiator between princes is one of openness and frankness, a practice that is very different from the dissimulation that is typical of such dealings. He speaks the truth without regard to the consequences, either to himself or to the matter in question. He will not bend the truth in order to accomplish any goal. His liberty and license are constant and inflexible because "the way of truth is one and simple" (VS795, F603).Truth is the social bond that is possible for free particulars. Free speech is the way in which diverse minds can be bound to each other in truth. There is no common essence to bind men together, and so society is brought about only through self-communication. The only way we can know each other is not through knowledge of a universal nature but through our words in which we communicate our thoughts and wills, that is, our judgments.

A character of a certain kind is required for the practice of freedom of speech, and Montaigne's character comes through especially clearly in his description of himself with respect to this practice. "I do not at all hate opinions contrary to mine. I am so far from being vexed to see discord between my judgments and others', and from making myself incompatible with the society of men because they are of a different sentiment and party from mine, that on the contrary, since variety is the most general fashion that nature has followed, and more in minds than bodies, inasmuch as minds are of a substance suppler and susceptible of more forms, I find it much rarer to see our humors and designs agree. And there were never in the world two opinions alike, any more than two hairs or grains. Their most universal quality is diversity" (VS785–86, F597–98).

In "Of the Art of Discussion" he elaborates on the attitudes that free speech requires. "I enter into discussion and argument with great freedom and ease, inasmuch as opinion finds in me a bad soil to penetrate and take deep roots in. No propositions astonish me, no belief offends me, whatever contrast it offers with my own" (VS923, F704). He is not offended nor does he respond with anger: "So contradictions of opinions neither offend nor affect me; they merely arouse and exercise me. . . . When someone opposes me, he arouses my attention, not my anger" (VS924, F705). Montaigne associates the inability to converse in this manner with a tyrannical disposition: "It is always a tyrannical ill humor to be unable to endure a way of thinking different from your own" (VS928, F709). In fact, in what may be the only instance in the *Essays* where he refers to himself as perfect, he says with respect to bantering and joking: "I am perfect in forbearance, for I endure retaliation, not only sharp but even indiscreet, without being disturbed" (VS938, F717).[39]

Montaigne removes self-esteem from discussion, thus removing the honor associated with winning an argument. His extreme tolerance for opinions different from his own is a necessary condition for a free society. Freedom of speech makes it possible for freedom-loving men to recognize each other and also provides one of the principal means of opposition to tyranny.

The Universal Church

In chapter 2 I argued that the Church is the basis for Montaigne's notion of society. The Church is the universal society that stands as an independent association which claims authority over the minds and hearts of men. While it is true that this authority can and did come into conflict with the authority of the state, causing civil unrest, it is also true that without such an independent authority, one of the principal limits on the coercive power of the state is lacking.

Like Socrates, Montaigne considers the whole world his city. "Not because Socrates said it, but because it is really my feeling, and perhaps excessively so, I consider all men my compatriots, and embrace a Pole as I do a Frenchman, setting this national bond after the universal and common one" (VS973, F743). But unlike Socrates, he is not entirely bound to his country: "What Socrates did near the end of his life, in considering a sentence of exile against him worse than a sentence of death, I shall never, I think, be so broken nor so strictly attached to my own country as to do. . . . That was a very fastidious attitude for a man who considered the world his city" (VS973, F743–44). Generosity is such that society cannot stop at the borders of one's country.

The conscience of Montaigne is different from the conscience of Socrates with respect to the degree of attachment that one owes to one's country. Socrates never left Athens, as he says in his *Apology*. He was content to remain always among his fellow citizens for he cared about them, if not exclusively, then at least much more than he concerned himself for the citizens of any other city. Montaigne, however, sets the national bond after the universal and common bond. This universal bond is grounded in the universal Church in which national origins do not matter. In Rousseau's description, Montaigne is the great cosmopolitan soul: "natural pity . . . no longer dwells in any but a few great cosmopolitan souls, who surmount the imaginary barriers that separate peoples and who, following the example of the sovereign Being who created them, include the whole human race in their benevolence."[40] Montaigne's invention of society, the philosophical act, effects the good of all mankind.

Conclusion

The Invisibility of Philosophy and the Light of the Good

Montaigne's philosophical project, I have argued, is nothing less than the invention of society, a new mode of association of free individuals. Yet, how can he produce such an astonishing effect when he himself warns us that he is nothing more than an accidental philosopher? Montaigne's transformation of philosophy and his invention of society are the same act: his epistemology and his political philosophy originate in the same act. The unity of the *Essays* is the oneness of this single act.

It must be admitted that the *Essays of Michel de Montaigne* do not look like philosophy: there are no first principles, no arguments, no conclusions, no evident philosophical teaching. True, there are hundreds of quotations from the ancients, but Montaigne's "own" philosophy, his own philosophical teaching, is nowhere to be seen. On the other hand, Michel de Montaigne himself is always visible: the *Essays,* as he often tells us, are all about him and only about him.

Yet Montaigne does describe himself as a philosopher, although only once, in the *Essays*. In fact, he is astonished to discover that he is "a *new* figure: an unpremeditated and accidental philosopher" (VS546, F409). Even in this passage—especially in this passage—where he describes himself as a new figure of the philosopher, his own philosophy is invisible. He simply uses the fragments of ancient philosophy to express what he is: a common, private man who claims no great learning or great deeds but who emerges into the public wearing only the fig leaf of ancient philosophy. Unpremeditated and accidental philosophy looks like nothing more than the articulation of the most familiar, the expression of prephilosophical presumption.

Montaigne's thought moves from the familiar, the knowledge of familiarity, and then back to the familiar, in astonishment at the familiar. The difference between his beginning and his end is simply the act of bringing the private into the public, bringing the familiar to light. In one sense this act is hidden: philosophy itself is invisible. Yet, in another sense, it is most public: the truth of the familiar is made visible. Philosophy is unpremeditated and accidental: the spontaneity of the familiar, the truth of what was already always there, is brought to light, accidentally, in the fragments of ancient philosophy.

The action of the *Essays,* then, might be described as bringing the private out into the public. Montaigne—a common, private, and weak man—presumes to bring out into public view everything that the philosophers and the great despise. By bringing the private out into the public, into visibility, he overcomes the shame of the private. Through this simple act of reordering, Montaigne transforms the human world by bringing into existence a new form of human association. In the telling of his thoughts and mores in public, philosophy becomes social. Montaigne subordinates philosophy to the everyday and thus invents society. This act of the subordination of philosophy to the everyday is the free act, the generous gesture, of the philosopher.

But what happens to philosophy itself when it descends, so to speak, into the everyday, the pre-philosophical? It seems to disappear. In becoming merely unpremeditated and accidental, philosophy has reimmersed itself in the pre-philosophical and now looks just like presumption, the pre-philosophical condition from which anything that can call itself "philosophy" must surely have to escape. What could be more unphilosophical than contentment with the pre-philosophical, with what is simply "one's own"? Unpremeditated and accidental philosophy does not look like philosophy but it does look like presumption. That is why it is invisible.

However, the pre-philosophical to which the philosopher returns, in which the philosopher reimmerses himself, is not exactly the same as the pre-philosophical from which he began, for it is now astonishing, the pre-philosophical without presumption. In the dialectic with presumption, philosophy itself is brought down to the most familiar. In the dialectic with philosophy, the most familiar is purified of presumption. What was simply and presumptuously one's own is now one's own in a new way. Judgment, which is "all one's own" and which makes the thing itself "one's own," introduces a new order. The act of judgment in which the philosopher subjects the thing itself and makes it his own is the same act in which he submits to the most common and lowly. That is how he makes the thing itself his own, bringing it back down to the original level of what was always already there, the most familiar. The philosopher can only come to know what he already knows. Judgment makes his own what was always already his own in the knowledge that is familiarity. In one sense, then, everything remains the same, but in another sense, everything is changed. Philosophy is the invisible power that brings the new out of the old, the possible out of the impossible.

The most familiar in which Montaigne begins is "the practice of everyday life." The practice of everyday life is the knowledge that is familiarity. Thus, the philosopher begins "at home" in the domestic and private. Philosophical presumption despises this beginning because it sees it as servile. Montaigne overcomes this philosophical presumption by subjecting the thing itself, that is, mastery itself, to the practice of everyday life, to his end, the domestic and private. In this way, he frees the most common human actions from servility and shame. He frees the slaves. That is, he refounds by replacing the old foundation of mastery with the new foundation of freedom. This is effected by the philosophical act: submission to the practice of everyday life is the subjection of mastery itself.

What happens to philosophy in the submission of the philosopher to the practice of everyday life? Philosophy becomes unpremeditated and accidental. What happens to the practice of everyday life in the submission of the philosopher? The practice of everyday life becomes the social, the space of the free self-revelation of free individuals. The philosopher is astonished at this transformation of the servile: actions that were instrumental are now good in themselves. Yet, the philosopher is astonished only at what he himself has produced.

In the single philosophical act of making the familiar astonishing, Montaigne both reforms philosophy by bringing it down from the heavens and refounds human association by freeing the realm of the domestic and private from its bondage to the servile. On the one hand, by descending into the pre-philosophical, philosophy itself is freed from philosophical presumption. On the other hand, the coming into existence of society requires the invisibility of philosophy because the social demands that the philosopher overcome his pride. As the philosopher disappears, the common man emerges into the light of the good. The philosopher must be the first to "step down" because it is the philosopher who orders the human world.

The spring of Montaigne's action is the desire for self-disclosure. At the same time, his settled inclination of judgment is the desire for the voluntary dissolution of his self. Montaigne is content to appear in public as weak. Yet this willingness actually shows his strength because he makes himself vulnerable and thus demonstrates that he does not fear death, that is, he is free. But because he looks weak, that strength is hidden.

The spring of the philosophical act is "the good," Montaigne's sympathy with all men, which looks weak because it is so different from Aristotle's striving for perfection. For Aristotle, the philosopher includes all men within himself because he is the perfection of the human form. Montaigne, the particular, the "new figure" of the philosopher, includes all men because, in the very act of self-disclosure, he willingly effaces himself for the good of all mankind.

Montaigne is the new figure of the philosopher: a merely unpremeditated and accidental philosopher. In this recovery of his common humanity, the philosopher gives up his claim to divinity and disappears into the anonymity of the crowd. At the same time, he emerges into the public as "the common man," as every man, in his concrete particularity. The *Essays of Michel de Montaigne* display, in this single act, the essence of unpremeditated and accidental philosophy as the selflessness of the philosopher and, therefore, as the transparency of philosophy to itself.

NOTES

Chapter 1

1. Hugo Friedrich, *Montaigne,* ed. Philippe Desan, trans. Dawn Eng (Berkeley: University of California Press, 1991), 55–56. However, Ullrich Langer, "Aristote," in *Dictionnaire de Michel de Montaigne,* ed. Philippe Desan (Paris: H. Champion, 2004), 61, shows the influence of Aristotle's *Ethics* on Montaigne's moral philosophy at a very deep level.

2. See Terence Cave, *How to Read Montaigne* (London: Granta Books, 2007), 9.

3. Descartes adopts a similar course which he recommends in a letter to Regius in 1642: "I should like it best if you never put forward any new opinions, but retained all the old ones in name, and merely brought forward new arguments. This is a course of action to which nobody could take exception, and yet those who understood your arguments would spontaneously draw from them the conclusions you had in mind. For instance, why did you need to reject openly substantial forms and real qualities?" Descartes says that, in his *Meteorology,* he did not reject or deny these but simply found them unnecessary for his explanations of things. Thus, he led his audience to see their uselessness and to reject them for themselves. *The Philosophical Writings of Descartes,* vol. 3, trans. John Cottingham et al. (Cambridge: Cambridge University Press, 1991), 205. My thanks to Keith Fennen for this passage.

4. See Philippe Desan, *Montaigne: Les formes du monde et de l'esprit* (Paris: Presses de l'Université Paris-Sorbonne, 2008), especially 9–15. As the title suggests, Desan argues that Montaigne does not believe in essences but insists on the plurality of forms.

5. Francis Slade, "Two Versions of Political Philosophy: Teleology and the Conceptual Genesis of the Modern State," in *Natural Moral Law in Contemporary Society,* ed. Holger Zaborowski (Washington, D.C: Catholic University of America Press, 2010), 235.

6. Thomas Hobbes, *Leviathan,* ed. C. B. Macpherson (reprint, London: Penguin Books, 1968), part 1, chap. 11, p. 161.

7. Ibid., chap. 46, p. 682.

8. Slade, "Two Versions of Political Philosophy," 241.

9. See Tzvetan Todorov, *Montaigne ou la découverte de l'individu* (Tournai, Belgium: La Renaissance du Livre, 2001), 22: "Montaigne's end is not to tell how he ought to be but how he is. The moderns, since Machiavelli, know how to separate the two." Zahi Zalloua, "Montaigne, Skepticism and Immortality," *Philosophy and Literature* 27 (2003): 54: "Montaigne defines *his* self-portrait in opposition to the ideal of *perfectio,* to the representation of a 'perfect face.' . . . Perfection is clearly not the project of the author's self-study."

10. Tzvetan Todorov, *Imperfect Garden: The Legacy of Humanism,* trans. Carol Cosman (Princeton, N.J.: Princeton University Press, 2002), 168–69: "Montaigne is modern also in that he does not regard the distance between the ideal and the real as a curse." Montaigne's goal is to tell not how he should be but how he is (148), for "each individual is already the whole man" (167). See also André Tournon, "Action imparfaite de sa propre essence," in *Montaigne: Scepticisme, métaphysique, théologie,* ed. Vincent Carraud and Jean-Luc Marion (Paris: Presses Universitaires de France, 2004), 37 and 41. Tournon provides many contrasts between Montaigne and Aristotle, especially concerning teleology, essence, and perfection. F. Rigolot, "Repentir," in *Dictionnaire de Michel de Montaigne,* ed. Philippe Desan, 868–69, argues that Montaigne's attitude toward repentance suggests that to repent would be to "form" the man according to an ideal model. Rigolot also discusses repentance as an attempt to escape the flow of time.

11. See William J. Bouwsma, *Waning of the Renaissance, 1550–1640* (New Haven, Conn.: Yale University Press, 2000), 86: prior to the Renaissance, the hierarchy of the cosmos and the hierarchy of human beings is the ontological foundation for political and social order and the legitimation of power. See also Cave, *How to Read Montaigne,* 48, on Sebond's theology and the "transcendental hierarchy."

12. Hannah Arendt, *The Human Condition* (Chicago: University of Chicago Press, 1958), 38.

13. Eva Brann, *What, Then, Is Time?* (Lanham: Rowman and Littlefield, 1999), 188. Brann discusses what she calls "aeviternity," which is a kind of agelessness, a kind of timelessness, which is somehow between eternity and temporality. She associates this with Vico's "imaginative universals." "They have a maker and a beginning; for all their poignant particularity they stand for a human type; they act in their own time and as individuals, and yet they are as indestructible as universals."

14. Francis Slade, "On the Ontological Priority of Ends and Its Relevance to the Narrative Arts," in *Beauty, Art, and the Polis,* ed. Alice Ramos (American Maritain Association, 2000), 62–63.

15. Ibid., 61.

16. Ibid., 66–67.

17. Michel de Montaigne, *The Complete Essays of Montaigne,* ed. M. A. Screech (London: Penguin, 1991), xxi.

18. Erich Auerbach, "Figura," in *Scenes from the Drama of European Literature: Six Essays* (New York: Meridian Books, 1959), 12–13.

19. Ibid., 28.

20. Ibid., 58.

21. Ibid., 42–43.

22. Ibid., 72.

23. Ibid., 59.

24. Ibid.

25. Peter Burke, *The Renaissance Sense of the Past* (New York: St. Martin's, 1969), 4.

Chapter 2

1. For an especially clear exposition of this view, see Terence Penelhum, *God and Skepticism: A Study in Skepticism and Fideism* (Dordrecht: D. Reidel, 1983), 22, 24, 56; and Penelhum's "Skepticism and Fideism," in *The Skeptical Tradition,* ed. Myles Burnyeat (Berkeley: University of California Press, 1983), 293, where he describes Montaigne as a "Catholic Pyrrhonist."

2. André Gide, *Essai sur Montaigne* (Paris: Jacques Schiffrin, Editions de la Pléïade, n.d.), 41–42, claims that Montaigne never speaks of Christ and may never even have read the Gospels. Arthur Armaingaud, "Montaigne: Etait-il ondoyant et divers? Montaigne était-il inconstant?" *Revue du seizième siècle* 10 (1923): 44, says that Montaigne sometimes hides his meaning. His contradictions must be interpreted by determining what is real and what is pretended. Armaingaud concludes that Montaigne's expressions of religious opinions are not sincere. On the other hand, Philippe Desan, in *Montaigne: Les formes,* 195, claims that it would be absurd to make an atheist of Montaigne.

3. For a thorough account of Catholicism in the *Essays* and the *Travel Journal,* see B. Petey-Girard, "Catholicisme," in *Dictionnaire de Michel de Montaigne,* ed. Philippe Desan, 140–43. For Montaigne, religious practice is anchored in tradition. Catholicism is for Montaigne a religion perfectly adapted to the needs of human beings of flesh and blood, as found in the Incarnation. M. A. Screech, "Montaigne: Some Classical Notions in Their Contexts," in *Montaigne in Cambridge, Proceedings of the Cambridge Montaigne Colloquium 1989,* ed. Philip Ford et al. (1989), 45–49, shows that many interpreters are not aware of the sometimes subtle indications of Montaigne's Catholic sensibilities. See also Malcolm Smith, *Montaigne and the Roman Censors* (Geneva: Librairie Droz S.A., 1981), 29. Smith offers an explanation of Montaigne's use of pagan terms, a practice which was of some concern to the censors. Smith examines the occurrences of these terms and shows how their meaning, within the context of the essays, is compatible with Christian teaching. Smith's exhaustive study of occurrences of pagan terms in the *Essays* leads him to conclude that Montaigne is "suffusing human language with the values of the Christian faith." Indeed, Smith regards the *Essays* as "the supreme example of a Renaissance author fusing the heritage of classical antiquity and the Christian faith." The *Essays* show how the values of classical antiquity are "absorbed and transcended" by Roman Catholic teaching (112). I agree with Smith's conclusion but I believe that it must be taken a step further. The new meanings that emerge out of this suffusion of human language with the values of Christian faith are, in my view, an absorption and transcendence of both classical antiquity and Christian belief. They are not reducible to the meanings of either ancient philosophy or medieval theology, for Montaigne brings forth new meanings.

4. See Thierry Gontier, "Montaigne, les humanistes et la doctrine des anciens," *Montaigne Studies* 21, nos. 1–2, pp. 26–31. Gontier reconciles Montaigne's submission to the Church and his independence from the theologians by claiming that what legitimates the discourse of humanists in "Of Prayers" is

not the subject matter (for "Of Prayers" is a theological subject matter), but the modality of affirmation: Montaigne does not claim authority.

5. See M. A. Screech, *Montaigne and Melancholy: The Wisdom of the Essays* (London: Penguin Books, 1983), 95: "Montaigne professed his complete submission to the Church of Rome. These professions increase in number and intensity in the final version" of the *Essays.* Screech also claims that Montaigne argued for the truth of Roman Catholicism (18).

6. Saint Thomas Aquinas, *Summa Theologica,* II-II, q. 2, a. 10.

7. The tradition, then, includes many important variants and developments from which Montaigne draws out intimations. Aquinas's Christian development, elaboration, and extension of Aristotle's teaching on the common good is in some ways taken up into Montaigne's notion of society and of virtue. See Mary Keys, *Aquinas, Aristotle, and the Promise of the Common Good* (Cambridge: Cambridge University Press, 2006), 96: "Aquinas does appear to privilege the generically *social* character of human nature over [Aristotle's] regime-relative political in several key respects. One may even say that while retaining an awareness of the importance of regimes and the virtues and vices they tend to promote, Aquinas *redefines* the political or civic character of human nature more fundamentally in the function of human sociality and its ethical requirements." Keys also discusses the role of goodness of will in Aquinas's notion of the common good (118–24, especially 123).

8. Josef Pieper, *Tradition: Concept and Claim,* trans. E. Christian Kopff (Wilmington, Del.: ISI Books, 2008), 35.

9. Ibid., 33.

10. Ibid., 40–43.

11. Malcolm C. Smith, *Montaigne and Religious Freedom: The Dawn of Pluralism* (Geneva: Librairie Droz, 1991), 81–82.

12. Francis Slade, "Was Ist Aufklärung? Notes on Maritain, Rorty, and Bloom with Thanks but No Apologies to Immanuel Kant," in *The Common Things: Essays on Thomism and Education,* ed. Daniel McInerny (American Maritain Association, 1999), 52.

13. Ali Benmakhlouf, *Montaigne* (Paris: Les Belles Lettres, 2008), 130, claims that the superiority of Catholicism over Protestantism is the fact that Catholicism does not forget our corporeal condition.

14. Eamon Duffy, *The Stripping of the Altars: Traditional Religion in England 1400–1580* (New Haven, Conn.: Yale University Press, 1992), 480. Although this book deals specifically with events that took place in England, Duffy's description of the Reformation applies to Christendom as a whole.

15. Ibid., 237.

16. Michael B. Foster, *Mystery and Philosophy* (London: SCM, 1957), 41.

17. Ibid., 28.

18. Ibid., 46.

19. For a more complete discussion of the dialectic of faith and reason, see my *Michel de Montaigne: Accidental Philosopher* (Cambridge: Cambridge University Press, 2003), chap. 5; "Montaigne and Scepticism," in *Cambridge Companion to Montaigne,* ed. Ullrich Langer (Cambridge: Cambridge University Press,

2005), 183–206; and "The Dialectic of Faith and Reason in the *Essays* of Montaigne," in *Faith and Philosophy* 18, no. 3, (July 2001): 323–36.

20. Frédéric Brahami, *Le scepticisme de Montaigne* (Paris: Presses Universitaires de France, 1997), 23.

21. T. S. Eliot, "The *Pensées* of Pascal," in *Selected Essays* (New York: Harcourt Brace, 1932), 363.

22. See my *Montaigne: Accidental Philosopher,* chap. 6.

23. T. S. Eliot, *Christianity and Culture: The Idea of a Christian Society and Notes Towards the Definition of Culture* (New York: Harcourt, Brace and World, 1949), 101.

24. Ibid.,198.

25. Ibid., 200.

26. Duffy, *Stripping of the Altars,* 91.

27. Neither Frame's nor Screech's translation captures this Eucharistic sense.

28. Duffy, *Stripping of the Altars,* 52.

29. Blaise Pascal, *Pensées et opuscules,* ed. Léon Brunschvicg, rev. ed. (Paris: Librairie Hachette, 1946), no. 789.

30. C. S. Lewis, *God in the Dock: Essays on Theology and Ethics,* ed. Walter Hooper (Grand Rapids, Mich.: William B. Eerdmans, 1970), 37.

31. Michael Oakeshott, *Religion, Politics and the Moral Life,* ed. Timothy Fuller (New Haven, Conn.: Yale University Press, 1993), 34.

32. Oakeshott, *Religion,* 59–60.

33. Duffy, *Stripping of the Altars,* 265.

34. Ibid., 298.

35. Roger Scruton, *A Political Philosophy* (London: Continuum, 2006), 112.

36. Michel de Montaigne, *Œuvres complètes,* ed. Albert Thibaudet and Maurice Rat (Paris: Gallimard, Bibliothèque de la Pléïade, 1962), 1236 (F961). References to the English translation of the *Travel Journal* are to *The Complete Essays of Montaigne,* trans. Donald M. Frame (Stanford, Calif.: Stanford University Press, 1943), and will be cited in the notes as (F, CW). This passage is from (F, CW 961). The Church, then, is the only multicultural society.

37. Pieper, *Tradition,* 55.

38. Etienne Gilson, "Where Is Christendom?" in *The Gilson Reader,* ed. Anton Pegis (Garden City, N.Y.: Doubleday, Image Books, 1957), 342.

39. Ibid., 343.

40. Ibid., 346. See also Bouwsma, *Waning of the Renaissance,* chap. 1: "The Cultural Community of Europe." Bouwsma devotes this chapter to a discussion of Christianity as the fundamental community of Europe at the time of the Renaissance.

Chapter 3

1. For a more complete discussion of both the skeptical aspects of the *Essays* and Montaigne's transformation of skepticism, see my "Montaigne and Skepticism."

2. See Benmakhlouf, *Montaigne,* 54–56, for a discussion of Montaigne as "the third possibility" with respect to the choice between two contraries.

3. In the versions of this passage earlier than the Bordeaux Copy, Montaigne had written: "Whoever wants to essay himself in the same way, and get rid of this violent prejudice of custom . . ." See François Roussel, *Montaigne: Le magistrat sans juridiction* (Paris: Éditions Michalon, 2006), 87–92, for a discussion of this passage and Montaigne's interior "reformation."

4. Those who form man are, presumably, the philosophers and theologians, "our masters" and "directors of conscience" (VS942, F720). See G. Defaux, "Représentation," in *Dictionnaire de Michel de Montaigne,* ed. Philippe Desan, 869–72. Representation is an image, copy, or likeness, that is, it is not form.

5. In *The Fabulous Imagination: On Montaigne's Essays* (New York: Columbia University Press, 2009), Lawrence Kritzman examines the role of the imagination in the emergence of the Western concept of the self. "In the *Essays,* the imagination acts as the generative core of an internal universe that influences both the body and mind and reveals itself as essential to human experience" (22). Philosophy is limited to the apprehension of static Being, of unchanging forms and essences, by the mind alone, separated from the body and the senses. However, a particular being that is constantly changing and becoming other can be approached only through the imagination. "As opposed to the universalizing ethos of reason, the imagination allows for an openness to the particular and the strange" (36). In "Of the Power of the Imagination" Montaigne says that his end is to tell, not what has happened, but what can happen. That is why "fabulous testimonies" serve him as well as true stories. "The essay, as Montaigne suggests, consequently becomes an exercise in approaching a horizon of possibilities" (4).

When we enter the realm of the possible, as distinguished from the actual and the probable, we encounter the unexpected and the self appears in all its strangeness. Kritzman argues that "at the core of Montaigne's writerly practice is the desire to domesticate the excesses and strangeness of the mind's activities. When the essayist explains the shift from reflection to writing . . . he recognizes the need to neutralize what he terms the 'monstrousness' within himself" (31). The *Essays* depict "imaginative experiences that test the limits of identity, knowledge, and ethics, such as the beyond of death, the ineffable nature of human desire, and the monstrousness of the self" (22). This picture of the self must be understood in contrast to the Aristotelian ontology in which human beings are directed to and find their completion and perfection in the naturally given end of happiness common to all. In "Of Cripples" Montaigne "demonstrates how the quest for causes engages us in a retrospective attempt to inscribe the teleological as the basis for a purposeful and predetermined development" (52). According to Kritzman, then, "the essaying process suspends the teleological thrust of Aristotelian metaphysics and its doctrine of ethics based on a principle of totalization" (161).

6. Todorov, *Imperfect Garden,* 49–50.

7. Søren Kierkegaard, *Philosophical Fragments; Johannes Climacus,* ed. and trans. Howard V. Hong and Edna H. Hong (Princeton, N.J.: Princeton University Press, 1985), 13.

8. Ibid., 11.

9. Ibid., 13.

10. Grahame Castor, *Pleiade Poetics: A Study in Sixteenth-Century Thought and Terminology* (Cambridge: Cambridge University Press, 1964), 171.

11. Ibid., 170.

12. Ibid., 178.

13. Ibid., 126.

14. Ibid., 106.

15. Ibid., 190.

16. Ullrich Langer, *Invention, Death and Self-Definitions in the Poetry of Pierre de Ronsard* (Saratoga, Calif.: ANMI LIBRI, 1986), 1–2.

17. Castor, *Poetics,* 103–104.

18. Ibid., 60.

19. Ibid., 62. In his *Montaigne dans tous ses états* (Fasano: Schena Editore, 2001), Philippe Desan discusses Montaigne's unpremeditated and accidental philosophy and links the accidental to contingency and thus to possibility. By contrasting Montaigne with Descartes and with Pascal, he shows why Montaigne is so difficult to locate within the parameters of modern philosophy. See especially 345, 348, 361–62.

20. This interpretation of what Montaigne means by reason is supported by Hobbes's explanation of his definition of philosophy: philosophy is the knowledge acquired by reasoning to possible causes. "By which definition it is evident that we are not to account as any part thereof, that originall knowledge called Experience." Hobbes, *Leviathan,* chap. 46, p. 682.

21. In *The Concept of Judgment in Montaigne* (The Hague: Martinus Nijhoff, 1968), 12, Raymond La Charité claims that "as far as can be ascertained, no tract of any kind, on psychology, existed which could have provided [Montaigne] with the semantic and ideational possibilities which he attributes to the faculty of judgment in the *Essays.*" See also Paul Mathias, *Montaigne ou l'usage du monde* (Paris: Librairie Philosophique J. Vrin, 2006), 84–90, for a helpful discussion of Montaigne's notion of judgment. Hassan Melehy, *Writing Cogito: Montaigne, Descartes, and the Institution of the Modern Subject* (Albany: State University of New York Press, 1997), 77: "The 'essays' are not of objects but of judgment—the objects enter indirectly, insofar as their constitution in the understanding comes under examination. And judgment is the 'tool' by which the limits of the understanding are scrutinized."

22. Georges Poulet, *Studies in Human Time,* trans. Elliot Coleman (Baltimore: Johns Hopkins University Press, 1956), 47–48. Poulet also shows the way in which Montaigne's notion of judgment is contrasted with memory.

23. La Charité, *Judgment,* 27: *juger* and *régler* (to order) are inseparable actions for Montaigne.

24. Ibid., 34: Judgment "always brings something to a close." Judgment stops the discursive and endless movement of reason.

25. Ibid., 38–40. Montaigne judges what is in him by nature. This can be seen clearly in the following passage from "Of the Resemblance of Children to Fathers" in which Montaigne discusses his natural aversion to drugs and medicine: "I have taken the trouble to plead this cause, which I understand

rather poorly, to support a little and strengthen the natural aversion to drugs and to the practice of medicine which I have derived from my ancestors, so that it should not be merely a stupid and thoughtless inclination and should have a little more form; and also so that those who see me so firm against exhortations and menaces that are made to me when my sickness afflicts me may not think that I am acting out of plain stubbornness; or in case there should be anyone so unpleasant as to judge that I am spurred by vainglory. That would be a well-aimed ambition, to want to derive honor from conduct that I have in common with my gardener and my muleteer!" (VS785, F597).

26. See C. Couturas, "Conscience," in *Dictionnaire de Michel de Montaigne,* ed. Philippe Desan, 201: the absolute refusal of the lie is for Montaigne the most constant quality of a conscience accountable for its acts.

Chapter 4

1. See David Hume, *An Enquiry Concerning Human Understanding* (Indianapolis, Ind.: Hackett, 1977), 4. "Be a philosopher; but amidst all your philosophy, be still a man." In his "Hume's Correction of Modern Political Philosophy" (paper delivered at Emory University, November 11, 2010), George Russell argues that the meaning of Hume's admonition is that abstruse philosophy destroys sympathy.

2. David Hume, *Essays: Moral, Political, and Literary,* ed. Eugene F. Miller (Indianapolis, Ind.: Liberty Classics, 1985), 534–35.

3. Pascal, *Pensées et opuscules,* no. 18.

4. Erich Auerbach, "L'humaine condition," in *Mimesis: The Representation of Reality in Western Literature,* trans. Willard R. Trask (Princeton, N.J.: Princeton University Press, 1953), 308.

5. Michael Oakeshott, *Rationalism in Politics and Other Essays,* ed. Timothy Fuller (London: Methuen, 1962; reprint, Indianapolis, Ind.: Liberty, 1991), 491.

6. T. S. Eliot, "Humanist, Artist, and Scientist," *Athenaeum,* October 10, 1919, p. 1015.

7. Robert Sokolowski, *Pictures, Quotations, and Distinctions: Fourteen Essays in Phenomenology* (Notre Dame, Ind.: University of Notre Dame Press, 1992), 32. See also Thierry Gontier, "Montaigne, les humanistes et la doctrine des anciens," 20–26, for a discussion of Montaigne's practice of quotation in relation to the humanists.

8. Sokolowski, *Pictures, Quotations,* 32.

9. For a discussion of the status of French and Latin in Montaigne's day, see Giovanni Dotoli, *La voix de Montaigne: Langue, corps, et parole dans les Essais* (Paris: Éditions Lanore, 2007), 237–38.

10. See Desan, *Montaigne: Les formes,* 60–62, for a discussion of Montaigne's "humanization of philosophy."

11. Hume, *Enquiry Concerning Human Understanding,* 71.

12. Here we can begin to see the influence of the *Essays* on modern science. See Francis Bacon, *Novum Organum,* trans. Peter Urbach and John Gibson (Chicago: Open Court, 1994). Bacon's new logic is a logic of discovery which

incorporates many of the features of Montaigne's mode of thought. For example, in book 1, aphorism 119, p. 121, Bacon writes: "In my opinion, in fact, nothing has hindered philosophy more than the failure to give time and attention to things of familiar and frequent occurrence that are accepted in passing, without any inquiry into their causes."

13. At the conclusion of the "Apology," the ancient philosophical contrast between being and becoming is set out through a long passage from Plutarch. "We have no communication with being" because we are in time, always somewhere between birth and death. There can be no communication between the temporal and the eternal because the eternal is unchanging and therefore truly is, whereas the temporal is always changing and therefore "never arrives at the perfection of being" (VS601–2, F455). Montaigne would have been relying on Amyot's translation of Plutarch's *Moral Essays,* in *Les œuvres morales & meslées de Plutarch,* trans. Jacques Amyot, vol. 1 (1572; reprint, The Hague: Mouton, 1971; New York: Johnson Reprint Corporation, 1971), 356. The Amyot text of this passage begins "nous n'avons aucune *participation* du vrai estre." Montaigne changes Amyot's "participation" to "communication." Participation in the divine is the transcendence of the human. The "Apology" concludes with the assertion that "it is for our Christian faith, not for [Seneca's] Stoical virtue, to aspire to that divine and miraculous metamorphosis." Man cannot raise himself above himself and humanity. He must be lifted up "by purely celestial means" (VS604, F457). Why does Montaigne replace "participation" with "communication"? The point of the passage at the end of the "Apology" is that transcendence of the human is not within our power and would have to come through the action of the divine. The Stoic sees himself as participating in divinity, as literally becoming divine. By changing "participation" to "communication," Montaigne shows that he is considering man without revelation. And that is what he had said he would do in the "Apology" from the beginning. But he is also suggesting that the temporal is the realm of communication. If there is any human universal in the *Essays,* it would be the ability of human beings to communicate with each other.

14. See René Descartes, *Discourse on Method,* in *The Philosophical Writings of Descartes.* vol. 1, trans. John Cottingham et al. (Cambridge: Cambridge University Press, 1985), 140. In part 5 of the *Discourse,* Descartes claims that there are two ways by which we could tell the difference between "true men" and machines that closely resembled men. The first is that "it is not conceivable that such a machine should produce different arrangements of words so as to give an appropriately meaningful answer to whatever is said in its presence, as the dullest of men can do." The second is that machines cannot act in all of life's situations in the same way as our reason makes us act. These are also the ways we can also know the difference between men and beasts.

15. Here again we see the way in which the tradition includes developments which are taken up by Montaigne. Mary Keys, *Aquinas,* 98, discusses the differences between Aquinas and Aristotle on the value and meaning of "servile" actions: "Christ's actions and example [of serving others] *had* to have

implications for a correct understanding of human nature and consequently the exercise of human authority, including political authority."

16. In his highly suggestive "*De l'experience:* Montaigne et la métaphysique," in *Montaigne: Scepticisme, métaphysique, théologie,* Vincent Carraud notes that the first sentence of "Of Experience" is a translation of the first sentence of Aristotle's *Metaphysics* (69). "Of Experience" is Montaigne's "first philosophy." It is here that he confronts Aristotle and departs from him. We do not recognize the importance of Aristotle for Montaigne on account of the traditional interpretation of Montaigne as a skeptic. But the first pages of "Of Experience" constitute a precise discussion of the beginning of Aristotle's *Metaphysics* (70–72) and the essay as a whole is Montaigne's subversion of the Aristotelian concept of experience. This subversion is the first condition for Montaigne's notion of the experience of the self (83). Montaigne's experience is of the union of soul and body, the experience that he substitutes for Aristotle's *Metaphysics* and *Physics* (84–85). Carraud suggests that it might even be possible to claim that, for Montaigne, experience is only experience of the self (87).

17. See Bacon, *Novum Organum,* book 1, aphorisms 24, 25, pp. 49–50, on the discovery of new particulars; and book 2, aphorism 2, p. 135: "Nothing truly exists in nature except separate bodies performing separate pure actions."

18. See Charles Gagnebin, *La philosophie critique de Montaigne* (Neuchâtel: Éditions de l'Aire, 2007), 161–63, for a discussion of Montaigne's "strong and generous ignorance."

19. See Sarah Bakewell, *How to Live, or A Life of Montaigne in One Question and Twenty Attempts at an Answer* (New York: Other, 2010), 17: "The trick is to maintain a kind of naïve amazement at each instant of experience." This is Montaigne's "desire to pay astounded attention to life."

20. See Michael Oakeshott's discussion of philosophy in *Experience and Its Modes* (Cambridge: Cambridge University Press, 1933).

21. In his *Montaigne en mouvement* (Paris: Éditions Gallimard, 1982), Jean Starobinski claims that Montaigne's purpose is to leave a record of ordinary life: this was what was so outrageous and scandalous about the *Essays* (51). This is "a truth closer to home that philosophy neglects" (282). Marcel Conche, "Montaigne, penseur de la philosophie," in *Montaigne: Scepticisme, métaphysique, théologie,* ed. Vincent Carraud and Jean-Luc Marion, 179: with Montaigne we rediscover the astonishment and the attitude of inquiry which are at the heart of Greek thought; we rediscover philosophy in its essence.

22. Todorov, *Imperfect Garden,* 167 (emphasis added). La Charité, *Judgment,* 48: Montaigne eventually substitutes *vie* (understood as temperament) for *jugement.* Thus "the faculty of judgment permeates the whole of one's psyche." Screech, *Melancholy,* 13: the last pages of "Of Experience" form the climax of all three books. "For Montaigne, at the end of his quest, had come to terms with melancholy and ecstasy—and so with religion, life and death, and with his being as a man." Tournon, "Action imparfaite de sa propre essence," in *Montaigne: Scepticisme, métaphysique, théologie,* ed. Vincent Carraud and Jean-Luc Marion, 34: concerning Montaigne's discussion of "vanité toute la sagesse," Tournon says that Montaigne opposes to this, not the wisdom of God,

but the deliberate choice of earthly life, here below, in its very inanity. Philippe Desan, "Essai (genre)," in *Dictionnaire de Michel de Montaigne,* 341: Desan's discussion of the sense of essaying as tasting (*dégustation*) fits well with this sense of experience and the practice of everyday life.

Chapter 5

1. Two major studies of Montaigne's political philosophy have been published over the past twenty years: David Lewis Schaefer's *The Political Philosophy of Montaigne* (Ithaca, N.Y.: Cornell University Press, 1990) and Alan Levine's *Sensual Philosophy: Toleration, Skepticism, and Montaigne's Politics of the Self* (Lanham, Md.: Lexington Books, 2001). Both have the merit of recognizing Montaigne's originality as a political philosopher and his status as a founder of modern philosophy. Schaefer claims that Montaigne's purpose is "a radical transformation of the political and social order" (32) and locates him in the line of philosophers of liberalism that begins with Machiavelli. Levine argues that Montaigne cannot be regarded precisely as a liberal because he does not insist on democratic government, the separation of powers, or the "rights" of individuals. Nevertheless, he sees Montaigne as a "protoliberal" (168) who lays the groundwork for liberalism and has a significant role in establishing the liberal ethos. Because they take Montaigne seriously as an original political philosopher, both Schaefer and Levine provide valuable insights into Montaigne's thought, and my own understanding of Montaigne has benefited from their work.

However, my study of the *Essays* is ultimately very different from each of theirs in emphasis and substance. First, I ground my interpretation of Montaigne's political philosophy in his rejection of Aristotelian form and final cause and, thus, in his rejection of the common good as the end of political association. I believe this is implicit in Schaefer and Levine, although it is not thematic. Second, Montaigne's notion of judgment is central to my understanding of his epistemology and his moral and political philosophy, whereas it is not for Schaefer or Levine. Third, I interpret Montaigne's refounding as the overcoming of natural mastery and, therefore, I see his liberalism as a radically new kind of rule. Montaigne does not insist on any premodern regime, including democracy, because he is instituting a more fundamental reform. In this I am indebted to Francis Slade's presentation of Machiavelli's "new form." Schaefer and Levine seem to understand Montaigne's innovation as a "lowering" of the end and thus of the standards of government, while I see it as a transcendence of the traditional hierarchy of weak and strong.

Fourth, then, both Schaefer and Levine argue that Montaigne is lowering the standard of morality. Schaefer claims that Montaigne initiates the morality of "bourgeois individualism" and that his preference is that "particular relations among human beings be governed by the cash nexus" (376). Levine argues that Montaigne's radically new conception of the subjective self is the basis for the liberal value of toleration. The best human life is radically private (167) and the character that Montaigne displays is a "sophisticated simplicity." Montaigne's argument for toleration, he says, appeals entirely to individual self-interest (e.g., 168, 200, 234). I agree that Montaigne introduces a strong sense of the individual and also that he values toleration on the grounds that the *common good* must be rejected. However, the character that he displays is that of the "self-ordered" individual, "strong in itself" and therefore capable of freedom. Montaigne's character is one of generosity and integrity and is not defined by self-interest. Again, his moral teaching can only be seen as a "lowering" of standards if one accepts the traditional hierarchy. My view is that Montaigne presents his new character as a "higher," because more fully human, possibility than the character of classical virtue. Montaigne restores philosophy to man: he considers the human as such, without linking it to the place of man in any traditional hierarchy. While this looks like a lowering of the standards of human thought and action, he claims that "it is an absolute perfection and God-like to know how to enjoy our own being rightly." I take this to be due to the fact that judgment, the overcoming of natural mastery, and his new character are all manifestations of the role of the will that transcends nature and thus makes possible a new kind of freedom.

Fifth, both Schaefer and Levine hold that Montaigne is not a Christian and that he seeks to undermine the power of religion and especially of the Catholic Church. Levine sees Christianity as the major source of the intolerance, oppression, and cruelty that Montaigne wants to overcome. I agree that Montaigne is highly critical of the Catholic side in the civil wars of France and of the cruelty of the Spanish conquerors in the New World. However, he does not blame Christianity, but rather blames the failure of men to live up to its teachings, for these evils. Also, there is good reason to believe that he did not really favor the toleration of Protestantism in France but that he ultimately accepted it as the only possible solution to the civil unrest. In contrast to Schaefer and Levine, I argue that Montaigne sees religion as essential to the social bond and that he views the Catholic Church as the basis for the possibility of a universal society that transcends the political realm.

2. Hobbes, *Leviathan,* chap. 15, p. 211.

3. Hobbes makes this explicit: "The difference of Common-wealths, consisteth in the difference of the Sovereign, or the Person representative of all and every one of the Multitude. And because the Sovereignty is either in one man, or in an Assembly of more than one . . . it is manifest that there can be but three kinds of Common-wealth." The names that Hobbes uses to identify these types of government are monarchy, democracy, and aristocracy. "There be other names of Government, in the Histories and books of Policy; as Tyranny, and Oligarchy. But they are not the names of other forms of Government, but of the same Formes misliked. For they that are discontented under Monarchy, call it Tyranny; and they that are displeased with Aristocracy, called it Oligarchy: So also, they which find themselves grieved under a Democracy, call it Anarchy." Hobbes, *Leviathan,* chap. 19, p. 239.

4. Hobbes's formulation of this relationship as "master-servant" and Machiavelli's formulation in terms of the opposition between "the great" and "the people" do capture the same idea that rule is not for the sake of the common good. However, I use the "master-slave" formulation in order to maintain the

connection with Aristotle's *Politics* where regimes that do not pursue the common good, and especially tyranny, are comparable to the master-slave relation in the household.

5. Jean-Jacques Rousseau, *Discourse on the Origin and Foundation of Inequality,* in *The First and Second Discourses,* trans. Roger D. Masters and Judith R. Masters (New York: St. Martin's, 1964), 173.

6. Benjamin Constant, "The Liberty of the Ancients Compared with That of the Moderns," in *Political Writings,* ed. and trans. Biancamaria Fontana (Cambridge: Cambridge University Press, 1988), 311.

7. Ibid., 310.

8. Francis Slade, "Rule as Sovereignty: The Universal and Homogeneous State," in *The Truthful and the Good: Essays in Honor of Robert Sokolowski,* ed. John J. Drummond and James G. Hart (Dordrecht: Kluwer Academic, 1996), 163.

9. Francis Slade, "Zeno's City" (paper presented at the annual meeting of the American Maritain Association, Notre Dame University, South Bend, Ind., October 2007), 1.

10. Ibid., 2.

11. Ibid., 16.

12. Hobbes, *Leviathan,* chap. 16, pp. 217, 220.

13. Thus, when Rousseau claims that the will cannot be represented, the result is that slavery is necessary for the full participation of the citizens in the activities of ruling. This shocking turn of the argument at the end of the *Social Contract* points to the fact that the "general will" is Rousseau's version of freedom as "neither master nor slave." Whatever Rousseau's reasons for asserting that the will cannot be represented, he displays the difficulties of bringing together political freedom and personal freedom. This difficulty cannot be resolved by requiring the individual to surrender his public will to a representative. Jean-Jacques Rousseau, *On the Social Contract,* trans. Judith R. Masters, ed. Roger D. Masters (New York: St. Martin's, 1978), book 3, chap. 15.

14. In his discussion of the difference between premodern and modern political philosophy, Francis Slade explains the nature of the new form of rule that is introduced by Machiavelli. Whereas, for classical political philosophy, rule is exercised by human beings who assert their claims to rule on the basis of their contributions to the city, that is, on the basis of political arguments, "modern philosophy turns itself into political philosophy in the strong sense. It aims to rule. It will advance . . . the only claim worthy of respect, the claim to rule of reason itself, a claim which equalizes and cancels all the other claims. Reason can make this claim because, according to modern philosophy, reason as such is rule. It is the essence of reason, as modern philosophy and the Enlightenment understand reason, to rule." See Slade, "Was Ist Aufklärung?" 58. The fundamental thesis of modern political philosophy is that "the political whole is the construct of reason." Slade, "Rule as Sovereignty," 179. I argue that, for Montaigne, reason inflexible and impassive settles the natural contest between masters and subjects because it is not merely private, self-interested reason but reason without a private will.

15. Oakeshott, *Rationalism in Politics,* 339.

16. Montaigne, *Œuvres complètes,* 1299–1300 (F1010).

17. Hobbes, *Leviathan,* part 1, chap. 15, p. 211. See Harvey C. Mansfield, *Manliness* (New Haven, Conn.: Yale University Press, 2006), 173: the laws of nature instruct men in sociability and are therefore particularly directed against pride or magnanimity. Mansfield points out that Hobbes nowhere in his mature thought praises manliness. In the *Leviathan,* he omits courage from the virtues.

18. Edmund Burke, *Reflections on the Revolution in France* (Buffalo, N.Y.: Prometheus Books, 1987), 175.

19. Plutarch, *Moralia,* vol. 10, trans. Harold North Fowler, Loeb Classical Library (Cambridge, Mass.: Harvard University Press, 1936), 815–16.

20. According to Tarn, there are three extant versions of the death of Betis, those of Hegesias, Dionysius of Halicarnassus, and Quintus Curtius. Tarn says that the version of Dionysius is the simplest: Alexander ordered that Betis be tied living behind a chariot and the horses driven at full speed, and so killed him. Hegesias's version is the earliest and Quintus Curtius relied on it to some extent. See W. W. Tarn, *Alexander the Great II: Sources and Studies* (Cambridge: Cambridge University Press, 1948), 267–68. Montaigne's principal source must have been Curtius's *History of Alexander,* 4.vi. According to Villey and Saulnier, this work was in Montaigne's library. More important, the punishment of Betis is not mentioned by the other historians of Alexander: Arrian, Diodorus, and Plutarch. Finally, Alexander's address to Betis, as found in "By Diverse Means," is almost verbatim from Curtius. See Quintus Curtius, *History of Alexander,* 2 vols., trans. John C. Rolfe, Loeb Classical Library (Cambridge, Mass.: Harvard University Press, 1946), 4, vi. David Quint, in *Montaigne and the Quality of Mercy: Ethical and Political Themes in the Essays* (Princeton, N.J.: Princeton University Press, 1998), 15, notes that Montaigne's source is Quintus Curtius and that, in the historian's account, Alexander is imitating Achilles. Quint also discusses the silence of Betis and the fact that Alexander finds it intolerable.

21. According to Curtius, when Betis was brought before Alexander, Alexander (who was "usually an admirer of valour even in an enemy") was "exulting . . . with insolent joy" (4.vi.26–27). Montaigne omits this description entirely. Curtius says that, in response to Betis's haughty silence, Alexander's "wrath changed to frenzy, for even then his new fortune suggested foreign customs" (29–39). Instead of reporting that Alexander's wrath changed to frenzy, Montaigne says that he turned his anger into rage (*tournant sa cholere en rage*), and he omits Curtius's explanation that Alexander was under the sway of foreign customs.

22. Quintus Curtius, *History of Alexander,* 4.vi.29–30.

23. Ibid. See Isabelle Pantin, "Montaigne lecteur de Quinte-Curce: Quelques réflexions sur la collecte de Dezeimeris," *Montaigne Studies* 17 (2005): 138, for a discussion of the story of Betis and Montaigne's omission of the comparison to Achilles. In the same volume, Philip Ford provides a thorough examination of the question of Montaigne's knowledge of Homer. See "Montaigne's Homer: Poet or Myth?" 7–16.

24. Quintus Curtius, *History of Alexander,* 4.vi.24.

25. Ibid., 4.vi.5–7. "Alexander, however, although trying to track Darius with all care, could not find out for what region he had made, because of a custom of the Persians of keeping the secrets of their kings with a marvelous fidelity; not fear, not hope, can elicit a single word by which confidences are betrayed. The ancient discipline of the kings had enjoined silence on pain of death. An unbridled tongue is more severely punished than any act of wickedness, and the Magi believe that no great cause can be upheld by one who finds it hard to keep silence, which nature has decreed to be the easiest thing for a man to do."

26. Ibid.,7.

27. See Etienne de La Boétie, *Le discours de la servitude volontaire,* text established by P. Léonard (Paris: Payot, 1985), 134–35. I have relied upon David Lewis Schaefer's translation of the *Discourse* in *Freedom over Servitude,* ed. David Lewis Schaefer (Westport, Conn.: Greenwood, 1998). This passage is found on p. 205 of Schaefer's translation.

28. Victor Davis Hanson, *The Soul of Battle: From Ancient Times to the Present Day, How Three Great Liberators Vanquished Tyranny* (New York: Free, 1999), 52. Hanson relies on scattered references in Xenophon, Plutarch, Pausanius, and Diodorus (52, 417).

29. Ibid., 118.

30. Ibid., 111.

31. Ibid., 57, 71.

32. Ibid., 53.

33. Ibid., 55.

34. Ibid., 53.

35. Ibid., 54–55.

36. Ibid., 107.

37. This is Cornelius Nepos's version of the story: "He was leading an army in the Peloponnesus against Sparta and had two co-commanders, one of whom was the brilliant Pelopidas. Because of the envious hatred of some men in Thebes these three leaders were stripped of their command, and others were sent out to replace them. Epaminondas disobeyed the order and, having persuaded his co-commanders to do the same, carried on the war. He was convinced that the inexperience of the new commanders would surely lead to the destruction of the army. Epaminondas did all of this under the shadow of a Theban law which punished with death all who kept their command longer than the prescribed period. Since he recognized that this law was enacted to preserve the state, and since he did not want the same law to ruin the state, he held his command four months longer than the people had originally directed. As soon as the commanders returned home, they were indicted on a charge of insubordination. Epaminondas allowed the other two officers to transfer all responsibility for their illegal actions to him. Such a line of argument freed them but made the case against Epaminondas so tight that no one thought he would even dare to speak in his own defense. During the trial he denied none of the charges, and having confessed to everything, admitted he deserved full punishment under the law. He did ask one favor of his judges, namely that they enter

the following statement in the trial record: 'Epaminondas was sentenced to death by the Thebans because he forced them at Leuctra to defeat the Spartans, whom they had never dared to oppose in battle before Epaminondas led them. In just one battle he snatched the Theban army out of the jaws of defeat and lifted the Spartan yoke off all Greece. He completely changed the earlier fortunes of Thebes and Sparta: Thebes now attacks Sparta and Spartans consider themselves lucky to escape from the battlefield alive. He did not cease his relentless pressure until Messene had been recovered and Sparta lay encircled by his troops.' When he had finished, a roar of laughter went up from the crowd, and no judge dared to indict him on any charge. The trial which had begun with accusations of treason, ended with exoneration and commendation." Cornelius Nepos, "Epaminondas (420–362 BC)," in *Lives of Famous Men,* trans. Gareth Schmeling (Coronado, 1971), 84–85. Hanson, *Soul of Battle,* says that Epaminondas reasoned that the law of a one-year limitation on the tenure of beotarchs was to prevent tyranny (83).

38. Hanson, *Soul of Battle,* 32.

39. Quint, *Quality of Mercy,* 17.

40. Hanson, *Soul of Battle,* 21, 116–17.

41. Nepos, "Epaminondas," 86.

42. Niccolò Machiavelli, *The Prince,* trans. Harvey C. Mansfield Jr. (Chicago: University of Chicago Press, 1985), chap. 12, p. 50. Epaminondas died in 362 BC. Philip became king of Macedon in 358 and occupied Thebes in 338.

43. James J. Supple, *Arms Versus Letters: The Military and Literary Ideals in the Essais of Montaigne* (Oxford: Clarendon, 1984), 249: Epaminondas shows Montaigne's increasing insistence on the primacy of virtue over valor and his shift from the worldly man to private conduct. See also 246–48 on the primacy of private values.

44. Niccolò Machiavelli, *Discourses on Livy,* trans. Harvey C. Mansfield and Nathan Tarcov (Chicago: University of Chicago Press, 1996), 1.21.3, p. 55.

45. Ibid., 1.17.3, p. 48.

46. Ibid., 1.55.4–5, pp. 111–12.

47. This was suggested to me by Francis Slade's discussion of the rejection of the common good in his "Two Versions of Political Philosophy," 248, in which he quotes Josef Pieper concerning his conversation with Carl Schmitt: "I asked . . . [Carl Schmitt] why, in his book on the 'concept of the political' . . . he had not written a syllable about the *bonum commune,* since the whole meaning of politics surely lay in the realization of the common good. He retorted sharply: 'Anyone who speaks of the *bonum commune* is intent on deception.'" Josef Pieper, *No One Could Have Known: An Autobiography: The Early Years* (San Francisco: Ignatius, 1987), 175.

48. Arendt, *The Human Condition,* 236–37.

49. Ibid., 241.

50. Ibid., 239–40.

51. Ibid., 237, 244.

52. Ibid., 238.

53. Ibid., 240–41.

54. Ibid., 239 n. 76 and 77.

55. Ultimately, of course, the question is whether or not these restraints are effective and sufficient. In particular, what kind of community is it possible to have in the absence of the standard of the common good? Keys, *Aquinas*, 41–56, considers the common good in relation to contemporary theories such as communitarianism and liberal pluralism, which seem to lack the solid moral foundation which the common good offers.

56. Simone Weil, "Méditation sur l'obéissance et la liberté," in Etienne de La Boétie, *Le discours de la servitude volontaire: La Boétie et la question du politique* (Paris: Payot, 1985), 95.

Chapter 6

1. Slade, "Two Versions of Political Philosophy," 254.

2. Ibid., 251.

3. The note on this passage in the Pléïade *Œuvres complètes* (1458) refers to Paul-Emile who, in *De rebus Francorum*, says that this nobleman would have borne the name of Gascon.

4. Biancamaria Fontana, *Montaigne's Politics: Authority and Governance in the Essais* (Princeton, N.J.: Princeton University Press, 2008), 27. See also R. Doucet, *Les institutions de la France au xvi siècle*, 2 vols. (Paris: Éditions A. et J. Picard, 1948), especially vol. 1, pp. 60–61, where the distinction and the relationship between common or customary law and written Roman law is discussed. Doucet shows that the question of the laws was a vexed issue in the sixteenth century and that no province of the kingdom enjoyed unity of legislation. I am grateful to Professor William Beik for his help in uncovering Montaigne's meaning and for suggesting the Doucet volume to me.

5. Fontana, *Montaigne's Politics*, 33. See also Desan, *Montaigne: Les formes*, 176–77.

6. Fontana, *Montaigne's Politics*, 28.

7. See Desan, *Montaigne: Les formes*, 171–73, for a very helpful discussion of the "new ethic" associated with the economic practices of the new merchant class which was developing in the sixteenth century.

8. Michael Oakeshott, "Political Education," in *The Voice of Liberal Learning*, ed. Timothy Fuller (New Haven, Conn.: Yale University Press, 1989; reprint, Indianapolis, Ind.: Liberty Fund, 2001), 173.

9. Ibid., 179.

10. Ibid., 175.

11. Fontana, *Montaigne's Politics*, 114.

12. Quint, *Quality of Mercy*, 20.

13. Ibid., 45.

14. Ibid., 26.

15. Ibid., 41.

16. Ibid., 104.

17. Ibid., 107.

18. See Emmanuel Faye, "Montaigne et la perfection humaine de Socrate dans 'De la physionomie,'" *Montaigne Studies* 21 (2009): 38: Montaigne goes

beyond the opposition between nature and education in the formation of Socrates's character.

19. See Desan, *Montaigne: Les formes,* 182: Montaigne ties the honor of the nobility to keeping one's word.

20. Within this context of the reordering of the virtues and vices, where does the virtue of justice find a place? Justice might be called *the* political virtue. Aristotle's understanding of the common good is inseparable from the virtue of justice: those regimes are just which aim at the common good and those which aim at the good of the rulers are unjust. Given Montaigne's rejection of the common good, what could he mean by "justice"?

Montaigne does refer to what he calls "justice itself." In "Of the Useful and the Honorable" he writes: "Justice in itself, natural and universal, is regulated otherwise and more nobly than that other, special, national justice, constrained to the needs of our governments" (VS796, F604). Here he denies the possibility of perfect justice established by human beings. In the "Apology" he expresses his dissatisfaction with the philosophical position that justice is simply a matter of obeying the laws of one's country. "Truth," he says, "must have one face, the same and universal." To say that we must follow the laws of our country is to say that justice has many faces. Montaigne's response is: "I cannot have my judgment so flexible" (VS578–79, F436–37). Yet there does seem to be a sense in which Montaigne sees obedience to the laws as the best that can be done given the imperfect forms of justice that men devise. "Laws," he says, "remain in credit not because they are just, but because they are laws. That is the mystic foundation of their authority; they have no other. And that is a good thing for them. They are often made by fools, more often by people who, in their hatred of equality, are wanting in equity; but always by men, vain and irresolute authors. There is nothing so grossly and widely and ordinarily faulty as the laws. Whoever obeys them because they are just, does not obey them for just the reason he should" (VS1072, F821). However, unlike Socrates, Montaigne's allegiance to the laws is conditional. If the laws threatened his freedom, he would instantly go and find others (VS1072, F821). This perhaps implies that freedom, not the common good, is the touchstone for evaluating the laws.

Montaigne's attitude toward justice may also have something to do with the fact that justice involves retribution or revenge, and that is the passion which he seems most concerned to suppress. Thus, in "Of Cruelty" he asserts that, even in "the executions of justice," whatever punishments go beyond plain death are "pure cruelty" (VS430, F314). It would seem, then, that the social virtues supersede the political virtue of justice in the reform of the nobility.

21. Fontana, *Montaigne's Politics,* 104.

22. Ibid., 105.

23. In *Montaigne: La manière et la matière* (Paris: Klincksieck, 1991), Géralde Nakam comments on these stories from "Various Outcomes of the Same Plan" and connects Montaigne with Machiavelli's *Discourses:* public peace rests on the confidence of the people (161–68). He also provides a very useful commentary on the symmetry of "By Diverse Means We Arrive at the Same End" and "Various Outcomes of the Same Plan" with respect to the terror exercised by tyrannies (169–71).

24. Montaigne, *Œuvres complètes,* 1289 (F, CW 1002).

25. Ibid.,1262 (F, CW 982).

26. Ibid., 1294 (F, CW 1006).

27. Smith, *Montaigne and Religious Freedom,* 81–82.

28. Ibid., 57, 61–63. Smith quotes from La Boétie's *Memorandum:* "It is impossible to couple together truth and falsehood, for one necessarily drives out the other. In ancient societies, any error easily gained acceptance, but as soon as the light of the gospel appeared and gave the lie to all the idolatry of the gentiles, it became manifest that the true religion and false religions were incompatible. The struggle between them did not cease until truth defeated falsehood and light drove out darkness. Now, just as our religion could not in any way accept paganism, in the same way it cannot accept diverse sects within itself, since truth is one, pure and simple, and never compromises with what is false and deceitful. And to imagine that our faith can have anything to do with what it rejects is to do violence to its inherent purity" (64).

29. Ibid., 105.

30. Ibid., 135.

31. Ibid., 86.

32. Ibid., 171.

33. Ibid., 178.

34. Ibid., 124.

35. Ibid., 102, 117.

36. Ibid., 112.

Chapter 7

1. Michael Oakeshott, *The Politics of Faith and the Politics of Scepticism,* ed. Timothy Fuller (New Haven, Conn.: Yale University Press, 1996), 76.

2. Ibid., 49. So also, William J. Bouwsma in *The Waning of the Renaissance* describes this as a time of unprecedented empowerment of princes, during which the pressures of central government were felt on individuals and intermediate bodies, such as guilds and ecclesiastical organizations. The justification of such power was now a major concern of political thought.

3. Michael Oakeshott, "The Masses in Representative Democracy," in *Rationalism in Politics and Other Essays,* ed. Timothy Fuller (London: Methuen, 1962; reprint, Indianapolis, Ind.: Liberty, 1991), 364.

4. Ibid., 365.

5. Ibid., 370.

6. Ibid.

7. Ibid., 366.

8. J. B. Schneewind, *The Invention of Autonomy: A History of Modern Moral Philosophy* (Cambridge: Cambridge University Press, 1998), 37.

9. Ibid., 45.

10. See Todorov, *Imperfect Garden,* 109–10: Montaigne is fleeing not society but servitude. Todorov argues throughout this book that humanism rejects the incompatibility of community and liberty.

11. For example, in the discussion of virtue in the *Summa Theologica,* Thomas Aquinas makes precisely that point (ST I-II, Q63, A1).

12. Quintus Curtius, *History of Alexander,* 4.vi.29–39.

13. See, for example, Thomas Aquinas, *Commentary of Aristotle's Nicomachean Ethics,* trans. C. I. Litzinger (Notre Dame, Ind.: Dumb Ox Books, 1993), book 7, lecture 11, p. 459: "Thus, sexual pleasure obviously very intense, impedes the mind to such an extent that no one is capable of exercising the act of understanding at the time of the act of pleasure, for the whole attention of the mind is drawn to it." Aquinas is commenting on *NE.* 1152b1–24, where Aristotle sets out arguments that pleasure is not the highest good.

14. Montaigne opposes cruelty in the executions of justice. Thomas Aquinas, *Summa Theologica,* 2.2, question 159, treats cruelty as a vice opposed to moderation, specifically with respect to punishment, and therefore the moderation of punishment comes under the rule of reason like all virtues. Cruelty for the pleasure of it is, for Aquinas, savage and bestial. But for Montaigne, cruelty is distinctly human; it cannot be brought under reason, for, more than any other passion, it tends toward the ravishment of reason. Also, Aquinas thinks that sexual pleasure is the best example of the ravishment of reason because at its height it interferes with thought. Montaigne thinks otherwise: the pleasure of the chase is a more appropriate example because it involves the pleasure of contemplation.

15. For a more complete discussion of Montaigne's practice of confronting the passions in their beginnings, see "Of Husbanding Your Will," especially VS1016–20, F778–80.

16. This is another instance in which we can see intimations of Aquinas's Christian development of Aristotle's ethics. Keys, *Aquinas,* 144, reads Aquinas "as offering a subtle yet far-reaching critique of Aristotelian magnanimity, one with roots in Aquinas's theology yet also comprising a philosophic reappraisal of Aristotle's account of human excellence." See also my *Accidental Philosopher,* chap. 7: "Montaigne's Character: The Great-Souled Man Without Pride."

17. René Descartes, *The Passions of the Soul,* in *The Philosophical Writings of Descartes,* vol. 1, trans. John Cottingham et al. (Cambridge: Cambridge University Press, 1985), part 3, article 161, pp. 387–88.

18. Ibid., articles 152 and 153, p. 384.

19. Ibid., article 154, p. 384.

20. Ibid., article 164, p. 389.

21. See Bernard Sève, *Montaigne: Des règles pour l'esprit* (Paris: Presses Universitaires de France, 2007), 319.

22. Flannery O'Connor, *Wise Blood* (New York: Farrar, Straus and Giroux, 1949), 5. In her "Note" to the second edition of *Wise Blood,* Flannery O'Connor asks: "Does one's integrity ever lie in what he is not able to do?"

23. John Kekes, *Enjoyment: The Moral Significance of Styles of Life* (Oxford: Clarendon, 2008), 146.

24. Ibid., 149.

25. Oakeshott, *Rationalism in Politics,* 339.

26. John Kekes, *The Morality of Pluralism* (Princeton, N.J.: Princeton University Press, 1993), 193.

27. Ibid., 196.

28. John Christian Laursen, *The Politics of Skepticism in the Ancients, Montaigne, Hume and Kant* (Leiden: E. J. Brill, 1992). See pp. 116–18 on Montaigne's inversion of the evaluation of the public and private realms. He places the private above the public. Further, religion is a public matter, not a matter of private conscience.

29. Kekes, *Enjoyment,* 237–38.

30. Ibid., 244.

31. Friedrich Nietzsche, "Schopenhauer as Educator," trans. William Arrowsmith, in *Unmodern Observations,* ed. William Arrowsmith (New Haven, Conn.: Yale University Press, 1990), 171.

32. Bouwsma, *Waning of the Renaissance,* 177: Montaigne "equated the highest grace in behavior with nonchalance." See Zahi Zalloua, "Montaigne, Seneca, and 'le soing de la culture de l'ame,'" *Montaigne Studies* 21 (2009): 163–64, for a very helpful discussion of Montaigne's nonchalance, especially in relation to politics.

33. Ullrich Langer, *Divine and Poetic Freedom in the Renaissance: Nominalist Theology and Literature in France and Italy* (Princeton, N.J.: Princeton University Press, 1990), 186. See also Zahi Zalloua, *Montaigne and the Ethics of Skepticism* (Charlottesville, Va.: Rookwood, 2005), 88, on the relationship between generosity and friendship.

34. See Todorov, *Imperfect Garden,* 130: this friendship is "not in the service of any external goal" and is "not reducible to any general notion." See also Todorov, *Montaigne ou la découverte de l'individu,* 9–10. Lorraine Smith Pangle, *Aristotle and the Philosophy of Friendship* (Cambridge: Cambridge University Press, 2003), 66: their friendship is "the freely chosen submission of each to the will of the other."

35. Etienne de La Boétie, *Le discours de la servitude volontaire,* 160 (Schaefer 220). For an illuminating discussion of friendship and tyranny within the context of Montaigne's friendship with La Boétie, see Michael Platt, "Montaigne, Of Friendship, and On Tyranny," in Schaefer, *Freedom over Servitude,* 31–85. See Starobinski, *Montaigne en mouvement,* 71–73, for a discussion of friendship, tyranny, and La Boétie's *Discours.*

36. Lewis, *God in the Dock,* 314.

37. La Boétie, *La servitude volontaire,* 134–35 (Schaefer 205).

38. Ibid., 135 (Schaefer 206).

39. In his *Montaigne: Des règles pour l'esprit,* Bernard Sève argues that generosity is necessary to discussion and that the intellectual capacities that produce discussion are necessary to the attitude of generosity (317). Generosity in discussion is shown in the refusal to be opinionated, the refusal of base interpretations of the actions of others, and the refusal of finesse and subtlety (326). Sève also argues that generosity is associated with Montaigne's hatred of lying because lying destroys communication. Generosity is one of the motives and persuasive forces of the *Essays* themselves (324). In "Un scepticisme sans tranquillité: Montaigne et ses modèles antiques," in *Montaigne: Scepticisme, métaphysique, théologie,* ed. Vincent Carraud and Jean-Luc Marion, 25–27, Charles Larmore argues that Montaigne transforms the skepticism that

he inherits: Montaigne's skepticism consists in avoiding enthusiasm which is imagining that one has discovered the definitive solution to a question. Larmore associates this version of skepticism with Montaigne's ignorance. Thus the true face of his skepticism appears in "the ethic of conversation" in essay 3.8, "Of the Art of Discussion."

40. Rousseau, *Discourse on the Origin and Foundations of Inequality Among Men,* 160–61.

WORKS CITED

Aquinas, Saint Thomas. *Commentary on Aristotle's Nicomachean Ethics.* Trans. C. I. Litzinger. Notre Dame, Ind.: Dumb Ox Books, 1993.

———. *Summa Theologica.* Trans. Fathers of the English Dominican Province. 5 vols. Reprint. Notre Dame, Ind.: Ave Maria, Christian Classics, 1981.

Arendt, Hannah. *The Human Condition.* Chicago: University of Chicago Press, 1958.

Aristotle. *The Complete Works.* Ed. Jonathan Barnes. 2 vols. Princeton, N.J.: Princeton University Press, 1984.

———. *The Politics.* Trans. Carnes Lord. Chicago: University of Chicago Press, 1984.

Armaingaud, Arthur. "Montaigne: Etait-il ondoyant et divers? Montaigne était-il inconstant?" *Revue du seizième siècle* 10 (1923): 35–56.

Auerbach, Erich. "Figura." In *Scenes from the Drama of European Literature: Six Essays,* 11–76. New York: Meridian Books, 1959.

———. "L'humaine condition." In *Mimesis: The Representation of Reality in Western Literature,* trans. Willard R. Trask. Princeton, N.J.: Princeton University Press, 1953.

Augustine, Saint. *The City of God.* Ed. David Knowles. Trans. Henry Bettenson. Middlesex, Eng.: Penguin Books, 1972.

———. *The Confessions.* Trans. F. J. Sheed. Indianapolis, Ind.: Hackett, 1992.

Bacon, Francis. *Novum Organum.* Trans. Peter Urbach and John Gibson. Chicago: Open Court, 1994.

Bakewell, Sarah. *How to Live, or A Life of Montaigne in One Question and Twenty Attempts at an Answer.* New York: Other, 2010.

Benmakhlouf, Ali. *Montaigne.* Paris: Les Belles Lettres, 2008.

Bouwsma, William J. *The Waning of the Renaissance, 1550–1640.* New Haven, Conn.: Yale University Press, 2000.

Brahami, Frédéric. *Le scepticisme de Montaigne.* Paris: Presses Universitaires de France, 1977.

Brann, Eva. *What, Then, Is Time?* Lanham, Md.: Rowman and Littlefield, 1999.

Burke, Edmund. *Reflections on the Revolution in France.* Buffalo, N.Y.: Prometheus Books, 1987.

Burke, Peter. *The Renaissance Sense of the Past.* New York: St. Martin's, 1969.

Carraud, Vincent, and Jean-Luc Marion, eds. *Montaigne: Scepticisme, métaphysique, théologie.* Paris: Presses Universitaires de France, 2004.

Castor, Grahame. *Pleiade Poetics: A Study in Sixteenth-Century Thought and Terminology.* Cambridge: Cambridge University Press, 1964.

Cave, Terence. *How to Read Montaigne.* London: Granta Books, 2007.

Constant, Benjamin. "The Liberty of the Ancients Compared with That of the Moderns." In *Political Writings*, ed. and trans. Biancamaria Fontana. Cambridge: Cambridge University Press, 1988.

Curtius, Quintus. *History of Alexander.* Trans. John C. Rolfe. 2 vols. Loeb Classical Library. Cambridge, Mass.: Harvard University Press, 1946.

Desan, Philippe, ed. *Dictionnaire de Michel de Montaigne.* Paris: H. Champion, 2004.

———. *Montaigne dans tous ses états.* Fasano: Schena Editore, 2001.

———. *Montaigne: Les formes du monde et de l'esprit.* Paris: Presses de l'Université Paris-Sorbonne, 2008.

Descartes, René. *The Philosophical Writings of Descartes.* 3 vols. Trans. John Cottingham et al. Cambridge: Cambridge University Press, 1985–91.

Dotoli, Giovanni. *La voix de Montaigne: Langue, corps, et parole dans les Essais.* Paris: Éditions Lanore, 2007.

Doucet, R. *Les institutions de la France au xvi siècle.* 2 vols. Paris: Editions A. et J. Picard, 1948.

Duffy, Eamon. *The Stripping of the Altars: Traditional Religion in England 1400–1580.* New Haven, Conn.: Yale University Press 1992.

Eliot, T. S. *Christianity and Culture: The Idea of a Christian Society and Notes Towards the Definition of Culture.* New York: Harcourt, Brace and World, 1949.

———. "Humanist, Artist, and Scientist." In *Athenaeum,* October 10, 1919, pp. 1014–15.

———. "The *Pensées* of Pascal." In *Selected Essays.* New York: Harcourt Brace, 1932.

Faye, Emmanuel. "Montaigne et la perfection humaine de Socrate dans 'De la physionomie.' " *Montaigne Studies* 21 (2009): 35–39.

Fontana, Biancamaria. *Montaigne's Politics: Authority and Governance in the Essais.* Princeton, N.J.: Princeton University Press, 2008.

Ford, Philip. "Montaigne's Homer: Poet or Myth?" *Montaigne Studies* 17 (2005): 7–16.

Foster, Michael B. *Mystery and Philosophy.* London: SCM, 1957.

Friedrich, Hugo. *Montaigne.* Ed. Philippe Desan. Trans. Dawn Eng. Berkeley: University of California Press, 1991.

Gagnebin, Charles. *La philosophie critique de Montaigne.* Neuchâtel: Éditions de l'Aire, 2007.

Gide, André. *Essai sur Montaigne.* Paris: Jacques Schiffrin, Éditions de la Pléïade, n.d.

Gilson, Etienne. "Where Is Christendom?" In *The Gilson Reader,* ed. Anton Pegis, 342–46. Garden City, N.Y.: Doubleday, Image Books, 1957.

Gontier, Thierry. "Montaigne, les humanistes et la doctrine des anciens." *Montaigne Studies* 21 (2009): 13–33.

Hanson, Victor Davis. *The Soul of Battle: From Ancient Times to the Present Day, How Three Great Liberators Vanquished Tyranny.* New York: Free, 1999.

Hartle, Ann. "The Dialectic of Faith and Reason in the *Essays* of Montaigne." *Faith and Philosophy* 18, no. 3 (July 2001): 323–36.

———. *Michel de Montaigne: Accidental Philosopher.* Cambridge: Cambridge University Press, 2003.

———. "Montaigne and Scepticism." In *Cambridge Companion to Montaigne,* ed. Ullrich Langer, 183–206. Cambridge: Cambridge University Press, 2005.

Hobbes, Thomas. *Leviathan.* Ed. C. B. Macpherson. Reprint, London: Penguin Books, 1968.

Hume, David. *An Enquiry Concerning Human Understanding.* Indianapolis, Ind.: Hackett, 1977.

———. *Essays: Moral, Political, and Literary.* Ed. Eugene F. Miller. Indianapolis, Ind.: Liberty Classics, 1985.

Kekes, John. *Enjoyment: The Moral Significance of Styles of Life.* Oxford: Clarendon, 2008.

———. *The Morality of Pluralism.* Princeton, N.J.: Princeton University Press, 1993.

Keys, Mary M. *Aquinas, Aristotle, and the Promise of the Common Good.* Cambridge: Cambridge University Press, 2006.

Kierkegaard, Søren. *Philosophical Fragments; Johannes Climacus.* Ed. and trans. Howard V. Hong and Edna H. Hong. Princeton, N.J.: Princeton University Press, 1985.

Kritzman, Lawrence. *The Fabulous Imagination: On Montaigne's Essays.* New York: Columbia University Press, 2009.

La Boétie, Etienne de. *Le discours de la servitude volontaire.* Text established by P. Léonard. Paris: Payot, 1985.

———. *On Voluntary Servitude.* Trans. David Lewis Schaefer. In *Freedom over Servitude,* ed. David Lewis Schaefer. Westport, Conn.: Greenwood, 1998.

La Charité, Raymond C. *The Concept of Judgment in Montaigne.* The Hague: Martinus Nijhoff, 1968.

Langer, Ullrich. *Divine and Poetic Freedom in the Renaissance: Nominalist Theology and Literature in France and Italy.* Princeton, N.J.: Princeton University Press, 1990.

———. *Invention, Death and Self-Definitions in the Poetry of Pierre de Ronsard.* Saratoga, Calif.: ANMI LIBRI, 1986.

Laursen, John Christian. *The Politics of Skepticism in the Ancients, Montaigne, Hume and Kant.* Leiden: E. J. Brill, 1992.

Levine, Alan. *Sensual Philosophy: Toleration, Skepticism, and Montaigne's Politics of the Self.* Lanham, Md.: Lexington Books, 2001.

Lewis, C. S. *God in the Dock: Essays on Theology and Ethics.* Ed. Walter Hooper. Grand Rapids, Mich.: William B. Eerdmans, 1970.

Machiavelli, Niccolò. *Discourses on Livy.* Trans. Harvey C. Mansfield and Nathan Tarcov. Chicago: University of Chicago Press, 1996.

———. *The Prince.* Trans. Harvey C. Mansfield Jr. Chicago: University of Chicago Press, 1985.

Mansfield, Harvey C. *Manliness.* New Haven, Conn.: Yale University Press, 2006.

Mathias, Paul. *Montaigne ou l'usage du monde.* Paris: Librairie Philosophique J. Vrin, 2006.

Melehy, Hassan. *Writing Cogito: Montaigne, Descartes, and the Institution of the Modern Subject.* Albany: State University of New York Press, 1997.

Montaigne, Michel de. *The Complete Essays of Montaigne.* Trans. Donald Frame. Stanford, Calif.: Stanford University Press, 1943.

———. *The Complete Essays of Montaigne.* Trans. M. A. Screech. London: Penguin, 1991.

———. *Les Essais.* Ed. Pierre Villey and V.-L. Saulnier. 3 vols., 2nd ed. Paris: Presses Universitaires de France, "Quadrige," 1992.

———. *Œuvres complètes.* Ed. Albert Thibaudet and Maurice Rat. Paris: Gallimard, Bibliothèque de la Pléiade, 1962.

Nakam, Géralde. *Montaigne: La manière et la matière.* Paris: Klincksieck, 1991.

Nepos, Cornelius. *Lives of Famous Men.* Trans. Gareth Schmeling. Coronado, 1971.

Nietzsche, Friedrich. "Schopenhauer as Educator." Trans. William Arrowsmith. In *Unmodern Observations,* ed. William Arrowsmith. New Haven, Conn.: Yale University Press, 1990.

Oakeshott, Michael. *Experience and Its Modes.* Cambridge: Cambridge University Press, 1933.

———. *The Politics of Faith and the Politics of Scepticism.* Ed. Timothy Fuller. New Haven, Conn.: Yale University Press, 1996.

———. *Rationalism in Politics and Other Essays.* Ed. Timothy Fuller. London: Methuen, 1962; reprint, Indianapolis, Ind.: Liberty, 1991.

———. *The Voice of Liberal Learning.* Ed. Timothy Fuller. New Haven, Conn.: Yale University Press, 1989; reprint. Indianapolis, Ind.: Liberty Fund, 2001.

O'Connor, Flannery. *Wise Blood.* New York: Farrar, Straus and Giroux, 1949.

Pangle, Lorraine Smith. *Aristotle and the Philosophy of Friendship.* Cambridge: Cambridge University Press, 2003.

Pantin, Isabelle. "Montaigne lecteur de Quinte-Curce: Quelques réflexions sur la collecte de Dezeimeris." *Montaigne Studies* 17 (2005): 135–54.

Pascal, Blaise. *Pensées et opuscules.* Ed. Léon Brunschvicg. Revised ed. Paris: Librairie Hachette, 1946.

Penelhum, Terence. *God and Skepticism: A Study in Skepticism and Fideism.* Dordrecht: D. Reidel, 1983.

———. "Skepticism and Fideism." In *The Skeptical Tradition,* ed. Myles Burnyeat, 287–318. Berkeley: University of California Press, 1983.

Pieper, Josef. *No One Could Have Known: An Autobiography: The Early Years.* San Francisco: Ignatius, 1987.

———. *Tradition: Concept and Claim.* Trans. E. Christian Kopff. Wilmington, Del.: ISI Books, 2008.

Platt, Michael. "Montaigne, Of Friendship, and On Tyranny." In *Freedom over Servitude: Montaigne, La Boétie, and On Voluntary Servitude,* ed. David Lewis Schaefer, 31–85. Westport, Conn: Greenwood Press, 1998.

Plutarch. *Les œuvres morales & meslées de Plutarch.* Trans. Jacques Amyot. Vol. 1 (1572). Reprint, The Hague: Mouton, 1971; New York: Johnson Reprint Corporation, 1971.

———. *Moralia.* Vol. 10. Trans. Harold North Fowler. Loeb Classical Library. Cambridge, Mass.: Harvard University Press, 1936.

Poulet, Georges. *Studies in Human Time.* Trans. Elliot Coleman. Baltimore: Johns Hopkins University Press, 1956.

Quint, David. *Montaigne and the Quality of Mercy: Ethical and Political Themes in the Essays.* Princeton, N.J.: Princeton University Press, 1998.

Rousseau, Jean-Jacques. *Discourse on the Origin and Foundations of Inequality Among Men.* In *The First and Second Discourses,* trans. Roger D. and Judith R. Masters, ed. Roger D. Masters. New York: St. Martin's, 1964.

———. *On the Social Contract.* Trans. Judith R. Masters. Ed. Roger D. Masters. New York: St. Martin's, 1978.

Roussel, François. *Montaigne: Le magistrat sans juridiction.* Paris: Éditions Michalon, 2006.

Russell, George. "Hume's Correction of Modern Political Philosophy." Paper delivered at Emory University, November 11, 2010.

Schaefer, David Lewis. *The Political Philosophy of Montaigne.* Ithaca, N.Y.: Cornell University Press, 1990.

Schneewind, J. B. *The Invention of Autonomy: A History of Modern Moral Philosophy.* Cambridge: Cambridge University Press, 1998.

Screech, M. A. *Montaigne and Melancholy: The Wisdom of the Essays.* London: Penguin Books, 1983.

———. "Montaigne: Some Classical Notions in Their Contexts." In *Montaigne in Cambridge, Proceedings of the Cambridge Montaigne Colloquium 1989,* ed. Philip Ford et al. (1989), 39–52.

Scruton, Roger. *A Political Philosophy.* London: Continuum, 2006.

Sève, Bernard. *Montaigne: Des règles pour l'esprit.* Paris: Presses Universitaires de France, 2007.

Slade, Francis. "On the Ontological Priority of Ends and Its Relevance to the Narrative Arts." In *Beauty, Art, and the Polis,* ed. Alice Ramos, 58–69. American Maritain Association, 2000.

———. "Rule as Sovereignty: The Universal and Homogeneous State." In *The Truthful and the Good: Essays in Honor of Robert Sokolowski,* ed. John J. Drummond and James G. Hart, 159–80. Dordrecht: Kluwer Academic, 1996.

———. "Two Versions of Political Philosophy: Teleology and the Conceptual Genesis of the Modern State." In *Natural Moral Law in Contemporary Society,* ed. Holger Zaborowski, 235–63. Washingon, D.C: Catholic University of America Press, 2010.

———. "Was Ist Aufklärung? Notes on Maritain, Rorty, and Bloom with Thanks but No Apologies to Immanuel Kant." In *The Common Things: Essays on Thomism and Education,* ed. Daniel McInerny, 48–68. American Maritain Association, 1999.

———. "Zeno's City." Paper presented at the annual meeting of the American Maritain Association, Notre Dame University, South Bend, Ind., October 2007.

Smith, Malcolm C. *Montaigne and Religious Freedom: The Dawn of Pluralism.* Geneva: Librairie Droz, 1991.

———. *Montaigne and the Roman Censors*. Geneva: Librairie Droz S.A., 1981.

Sokolowski, Robert. *Pictures, Quotations, and Distinctions: Fourteen Essays in Phenomenology*. Notre Dame, Ind.: University of Notre Dame Press, 1992.

Starobinski, Jean. *Montaigne en movement*. Paris: Éditions Gallimard, 1982.

Supple, James J. *Arms Versus Letters: The Military and Literary Ideals in the Essais of Montaigne*. Oxford: Clarendon, 1984.

Tarn, W. W. *Alexander the Great II: Sources and Studies*. Cambridge: Cambridge University Press, 1948.

Todorov, Tzvetan. *Imperfect Garden: The Legacy of Humanism*. Trans. Carol Cosman. Princeton, N.J.: Princeton University Press, 2002.

———. *Montaigne ou la découverte de l'individu*. Tournai, Belgium: La Renaissance du Livre, 2001.

Weil, Simone. "Méditation sur l'obéissance et la liberté." In Etienne de La Boétie, *Le discours de la servitude volontaire: La Boétie et la question du politique*, 87–95. Paris: Payot, 1985.

Zalloua, Zahi. *Montaigne and the Ethics of Skepticism*. Charlottesville, Va.: Rookwood, 2005.

———. "Montaigne, Seneca, and 'le Soing de la Culture de l'Ame.' " *Montaigne Studies* 21 (2009): 155–68.

———. "Montaigne, Skepticism and Immortality" *Philosophy and Literature* 27 (2003): 40–61.

INDEX